# The Art of Being a Boss

# The Art
## of
# Being a Boss

Inside Intelligence
from Top-Level Business Leaders
and Young Executives
on the Move

**by Robert J. Schoenberg**

J. B. Lippincott Company
Philadelphia and New York

*With love,*
*to Shirley, Art and Ted,*
*and to the memory of our parents*

U.S. Library of Congress Cataloging in Publication Data

Schoenberg, Robert J., birth date
    The art of being a boss.

    Includes index.
    1. Executives. 2. Executive ability. 3. Super-
vision of employees. I. Title.
HF5500.2.S326        658.4        78–15150
    ISBN–0–397–01291–8

# Contents

# Preface

*Whenever he felt like it, crippled newsboy Billy Batson had only to utter a single magic word and* SHAZAM! *he was Captain Marvel. Much of the literature on how to get ahead, especially in business, urges belief in the same basic style of operation. All we have to do, such books assure us, is understand one key concept—power, intimidation, assertiveness, overachievement, politics, objectives, motivation, transactional analysis—learn whatever this month's one true magic word happens to be, and we will unfailingly become . . . Captain Success!*

*What a pity it is not really that simple.*

*This book was born of the recognition that being the kind of better boss who gets to be a bigger boss is an art, with all that word implies about the need for multiple talents, techniques, knowledge and disciplines. Discoverable, teachable skills are involved; but there is no magic word, no abrupt and secret path, no royal road to success in being a boss. Many things are important to know, and no one or two or dozen or score are enough.*

*But the writers of business books typically have an idiosyncratic and fiercely held notion about what is important. They have an ax to grind, a point to prove. If their thesis has evolved from their own success in business, they are understandably convinced that theirs is the way, all you really have to know. If they are business consultants, they tend to be even more dogmatic because they are selling something. In either event, everything is sure to be angled to make their case. What's more, no one who sets up as an authority can very well make the rounds of other authorities, checking perceptions, guided by consensus.*

*There is another restriction. It should be no surprise that any book on business success (including this one) is prescriptive in its answers. But an executive or consultant, basing his advice on his own experience, will also be prescriptive about questions. He tells you not only what you should know but what you should want to know, because that is what has been important in his own career.*

*This book is different. I have no pet theories, no techniques or cause to champion, no system I want to see established or publicized. Furthermore, I had no ego problems in asking a wide variety of people for their views, no bias in compiling, cross-checking and evaluating their answers. I was disinterested in the very best sense. I did not even have preconceptions about what questions should be asked. As you will see, the topics in this book emerged from group interviews with precisely the sort of people best calculated to benefit from such a book.*

*Fact is, I am about to disappear. I did the interviewing, the selecting, even the synthesizing of questions and answers, and wrote the narrative. But the true authors are the more than a hundred men and women who framed those questions and provided those answers.*

*You will find a lot of questions and answers, a lot of vitally useful advice. You will not find* SHAZAM! *On the other hand, the sum of what you will find is pretty nearly magical in the way it can make anyone succeed as a boss.*

*Guaranteed?*

*Maybe. While interviewing the chairman of Savin Business Machines, I said that there obviously was no magic formula for success.*

*"Of course there is!" said Paul Charlap. "I have a four-point magic formula that can make anybody successful. Want to hear it?"*

*I nodded eagerly. This was going to be an easy book to write after all.*

*"First, you have to work hard. Not just moving papers back and forth. Do you know how many people I watch moving papers back and forth until the paper's out of date, so that then they can throw it away and get another paper?*

*"Then you have to work smart. If you're selling one of our machines, don't waste your time teaching people what they should use; go to the people who are already using something like it and show why they should use ours. Let IBM teach; we'll go get the business. That's working smart.*

*"Third, you have to demonstrate with enthusiasm. Whatever you have. Because enthusiasm is catching. Car people know that. They'll say, 'Ooooh! Is this a machine! Listen!' and they'll slam the door. You say, "Wow! That really does slam! I'll take it!' It has nothing to do with anything except enthusiasm.*

*"Fourth, you have to give service, not try to beat people. In Business Week, back in 'seventy-five, somebody asked me about one of our machines and I told him, 'The machine's a disaster.' Everyone here got mad at me. But if we don't recognize a disaster when it happens and tell the customer we know and say, 'We're going to do better,' how is he going to trust us next time? So the object is not to beat people, but to serve them so they come back to you.*

*"If you do those four simple things, you will be successful."*

*Guaranteed. In fact, the rest of this book is really a detailed explication and demonstration of that "magic formula." But no tricks or ploys, no SHAZAM.*

*After a long and searching interview, the chairman of Consolidated Foods, John Bryan, said that a couple of days earlier he had been talking on a jet with his seat mate, a salesman. The fellow allowed that he had discovered the secret, the sure way to success. After every contact with a customer, long-term or potential, he immediately wrote a short note: Thanks for your time and trouble, etc.*

*"You aren't going to tell them that kind of trash, are you?" asked Bryan.*

*I said I would not. And I won't.*

# Acknowledgments

Start with my total indebtedness to the many men and women who sat and talked with me, often for a considerable time, and for attribution—a sure guarantee to the reader that these people thought hard about what they meant to say, and mean what they did say.

I wish there were room enough (about 3,000 pages) to quote each of them in full. As it is, no one person is quoted very often. But inevitably some are quoted more often than others, a few hardly at all. It has nothing to do with their rank or prominence, the originality of their ideas, felicity of expression, or even soundness of advice. Many people often made essentially the same point, and where a quote was needed to illuminate the point, it was a question of choosing the one of many that most aptly fit the way I synthesized the consensus.

Where I synthesize without quoting anyone, it may seem that I am advancing my own ideas, but I am not. What these people said, even when not quoted directly, informs every paragraph of this book. No part of anyone's interview was "wasted."

I also want to thank some individuals.

A. J. Langguth—for his advice, criticism, friendship and encouragement all the way through.

Jim Keefe, Mac McIntosh and Lou Parris—for some very helpful suggestions at some very critical points.

Sam and Anita Kane in Chicago, Burt and Shirley Wellenbach in Philadelphia, Nick and Janet Wedge in Ossining and Craig Moodie in New York City—for extended hospitality while I was researching this book. They made fun and easy what could have been lonely and hard.

Ed Burlingame and colleagues—for a big idea and a big chance.

And Don Congdon—without whom, not.

# Introduction

The plan of this book was to start with no preconceptions about questions or answers and with only one assumption: that the reader is most likely a junior or mid-level executive (or someone about to become one), eager, apt and willing to learn, with at least a taste of being a boss, hungry for more and avid for information on how to get better at it.

That seemed a pretty safe assumption. But what, exactly, would such a person want to know about the art of being a boss? What subjects, and what questions within broad subject areas, would he or she want covered? There is a reasonably simple, astonishingly accurate way to find out called the "focus group interview."

Most advertising research techniques are blendings of moonbeam and cowpat, designed to prove to the client, after the fact, that whatever the agency decided to do was the right course. Focus group interviews are different. The idea is that if people with some common interest are gathered together and encouraged to exchange views on that interest (with a moderator *focusing* their attention), the interplay of their ideas and concerns will expose all the important attitudes shared by large masses of people toward the subject. Invariably it works. So the first step was to hold focus group sessions with representative young executives, most of them first-level supervisors from a range of companies, to find out what subjects should be covered. The people in the focus groups, and their company affiliations, are listed at the end of Appendix II, List of Companies, under "Focus Group Panelists."

Throughout the rest of this book, quotations are attributed by name, on the theory that someone's position, rank, age and other deducible details of outlook, including what else he or she is quoted as having said on other matters, are all part of establishing the validity and value of any particular idea. But a basic rule for focus groups is that panelists must feel the absolute freedom of anonymity in exposing their thoughts. That seemed particularly important in this case. Juniors would be opening up, saying what was really bothering them, in effect admitting an important lack of knowledge and confidence. To induce candor, they were assured that no one would be quoted by name and that no areas of concern would be identified with any particular person, though each individual in the panel would be named to encourage a sense of seriousness and thoughtful responsibility.

It turned out to be a workable and liberating compromise. For example, the important point emerged that young executives would not be content to hear answers only from people at the very top. One panelist said, "I read a book that was written by the president of our firm about thirty years ago on controllership. It was relevant then; now the problems have changed. I could learn from him, right now, how to put together a board of directors and a topflight management team. But I don't know that he'd have much to tell me about running an accounting department at my level. A lot's changed since he did it." That started a discussion—and, as a result, answers in this book are as likely to come from identified young comers in an organization as from the chairman. But can you imagine a very junior executive saying such things for attribution?

Another important topic developed because a panelist was sure his subordinates would never find out what he thought of them. The talk had been about problems faced by those in the group who regularly dealt with highly trained and talented people—what eventually became the section, "Handling Talent and Temperament." One young man broke into the conversation impatiently.

x: "That's a *tough* problem? I wish I had it! My problem right now is, How do you motivate the *marginal* employee? Don't say I call them that, but that's about all I've got. And I think that's the hardest problem: to keep employees like that motivated. We always worry about the guy who's maybe B+ and you want him to be A. What do you do about the guy who's a C—a good C? How do you keep him there all the time, or maybe get him up to C+?"

w: "Yeah, there's a lot more of them than there are geniuses you have to handle. How much time should you devote to it? There's a school of thought that says you shouldn't devote too much. Work with the high achievers, and make them even higher achievers."

x: "What *do* you do? Ignore them? I disagree, but I don't know what's *right* to do."

Come to think of it, he probably would have been as slow to let his management in on such doubts as he was to let his people know he considered them, at best, C.

A valuable bonus of the focus group technique was that, in discussion of even fairly obvious points, a new or unexpected slant helped frame questions for the later interviews. A panelist said, "One topic that might be interesting is how you get recognized as a manager instead of just 'one of the boys' who happens to be in charge of the rest of the boys." Obviously, "Standing Out" would have to be a section. But then the following exchange took place:

A: How do you impress your superiors not only that you can get the job done, but in the way they want to see it done?

B: No! If you do the job, if you get it done, the impression will take care of itself.

After the derisive laughter died down, other points were raised:

C: Well, I've sure seen it happen where two people in the same department will get a job done, but one doesn't say the things people want to hear, and doesn't do things the way people want them done, and that one kind of languishes, while the one down the hall who's maybe not even turning in as good a job, is suddenly a manager. What happened is the first one's impressing people the wrong way.

A: But is there a common thread that people are looking for? I'm not sure. The two companies I've been with, there was a certain style they're looking for. Is that generally true?

There was plainly a lot more to find out about standing out than just turning in a good performance. In fact, in another focus group session, someone had a totally different slant on excellence of performance:

Y: How do you maintain mobility? You can be extremely good in your own little area, and you're immediately written off for any moves. It happens all the time in my company. They say, "Oh, my God! We'd have to replace so-and-so!" And you're stuck.

Z: You have your own personal plan.

Y: But how do you do that? Continue to do an extremely good job where you are, because you have to, but not keep yourself out of an opportunity somewhere else?

A repeated theme, cutting across most areas of questioning, was that young managers want specific hard information about the various topics of interest, not just theoretic vaporing, no matter how authoritative the source. "One main question I would have," said a panelist, "is, How do you evaluate performance? There's a lot of talk, a lot of seminars, dealing with standards of performance, but how do you make it work, tied in with developing people and rewarding them and so forth? I'm talking about successful techniques that are actually used. That's a lot more useful than a lot of the usual 'philosophy' of performance evaluation."

There was much more. Here is a sampling of some of the concerns expressed, which you will find mirrored in the subjects treated in the book:

"My main problem in being a boss is: How do you control what people do? Control. That's the whole thing."

"The biggest single thing I do every day is decide what we should do and what can wait. How do you set priorities?"

"The toughest job I find I have is this: How do I get people to cooperate and do exactly what I want them to if they're in other departments and I have no direct control over them?"

"One of my people just quit. But, really, I should have canned him months ago. How do you develop the right attitude that lets you fire people when you should? And how do you know *when* you should?"

"I'd like to see something on how to communicate what you want done. I've seen supervisors go about it in such a way that they create an adverse effect so that people are thinking, "How am I gonna screw this guy?" They're not out to hurt the company, just get back at the supervisor; they're mad because of *how* they've been given orders."

"I'd like to know from upper-level people how much they think it was luck? How much innate ability, intelligence, et cetera? How much strategic planning? And how much was methodical plodding away—plain hard work? How do you tell which characteristics are most important?"

Finally, there were practically explicit directions about where to go for answers. One panelist said, "I think a very important topic is developing people, because that includes things like motivation, and it ties in with performance. I'd like to hear about that."

"Any particular people you want to hear from?" asked another member of the panel.

"Well, not specific people by name, but people from certain corporations. IBM, Hewlett-Packard, Litton Industries —companies that have been successful because they develop people. The ones responsible for development in any companies that are *known* for their ability to develop people would be a very good source for information. How do they make sure they see the high-potential people in their organizations? And what do they look for?"

It was not so much, then, a question of personalities or rank but of people who had recently demonstrated some particular mastery of each subject. Leads came from stories in the business press. For instance, for "Standing Out," a story about William George, who took over at Litton Microwave at age thirty, provided one kind of lead; another story that mentioned Edgar Speer's step-by-step climb to the top at U.S. Steel, with a career in production that spanned more years than William George had been alive, suggested a lead for a different sort of perspective on how to stand out.

A story about John Bunting, flamboyant chairman of the First Pennsylvania Corporation, suggested that he would have a lot to say about style. One about Arthur Larkin pointed him out as someone to ask about handling mistakes; he had recovered nicely from a $46-million beauty. William Roesch had made a career out of going into new situations that were bad and turning things around; what's more, he would probably supplement Edgar Speer's views on standing out, having risen gradually to the top in Jones & Laughlin, up from (literally) the coal mines.

And so it went. Except that many had as much or more to say about other topics as about the specific one they were contacted for.

After the interview many were asked to identify young comers in their organization—middle-management or even more junior—who could also be interviewed. Where you find only one person in an organization quoted, it is not for lack of cooperation but rather lack of time or conflicting schedules. Every chief executive who was asked willingly supplied subordinates for interview.

In all, over one hundred people were interviewed, from more than forty organizations ranging in size from the country's biggest, Exxon, to ones grossing less than $50 million (though the concentration is on larger corporations). The interviews were tape recorded, and although the quotations have been edited, they are as nearly verbatim as possible.

The result is the art of being a boss—as developed by people at all levels who have shown by their success that they know this art and how to practice it.

# I  *QUALITIES OF A BOSS*

*Many qualities make an attractive, happy human being, qualities that any of us would rejoice in for ourselves and certainly appreciate in our neighbors. But for any given calling only a few qualities are really necessary.*

*What are the qualities of a boss? Not what are "nice" or useful to have—popularity, say,—or even what most bosses do indeed seem to have—such as personal integrity. Such qualities are not central to the nature of a boss. Being popular makes it easier to lead, but it is a notoriously frail reed. And although personal integrity saves time and trouble, a boss can get along without it by calculating the effect and consequences of acts beforehand and avoiding those (like betrayal) that figure to be eventually counterproductive.*

*The qualities of the boss we shall examine are specifically related to how bosses must function* as bosses, *and they range from useful to essential. "There are certain minimum standards you must meet in order to be anything," says business consultant Milton Rock. "For instance, your chances of being an Olympic high jumper,"—he looked appraisingly at his rather stumpy interviewer—"are nil no matter how hard you might try, because you're short— compared to a high jumper. It's the same with being a boss. If you happen to have an IQ of only a hundred, you are not going to be chief executive officer, even if your father owns the business."*

*But assuming acceptable basic intelligence, there* are *things you can do to acquire those other qualities of a boss that you need.*

# 1 *Do You Have What It Takes?*

"If he has the qualities of a boss he will thrive; if he doesn't, no matter what he does or says, he is not going to thrive." So says Milton Glass, treasurer of the Gillette Company.

That thought was echoed in one form or another by nearly everyone quoted in this book, but it is reassuring to know that not one of them believes those necessary qualities are superhuman. "I used to be in awe of people at the top," says Evelyn Berezin, founder and president of Redactron Corporation. "But as I've gotten to where I've met some, I'm astonished at how rare it is to find the really extraordinary person. Maybe I had an exaggerated idea of what people in those exalted positions would be like."

More likely, she sees in them only qualities she recognizes in herself, and finds those the unremarkable and necessary freight of any successful boss. Although good bosses come in all shapes, sizes, powers of intellect, character and personality (some are even extraordinary), there are common threads in their qualities. But only one quality is absolute and universal: The desire to succeed. Given that, the lack of almost any other quality or capacity can be compensated for by strengths in other areas. Being a successful boss, though, takes so much concentrated hard work that only a consuming desire to succeed can sustain the necessary drive.

Other, almost as vital, qualities directly relate to how a good boss operates. They are necessary because they affect the boss's ability to take hold of a group and the group's acceptance of the boss's leadership. Furthermore, most of the qualities are interlocking, one affecting the other.

For instance, three qualities that bosses widely agree on

as necessary are aggressiveness, self-confidence and articulateness (which has come to mean fluency). Aggressiveness is needed to take the lead, to get out in front of situations. But that is an exposed position, demanding self-confidence, which you cannot rightly hope to have without an aggressiveness that pushes you to master your field, and an ability to present it and yourself clearly and persuasively, with an assurance born of knowing you are right, so your people will gladly follow your lead. Conversely, knowing you have all that in hand does wonders for self-confidence.

Notice that none of the qualities means much alone. (Unsupported, each can even be a danger: Just think where unjustified self-confidence leads.) In concert, they amount to being in command—of yourself, your subject, your subordinates, the situation. And it is inconceivable that the boss *not* be in command.

There is another aspect to the pragmatic nature of the necessary qualities. Take fluency. The immediate and obvious need for it involves communication, but it is for the lucid transmission of solid ideas, not elegance, that fluency is prized; mere glibness is nothing. For instance, when writers are assigned to compose speeches for top executives, the writers' early drafts may read well, but the speeches often lack depth, substance and insight, reaching no novel conclusions until the executives insert their own ideas into later drafts. A speech worth listening to is the result of the ability to dig into an issue and think innovatively about its solution, which is what makes people top management, and they'd rather be managers than speech writers.

Furthermore, the necessary mastery of subject matter is attainable only by people with an advanced capacity to become immersed in their work, a quality that starts with the realization that they have a limited number of chances to prove themselves and a limited time in which to do it. "If you blow your first assignment, you'll probably get another chance," says

Richard ("Dick") Jackson, vice-president for finance at Litton Microwave. "Blow that and you might not get another. Young MBAs tend to feel that they can fall back on their degree, that whatever they do is right. They don't go into assignments with a sense of urgency."

That "sense of urgency" pinpoints a major difference between the kinds of qualities needed by subordinates and bosses. It is a commonplace of success literature that one must "accept responsibility." True. But a sense of urgency will not permit an aspiring boss to be content with anything so passive. Only a natural-born subordinate would wait around to be offered responsibility. "You have to usurp power," says Savin Business Machines chairman Paul Charlap. "It doesn't come to you except by usurping it. But it's easy to do because the lazy ones sit back and let you."

Even in the most formally structured company it is always possible to usurp a little more power. In some circumstances it is even required—for anyone who hopes to be a boss. "I threaten people here," Charlap continues. "If I catch you saying, 'It's not my fault; it was *his* responsibility,' with the fingers pointing around the circle, I'll fire you, because if you don't have enough interest in the company—if you're willing to stand there and watch a drunk get in a car, or let a two-year-old without a life jacket play on the end of a dock alone—well, you're not allowed to do that. You are required to run and protect that two-year-old." Just as you are required to protect the interests of your company, even in areas not your "responsibility," because it *is* your responsibility if you want to be boss. And nothing can more surely or quickly persuade management that you are boss material than the reputation (which does get around) for being someone who aggressively looks for and seizes opportunities to further the company's interests regardless of "responsibility."

It comes down to a matter of good judgment, another prime quality of the boss. This may be the most elusive one, hard to define because it encompasses so many others. But two especially important ingredients, without which you cannot exercise good judgment, are intellectual honesty and decisiveness.

Except for willful wrongheadedness, the thing most subversive of good judgment is wishful thinking, the reverse of intellectual honesty. "You want people who can be honest with themselves in analyzing a situation, making judgments and evaluating projects," says Donald Seibert, chairman of J.C. Penney. "It means being completely objective when you look at an array of facts, resisting your own bias toward what you hope to find. If you start reading facts to support the 'right' outcome, you are likely to come up with a distorted picture."

It is not enough to face reality; you have to do something about it. Indivisible from good judgment is the realization that, while close decisions can generally go either way with no dramatic difference in result, there must *be* a decision, made with no vacillation. So the quality of decisiveness is looked for early and in every episode of conduct.

"We hired a bright, twenty-eight-year-old portfolio manager from a bank in Wisconsin," says Gordon Crosby, chairman of USLIFE Corporation, "and within three weeks, maybe four, he had sold his home in Madison, purchased a new home in Summit, New Jersey, and was on the job. We had another situation, an internal transfer, where it took the man almost nine months to make the move. Now that told us something." On one hand, there was a model of decisiveness and organization. On the other was a man who, however otherwise valued, showed he lacked any urgent sense of what was important. "He had a tendency to get caught up in the nitty-gritty," says Crosby, "and lose sight of the big picture."

Look at how lack of intellectual honesty and decisiveness defeated good judgment. The second man could not face the realities of the transfer. Was it good for his career? His family? Was it to his liking? Clearly the company wanted him to move, so it could not possibly be smart to do so with foot-dragging reluctance. But maybe if he ignored that reality, everything would somehow come out right. His only "decision" was not to be decisive either way, neither to move nor to say "no, thanks" to the transfer. So he got the worst of both decisions, plus a damning residual reputation as a vacillator, which can hardly be reckoned an exercise in good judgment.

Another matched pair of qualities are dependability and consistency. Dependability is what you display to superiors; consistency is the same quality, displayed to subordinates.

When looking for promotable people, management wants a person who always achieves the expected results—or better. Expectation is the key. We give the project to Sue's group because we *know* we will get good results. From Sam's group maybe we will and maybe we won't; all we can expect is that they will be a day late and a dollar short. From Pete's group we expect results that may be sensational or horrible, depending on whether Pete likes the project or not. So Sue gets it. Brilliance is gravy, but your superiors must know they can count on you every time for at least reasonable results.

Your group should feel the same way about you. For them to put out the sort of work that persuades management of your dependability, your people need the assurance of your consistency. This means never being arbitrary or capricious, but applying the same even-handed standards today and tomorrow. If a subordinate does a laudable job, it does not suddenly become inept because they hated it upstairs. A subordinate who needs a decision gets one that is timely and fair, not trimmed to political winds. If you tell a subordinate one thing today and, tomorrow, management decides on a 180-degree change, you do not try to pretend that is what you meant all along. Certainly not if you, not management, decided on the new direction. "When you make a mistake you have to have self-possession," says Academy Award–winning film director George Cukor. "Actors will say, 'Well, yesterday you said do it *this* way!' I say,

'Did I say that yesterday? Wasn't that terrible! An aberration! What are you going to do, shoot me? I was wrong yesterday, and I don't mind saying it. That doesn't mean I'm wrong *now*, when I've had a chance to think it over.' "

It all adds up to a decent regard for people, another quality of the boss.

Before Donald Port became a project manager in the chairman's office at Gillette, he was with the safety razor division, where one major task was looking for floor supervisors. "A supervisor," he says, "has to regard those on the line as 'our people,' not part of the fixtures. If you're not capable of doing that, I can't use you. The last thing I need is the Marine-sergeant type, hassling the troops. It's got to be somebody who can empathize and relate to people. Skills—other kinds of skills—we can teach you." The "people skills" are really no more complicated than a corporate version of the Golden Rule.

"You can't get to the point where you're so demanding of people that you think every time you press a button the whole world's going to jump," says Wallace Timmeny, associate director of enforcement at the Securities and Exchange Commission. "On the other side of the button there's a human being."

Let's pause and see where we are. The only absolute essential is a desire to succeed. Beyond that, you need aggressiveness, self-confidence and fluency; a sense of urgency about your work and your career; good judgment, including intellectual honesty and decisiveness; and dependability and consistency, leading to general "people skills."

What if you *don't* have what it takes?

# 2 *What to Do If You Don't Have What It Takes*

After the desire to succeed, the only other truly indispensable quality is enough intellectual honesty to recognize in yourself a lack of the other important qualities. Because you *can* do something about it.

It is not necessarily true that signs of success are visible from the very start of a successful career. If you can discern promising patterns in your background, fine. But the past is predictive, not prescriptive, and certainly not proscriptive. You will not surely succeed as a boss because of early leadership qualities any more than you must fail as a boss because you were not elected fifth-grade hall monitor. It all depends on what you do about it now.

If you lack some of the qualities necessary or desirable in a boss, you can compensate by stressing other qualities, or set about filling the gaps, or both. And if it does not come naturally, that just means you have to work harder at it. "I always liked being at the top," says William Spoor, Pillsbury Company chairman. "It was the role I was most happy with. Not that I'm smarter; I'm not. A very smart person will take six months to get something that takes me a year. But I never lose my span of attention. I'm willing to stick with it as long as it takes."

It takes tremendous self-discipline. "I hate war," says Paul Charlap, "but I love the *idea* of an army. Everybody should spend a year in the Marines because you learn that 'the spirit's willing but the flesh is weak' is a crock! You learn, 'I *can* march that extra fifteen miles with a pack on my back.' It's discipline, like a checklist in your head. You say to yourself, the night before, 'I'm going to do this amount of work, make this number of phone calls, this number of calls knocking on doors, this number of demonstrations'—and you don't go home until you do it. After a while, with anything, it becomes automatic. At a level where somebody else has to put out all kinds of effort, you pass by like it's nothing!"

When you think about it, no one starts life with *any* of the necessary qualities. Each is picked up en route, some sooner, others later, with varying degrees of ease. But at some point—now, for instance—you can make an inventory of your assets and determine to increase the stock, following up with self-discipline.

How do people attain fluency? Demosthenes stuffed pebbles in his mouth and orated. William Spoor stuffed as much meaning as he could into cablegrams at a dollar a word when he was exporting flour and had to learn concise exposition. Evelyn Berezin stuffs a pocket dictating machine into her handbag and practices over and over.

How can you do it? Take a public speaking course. Join a theater group, a debating society, a lunch-discussion club; talk to yourself. A moment's reflection will reveal any number of effective and practical ways that want only your determination and self-discipline to realize. It is the same for all the necessary qualities. You are ahead of the pack knowing that, yes, it is important to have certain qualities and, yes, it is within your power to acquire those you lack.

The ability to recognize what you lack is a matter of sensitivity to your surroundings, a combination of quickness to pick up the subtleties, the innuendo of situations, and the realistic courage to face the conclusions you draw from them. William Spoor once pushed through a hefty raise for a young comer who seemed to have only one drawback. "He dressed in suits that looked like he'd paid twenty-five bucks for them back in the forties," says Spoor. "Clothing wasn't important to him—and it isn't to me, either. But people looked at him and said, 'Well, if he'd only sharpen up. . . .' So when I told him about the raise I also said, 'The directors voted you an extra hundred so you can buy four more of those suits you wear.' A couple of days later Wally came in and said, 'Here's my first new twenty-five-dollar suit. How do you like it?' He was gorgeous! Just a word was all it took." That is all it should take. A word —if to the wise.

But when it comes to the basic qualities (which dressing well certainly is *not*), no one should have to point out a lack. Even cursory self-analysis should be enough to flag the danger areas, the points needing effort.

Take "people skills." In today's business world it is a byword that "this is the people business"—which basically means caring about people. Not soppily, or with the outlook of a social worker, but with a constant awareness that people are your company's most important resource and that your personal advancement at every stage will turn on how people react to you and perform for you. *You* are, willy-nilly, in the people business.

Realizing that, and being realistic about yourself, you can spot potential trouble areas. "Some people have personality problems," says Victor Kiam, Benrus Corporation chairman. "If you're a tremendous introvert you'll have a terrible time in management because it takes you so much longer to reach the people you're working with. An introvert, by nature, is not going to develop the necessary communication and relationships as quickly as an extrovert." Certainly you will have a harder time being interested in your people and concerned about them. It will take conscious effort to notice them, maybe an act of will even to remember to be civil. But, knowing that, you can discipline yourself to make the effort.

Robert Hinman, VP in the chairman's office of Gillette, says that since the company has grown to a 30,000-employee multinational, it is an awesome task "to retain the same spirit the company had when it was over in South Boston." Yet that spirit is thought to be a key to Gillette's success. It traditionally derives from a feeling that the chairman is close to the people in the ranks—something the incumbent has to work at. "Colman Mockler is a somewhat private man," says Hinman, which is like saying that Wilt Chamberlain is a somewhat lengthy man. Mockler must take particular care to make it clear that he does have the welfare of his people at heart. Hinman says he was indelibly impressed, back in 1971 when wage and price controls were ordained, by the priorities Mockler set. The immediate application for pay increases was for so-called "nonexempt employees"—factory workers, office help and the like—getting permission for their wage hikes. Next he turned to getting raises for middle management. Only at the end did he worry about such matters as the stock-option plan. "It left an impression on me," says Hinman, "because that is what makes the company work, thinking in terms of the employees."

Anyone to whom personal relationships come easily has the edge, but if you're not one of them, you can work to become one. Heath Larry had a coterie of backers for the chairmanship of U.S. Steel. Edgar Speer got the job, and Larry says it was an understandable decision. It isn't the steel business, you see, it's the people business. "And Ed is more oriented to people than I am," says Larry. "I started as a lawyer, and to some extent I still tend to become wrapped up in ideas, in concepts, in things. Ed's an old production man—and production is pure people." Nevertheless, Larry did work at it and became vice-chairman of U.S. Steel and head of the National Association of Manufacturers—not a bad reward for effort.

This discussion started with a reassurance that to be a good boss you do not have to be superhuman. In fact, it does not really matter much *what* kind of human you are. Although many of the necessary qualities of the boss can roughly be called "personality traits," they have nothing to do with personality in the usual sense, certainly nothing to do with what sort of person the boss is. He or she can be one of God's sweet angels and be confident, honest and fair; he or she can also be an irascible son of a (or plain) bitch and be confident, honest and fair. And a good boss in either case. He or she can be tall or short, fat or thin, of any race, creed or place of national origin. It would be idle to pretend there is no bias in business today. But it would be wrongheaded to ignore the devoted effort business is making to eliminate it. The cynic may claim the effort is mostly lip-service. But you have to have the subject in mind before you talk about it. Besides, as Arthur Howe, director of public affairs at INA Corporation points out, "the verbiage has to come first."

Old stereotypes and knee-jerk considerations of "image" and personality are breaking down along with more official discriminations. The socially less acceptable are coming out of the closet (anyway, the back room), too. If you have a serviceable talent, it is beginning not to matter whether you match the look and manner of past stars. Performance is getting to be the sole criterion for advancement. Consider this set of statements from people at U.S. Steel:

Chairman Edgar Speer: It doesn't matter how a man parts his hair; it's what kind of job he does.

Staff Assistant Drummond Bell: At one time U.S. Steel had an image situation where you had to be six-foot-two, eyes-of-blue and drink a lot. That was the "Steel Image." Ed Speer's changed it; he's performance oriented. We know from our bosses he's saying the people who are going to go someplace in this company are the people who perform.

Executive Assistant Peter Mulloney: Drummond Bell is—and I say this with no disrespect—a funny-looking little fellow whose clothes never fit, who's generally unpressed, and so on. But Drummond was noticed in every job he's been in because he was able to analyze each job, then do it better than most people can. He also has a sense of humor and is a pleasant, interesting person, but that's not the main thing. The main thing is that he's been able to produce.

The important qualities, the ones that mean advancement, are the ones that let you produce. The humor, the pleasant personality, the good looks and social grace—that's all extra. You can make up for their lack if you have what it takes. And if you do not have it, you can get it.

# II  *STARTING OUT RIGHT—AT ANY POINT IN YOUR CAREER*

*"Positioning" means a lot more than just what job you happen to have in a company, or even what job you should try for next. It means your relationship to a company in light of your talents, tastes, ambitions, probable future—even what kind of company it is and its probable future.*

*Proper positioning is something that can start at any point in your career; it is never too late. But it is essential to position yourself correctly as soon as you know how. Once you understand correct positioning—what to look for, what to beware of—you can maintain the right position and jockey to improve it as your career blossoms.*

*What are the elements of proper positioning? What kind of company should you look for, and what sort of place in the right company? What factors in your makeup contribute to proper positioning? Most of all, what do you need to arrive at proper positioning, and how do you know when you get there?*

# 3 *Getting in the Right Position*

Just because you happen not to be at the start of your career does not mean your positioning is already irrevocably set. *Useful* positioning does not involve charting a route to the top, step by step, then resolutely scrambling for each predetermined foothold. Ask any mountain climber. Or ask successful bosses, most of whom will tell you they never pointed for specific jobs on the way up. Instead, they got themselves into the strongest possible position as early as possible, one congruent with their tastes, skills and strengths, then vigorously attacked whatever targets of opportunity came along. They found a business that strongly interested them and looked for some facet of the business that allowed full play to their particular talents and needs.

You cannot hope to perform at peak if you have to fight an innate distaste for what you are doing, any moral or ethical reservations about its worth, propriety or importance, or the slightest disparity between the job and your natural abilities. "You'd better be honest with yourself as to just what your strengths and weaknesses are," says Donald Petersen, Executive VP of Ford Motor Company "and avoid like the plague trying to create something artificial, because it just won't stand up. The people who go with their strength have a lot more staying power and operate in a more natural manner."

Proper positioning starts with acute and thoughtful self-knowledge. You must study the sum of the education, experience, even quirky biases that comprise you and ponder how that package of abilities and flaws, likes and loathings, will fit into any given place or condition of work.

How do you go about it?

Whether you are just starting out or in mid-career, you might go to a company like Bernard Haldane Associates. Critics of such services argue with their specific utility in job-hunting, but no one can question the basic soundness of the approach. "Our concern," says the company's founder, Haldane, "is to find out what are the skills and talents a person has that enable him to say, 'This is me; this is what really turns me on as a person; this is the direction in which I would like to develop and continue to grow.' " Certainly a little psychological testing —like a little chicken soup—cannot hurt. But it may not be needed if you are capable of honest self-examination. "Unfortunately, most people are not honest with themselves," says Herbert Patterson, senior adviser in the consulting firm of Marshalsea Associates and onetime president of the Chase Manhattan Bank. "They don't see their own face in the mirror when they shave, they see what they would like to be. But when you wake up around four o'clock in the morning . . ." Patterson laughs. "Beats psychiatry all to hell!" What it takes is a relentless determination to look at yourself without defenses; to examine, not attack yourself. And to match what you come to realize about yourself with the known realities of the business world.

Armed with self-knowledge, you can insouciantly turn down what most others might consider irresistibly mouth-watering offers—if they are incongruent with your proper positioning. "I've already said no to the opportunity to be a fifty-thousand-a-year consultant to the tire and rubber industry," says Richard ("Rick") Jackson, manager of business analysis at Litton Microwave. "I also turned down a chance to be a consultant to the government of Iran." His experience in the Air Force, then as a civilian in the Department of Defense, showed him how and where heroic amounts of money could be saved. "But I don't like what I'd have to become. I don't want to live my life as a consultant, always on the outskirts of the action." He knew he wanted to be in the thick of it, in management, and wanted a chance to grow with a vigorous, growing, consumer-goods outfit, a description fit neither by Firestone nor the Shah, no matter how good the pay.

It is obviously better to be right about yourself at the start of your career. But just as obviously, it is better at any point to act on dawning self-knowledge rather than struggle on (with invariably indifferent success) against your natural bent.

Andrew Ackemann of Leisure Dynamics is a vivid example of someone who knows who and what he is, what he wants, what he lacks and how and where to get it. What's more, he knew enough to act on the knowledge with successive congruent positionings. "I'm not content to be a small fish in a big pond," he says. "In the Navy I had a chance to be assistant to the assistant to the navigator of an aircraft carrier, or to command a minesweeper, the smallest capital ship. I chose command." It was the same when he got out. He went to work for a bank—but in a small branch, where he could run some trust accounts on his own. Next he joined Xerox, "in a small, highly refined area that allowed me to exercise a good deal of autonomy." After a while he ran his own company, Permacraft, which meant all the autonomy he could use but not enough scope. He wanted to run something bigger than Permacraft, "but I needed more training and more breadth of experience before I could do that." He became administrative assistant to the chairman of Leisure Dynamics. "My proximity to Bo Polk and the other managers make this an ideal training ground. Also, when I'm ready to take line responsibility for a twenty- or thirty-million-a-year business, I can find it right in Leisure, without jumping around. Nine years out of college, my résumé looks a little busy, and I need to get it calmed down. It took a long time to find the right channel for my personal goals consistent with the needs of someone who was in a position to employ me." Put another way, knowing himself, he repositioned himself congruent with opportunity.

A debating point of career planning has always been

whether to go with a large or a small company. In the context of self-knowledge applied to correct positioning, the decision is transparent, controlled by the logic of what people want matched to the implications of their choice.

William George always knew he wanted to be "in general management." After an industrial engineering degree from Georgia Tech and a Harvard MBA, he decided to go into government. There were two reasons. First, he felt he could better deal with the pervasive effect of government on business after working within government. More important, he knew that in government service, people can achieve resounding titles and high-powered general management responsibility despite quite young age.

Sure enough, after a couple of years as assistant to the controller in the Department of Defense, he was offered a chance to be special assistant to the Secretary of the Navy. Two more years and George was ready to make his move, positioned as someone fully trained and educated, with a demonstrated ability to function at a high management staff level. The logic of his positioning continued. He joined a division of Litton Industries—a company large enough to have within it units of a size that might plausibly be entrusted to young men, while young and dynamic enough itself not to make age a shibboleth.

Four years later, at age thirty, George was president of Litton Microwave.

If he had done everything the same way but had elected to stay at the Litton Industries corporate level, he would not today be corporate CEO. For one thing, the position is already amply filled. But, anyway, a corporation the size of Litton is not going to have a thirty-year-old chief executive no matter *what* his attainments. It is not only a question of the top job. If you want general management responsibility and do not want to wait for it, you should go with a smaller outfit where positions regularly become available as the company grows, and where, furthermore, there are fewer (or no) fixed standards to measure you against. "A lot of things are uncharted here," says Richard ("Rick") Shriner, manager of range engineering at Litton Microwave, "so you get a chance to do them. The way to be noticed is to be sure you're in an area that's new and opening. It's harder to evaluate people in an organization like IBM because the tasks and records of accomplishment are so similar, whereas in an environment like this the tasks are what you want to make them and go as far as you take them."

Then shouldn't everyone work for a dynamic smaller company? Not at all. You have to be exactly sure what you want and what you are doing and know exactly how to get where you are going with little help and few mistakes. Visibility is no boon when you are still experimenting; in smaller companies there is not much room for error or maneuver. "We watch guys fall by the wayside," Shriner continues. "Here, if you can't grow, you're going to get kicked out the door, whereas in a huge organization you could drift. I was at Corning—which is big enough to see that happen."

Of course, what seems like "drifting" to Shriner might be a process of self-assessment and positioning for a less positive careerist. "Let's say we hired a person as a systems engineer," says Edward Krieg, IBM director of management development. "That's a technical-support job. And assume the person showed signs of wanting to be a marketing representative. You'd say, 'Let me expose you to a few sales presentations; let me send you to a class; let me give you an assignment that pushes you more into the area where I think your real strengths are.' "

Such things are not in the vocabulary of smaller companies. It takes the scale of an IBM to allow such freedom, and not just at fledgling levels. In a large company, new divisions, whole new businesses are born, and if a leader wants to do something, both the freedom and the opportunity are available. Undeniably, there are more resources and backing and clout, greater diversity and choice of activity. There can also be plenty of excitement and sense of moment in jobs below the top level in a large outfit, and there are more jobs that pay better, with more security and total responsibility, than at a comparably below-the-peak level in a smaller company. Finally, do not overlook the psychological income: The considerable pride and prestige in being connected with a big, powerful, well-known company, in not having to define and explain when someone asks where you work.

So which is better for you, big or small? You decide. But *decide*—don't let it be an accident. The results of incongruent positioning can be too horrendous.

Fortunately, there is a remarkably simple test to tell if you are correctly positioned. Ask yourself if you enjoy what you're doing, if you like coming to work most mornings. If your answer is no, you're in the wrong job or the wrong company.

You ought to be having fun. Otherwise you cannot hope to put in the kind of effort necessary to succeed. "About seventy percent of every job, no matter at what level of the organization, is made up of things that one would rather not do," says Gillette's Colman Mockler. "The other thirty percent has to really give a sense of satisfaction and excitement. Otherwise one will not be able to do the other seventy percent effectively. So a prime characteristic of the manager is that he basically enjoys what he's doing."

That does not mean that your office habitually rings with irrepressible glee. "Fun" is shorthand for a passion that runs deep. "If you really want to do well," says Milton Rock, managing partner of the consultant firm, Hay Associates, "you have to be committed; you must be relatively interested and happy—and 'happy' is not 'pleasurable.' Happy to be willing to survive the time it requires, and practice it takes, and the continuing education." All of which is the key to congruent positioning.

"It's having joy in what you do that, in part, leads to your getting this job of being boss," says Erik Jonsson, founder of Texas Instruments. "If people don't think it's reasonably good fun, they're in the wrong job. If they wake up in the morning and hate to go to work, they're in the wrong job. But if they struggle with it and always want to take one more try, or think of something new they want to tackle today because it would be great to succeed with it, then I think these people are going to be leaders whether they ask for it or not."

# 4 *Probable Opportunity Paths*

Assuming that your goal is to move eventually into management, congruent positioning requires that your job be one the company considers integral to its line operations. You must be on what Chevrolet's director of salaried personnel Richard McIlvride calls "the most probable opportunity path." For instance, he says, "There are relatively few examples here of people moving from personnel to plant manager, or even from district sales manager to plant manager. So the most probable opportunity path to become plant manager would be production and related areas of plant operation."

Furthermore, companies tend to elevate some functions in prestige at the expense of others. You should be doing whatever the company prizes most and stay away from what it considers peripheral. No one will notice what a splendid job you are doing if no one particularly cares whether the job gets done or not.

In most companies, for example, anyone with management ambition would be wrong to head for the advertising department—except in, say, a cosmetics company or an ad agency, where it is of course the front line. The same is true, more subtly, for merchandising or marketing. They are fine, expandable positions in a consumer-goods outfit and dead ends in a basic industry. "Exposure to top management comes in the selection of the company you work for, the style of the company," says Robert Iverson, marketing director of bakery products at Sara Lee. "One of the things I like about Sara Lee is the exposure I had to top management, even at a much more junior level." It did not hurt that the president of Sara Lee is a marketing man. "Tom Barnum is very interested in what my department does" is how Iverson puts it.

There may be a marketing department at U.S. Steel. Somewhere. That is not to say *sales* are not important at Steel, but that is quite distinct from marketing. The distinction—and the lesson about congruence—is good to keep in mind if you are a marketing man of vast ambition and you hear about this swell opening in Pittsburgh.

Whatever you decide is your most probable opportunity path, it *must* involve specific skills. You cannot hope to be some vague, free-floating boss type. "I don't think people buy that," says John Bunting, chairman of the First Pennsylvania Corporation. " 'Boss type' just means you come from the right social background and your family got you in here and therefore we're moving you along. That's the reputation banks have. They take second sons of wealthy families and make them vice-presidents after a suitable time period. That does not play anymore—being someone who never was really good at anything except bossing people around. You have to be good at something, to have made a reputation somewhere." Otherwise your subordinates, the people you must rely on to enhance your reputation as a boss, simply will not respect you enough to put out any effort. Bunting says you must be either "very good at whatever the function of that unit is, or known as expert at something else—but someone to whom top management is obviously giving experience. That's O.K. People will accept that, as long as you have been good at *something.* "

You need specific expertise all the more to impress peers and supervisors. You must put yourself in a position where they depend on you to get their own jobs done. "For instance," says Robert Baker of American Airlines, "I positioned myself, by design, as the technical operating expert of the marketing department, so whenever an operating decision came up I would be the primary input."

From director of ramp services, Baker was promoted to assistant VP for marketing administration, reporting to Robert Crandall, senior VP for marketing. "If you look at the backgrounds of our vice-presidents," he says, "I'm the only one with operating experience, the only one who's gotten an airplane off the gate. So when I say it's feasible to operate in a certain way, to do this or don't do the other thing, they can't get in my game. Even Crandall can't, because he's never had that operating experience. It's a case of positioning yourself with your boss where he depends on you."

Baker's operating expertise started fortuitously. He took a high school summertime job as a "bag smasher" with United and continued summer work with airlines during college just as a job. But a conscious positioning plan took shape in graduate school at Wharton. He sought work specifically with a "ground-handling company"—the kind that does everything for nonscheduled airlines except sell tickets, fly planes and offer coffee, tea or milk—because he knew it would give him a marvelous range of experience. "At that time—'67, '68—MBAs were a glut on the market," Baker explains. "It was going to be a bad year to get a job, and I thought work experience would weigh heavily."

It did. Hired as part of a program American was then running to utilize MBAs, Baker examined the opportunity paths, decided what the company considered integral to its business, and positioned himself accordingly. His entry-level job was as freight supervisor at Newark Airport, which he describes (with restraint) as "the outpost of the world." The people running the program were taken aback that a bright-eyed MBA *wanted* to be on the line and not on staff. But starting without a recognized and prized specialty is, in effect, trying to be a boss type with nothing that peer or superior must rely on, a lamentably common error. "Most MBAs don't like the roll-up-the-sleeves fieldwork of business," says Baker. "They want to be on staff, making million-dollar decisions in thirty days. There's a very negative reaction to this approach within American—and within industry in general." The proof is that Baker is the only MBA left at American from the program. But he has flourished.

It is an excellent principle. "Be the diamond in the rock pile," advises Louis Ross, VP and general manager of Tractor Operations at Ford. The drabber the background and the dimmer the competition, the brighter your own gemlike fire gleams. You need not insist on immediate transfer to Janitorial Services; just remain alert to possibilities in the most prosaic posts, if they fit a reasoned positioning plan.

Remember that Litton's William George wanted to be in general management as soon as possible and needed an early showcase for his management talents. Even so, he first positioned himself as a technical specialist; the controller's office in the Department of Defense was *his* rock pile.

There is another point to remember about choosing the right avenue for your positioning: it changes. You must constantly modify and update your perception of congruence. Have things changed in the company? Have you changed? Does your path look as promising as it did a year ago?

Dick Jackson started at the corporate level of Litton Industries as a financial analyst concentrating on acquisition studies, an expertise of first importance to Tex Thornton and everyone in control. "I was able to get high-level attention within two or three months," Jackson says. But he realized it was a dead end; he was too junior an individual performer in too senior an environment to hope for supervisory experience. "A job opened up," he says, "which meant moving from staff to a line operation—and that was really the next step for me, to be responsible for motivating and supervising other people. The way management looked at me and measured me became more vague, but it was just as important that everything I worked on be successful."

That means he had to work hard at it. Even when your positioning is perfect at each stage, the next imperative step is to work like blazes. Hard work can make up for any reasonable deficiency, and it magnifies any particular strength.

Actually, practically all the techniques for success discussed in this book are predicated on your willingness to work extraordinarily hard, and time and time again this is reflected in the words of top managers. The chairman of Pillsbury says he made up for not being awfully smart by working hard. The chairman of General Mills says no, Bill Spoor is plenty bright; it's he, James McFarland, who is only average. But he makes up for it by working hard. William George at Litton Microwave and Robert Crandall at American Airlines both admit (if pressed gently) that they *are* quite smart, but they say brains alone were not enough to make them shoot to the top at remarkably young ages. They had to work hard.

The fact is, management considers hard work a virtue in itself. "If people can do their work in half a day," says Peter Mulloney, an executive assistant at U.S. Steel, "then we should give them more work." In fact, they should ask for it, not simply take it easy the rest of the day, no matter how well they did earlier. Even good results are not enough to make up for a lack of hard work. "I don't like a guy who's a loafer, even if he performs extremely well," says Benrus chairman Victor Kiam. "I have a guy right now who'd be a world-beater if he'd work, but he's always looking to chisel on the time he puts in. He probably pays for himself, and more, as it is—but I won't keep him with the company."

There are four reasons management prizes hard work so highly. First, obviously, if you are a hard worker, management naturally sees you as the instrument of greater output—magnified, since your hard work will predictably inspire, impel or at least shame your subordinates into working harder. Certainly the odds are against getting subordinates to work hard while you loaf, which is the second reason for hard work. "You set the standards for the group you're running," says Victor Kiam. "You can't just say to them *Work!*—and sit on your ass and not do a goddamn thing." Third, since a major criterion for judging competitors is who accomplishes most, the only sensible strategy is to work as hard as you can and accomplish as much as possible. Finally, hard work broadcasts to management an enthusiasm for something they consider so engrossing they have devoted their lives to it. Conversely, disobliging grumps who will not work hard effectively proclaim that in their estimation management's life's work is not worth spending more time on than is absolutely necessary.

Of course, it pays you to recognize and display what management considers the most conclusive signs of hard work. For instance, Leonard Berlin, senior financial analyst at Exxon, has established a reputation as a particularly hard worker, in part because he routinely is at work a half hour early. "That's a big thing to my boss," says Berlin. "It doesn't matter that I leave at the regular time; getting here early shows an interest. I think that if I stayed to seven every night it would make less impression."

If this sounds merely cosmetic and manipulative, remember the issue is not your willingness to work hard, but the effectiveness with which you flaunt the genuine article. If getting in early says more about enthusiasm ("I can hardly wait") than does staying late ("I didn't get everything done") you would be foolish not to transmit the more cogent signal. Whatever it is.

You would be even more foolish not to avoid whatever are considered special telltales of indolence—even if arbitrary or downright crotchety. Alex Novak, controller of Benrus, was enlarging on what chairman Victor Kiam had said about setting an example of hard work. "It's hard to get subordinates to break their ass for you," Novak said, "if they see you with your feet up on the desk." Kiam was just out of the hospital after a back operation and his feet were up—doctor's orders to relieve strain. Senior VP for operations Nicholas Mercurio pointed sternly to the offending feet. There was a round of laughter. But almost at once down came the feet—strain on the back be damned.

You have to work hard. And it does not end when you have gotten yourself into the right position on the most probable opportunity path. It takes hard work to improve your position, and to make the most of the opportunities that come along, even though you have done well to put yourself in their way. It takes your maximum effort to continually increase your value to your company.

# 5 *Improving Your Position*

Positioning is never static. You must constantly adjust your position to advantage by upgrading personal and professional qualifications. That is not the same as getting better in your job. It involves skills, personality traits and kinds of knowledge so fundamental they may seem extraneous. So first you have to realize that certain things are important and then face up to the fact that you lack them, if you do.

For instance, you need an ability to read quickly, with good comprehension, and to write clearly with good syntax and spelling. You should have a good memory. You should survey the adequacy of such basics as vocabulary, arithmetic and handwriting. If your job involves taking a lot of notes, you should know shorthand; if you must write a lot, you should know how to type; if you have to help others visualize design concepts, you should be able to sketch. Everyone in business should know enough accounting to read a balance sheet.

You can make your own list of fundamental tools, remembering three rules: If you wonder whether any skill is important, it is; if you think you can get by with whatever skills or level of skill you have, you can't; and if you wonder if you need more, you do.

The situation with basic personality traits is identical, though more complex.

At first glance, Robert Ludwig seems an improbable candidate for leadership, a gangly and rather unprepossessing twenty-five-year-old accountant working for controller Stanley Gondek at Sara Lee. Given Gondek's emphatic views on professional competence, Ludwig's credentials are unarguable. But his manner is so slight, shy and tentative, it is hard to credit that a bluff mesomorph like Gondek would tap him as a young comer. It would be easy for people in such circumstances to tell themselves they are such whiz-bang accountants that personality factors do not *really* matter. After all, the only thing that really counts is technical excellence, isn't it? No. "I know," says Ludwig, "handling people is going to be more and more important if I'm going to get anywhere. So I'm taking a course in personnel management." He realized the importance and recognized a lack. "I'm on the quiet side and maybe that's a weakness. School is helping me bring myself out more, making me more outgoing and confident."

It is a cinch today to find help in any area of personality development, sensitivity training and the like. But you have to recognize the need for help, even when defects are deep-seated and subtle.

As illustration, Warren Anderson, executive VP of Union Carbide, started as a chemical engineer and then went into sales and marketing. While continuing to work full time he also went through law school—not to practice law but to practice a new way of thinking. "In science," says Anderson, "you're either right or wrong. After my first law exam, the professor said, 'Do you have a technical background? I was reading your exam and I thought you were sending me a telegram.' He would ask these long, complex questions, and I'd say, 'Not guilty.' You can't do that." Not in law and not in the upper reaches of responsibility and power in any business. For Anderson, law school was remedial thought training.

Recognizing such subtle needs in oneself takes extraordinary self-analysis backed by the energy and resolve to follow through. But it pays. Actually, just the blatant determination to acquire skills or correct evident drawbacks is itself one of the most convincing signs of a young comer, a plus on your record.

You must also do something about evaluating your professional qualifications for each job at each level. That may mean as little as a few extension courses or on-the-job training; it may mean much more. Early in his career, Stanley Hunt found himself supervisor of the controller's group at a General Mills chemical plant in Kankakee, Illinois—"an accounting supervisor without a real accounting background," he says. He had been made supervisor because, with a B.S. in business administration from Kentucky, he was the only college graduate in the group. "But I decided that if I was going to stay in accounting control, I'd better learn a little about accounting," Hunt says. "So I went back to Northwestern and got my master's degree." It comes in handy since he's now assistant controller of General Mills and director of corporate accounting.

Do you need any more advanced training or credentials? Often the company will help you, if only with a leave of absence. In any case, it is finally up to you to do whatever is necessary, even if it means interrupting your career to go back to school for supplementary training or an advanced degree.

Whatever particular qualifications you need, there is a general one that is essential for every boss. It is an *executive* knowledge of what your job is and how it meshes with the company. "Let's say you've got a young salesman," says Peter

Mulloney of U.S. Steel. "A customer says, 'Youngstown is giving me five dollars off on sheets.' Well, that salesman should be able to say, 'I'm sorry, we're not going to meet that,' then give the customer convincing reasons why it's unwise to take the other offer. Now you can't do that when you're brand new. But at a certain point you should have accumulated enough knowledge so that for most questions you *are* U.S. Steel in the customer's eyes. That's rare. But that's the best way young people can surface: when their management says, 'Gee, we've got someone out there who's . . . us!' "

How do you come by this deeper executive knowledge? "Be analytical and realistic," says Mary Roebling, chairman of the National State Bank of Trenton. "Figure out what makes your company successful in the economic world and what makes your department successful." You must also be aware of how those successes interrelate and what your role in them should be. It takes analysis, questioning and thought. It takes time. Above all, it takes awareness that it is necessary, which is what most people in any company lack. They are the plodders who imagine that just doing a "good job" is enough. It is not enough beyond the first few desultory promotions; it is not enough for leadership. How can you lead if you don't know where you are going? Or if you don't know what's going on when you get there?

After you have achieved an executive knowledge of your job, the final step in improving your position is to get an approximation of the same knowledge about other job areas in the company. The process is called broadening.

"A business has to try to determine what kind of potential you have for solving problems you've never been exposed to before," says Glenn White, Chrysler VP for personnel and organization. "So the basic questions for a bright young employee are 'How do I get into my background accomplishments that will make me attractive for bigger jobs and more responsibility?' and 'How do I get exposed to the kinds of problems that, if I help solve them, will make me look like a desirable commodity?' "

Both broadening and promotion can be defined as *an opportunity for further useful learning—by a demonstrated fast learner,* and the most convincing way to demonstrate fast-learning abilities is to leap into new situations, early and often, even when you are plainly in over your head. "I call it the 'risk-taking' of leadership," says General Mills chairman James McFarland. "Many people say, 'Yeah, I want to be a boss,' but they are not getting themselves positioned in different jobs. They'll say, 'I don't want to get out of the mainstream,' and all that. That's the worst decision for them to make in their lives."

The reason broadening is so important is that a prime role for the boss of anything from a section to a multinational corporation is to act as moderator. "The CEO has to be enough of a generalist to understand problems as specialists in each department present them," says Goodyear chairman Charles Pilliod, "and help them reach solutions—if by nothing else than being able to judge them on a reasonable basis. You can't possibly be an expert in all fields, but you should be fairly well versed in the main segments of your operation."

Before Pilliod became chairman, he was general manager of Goodyear's European operations. He felt his successor should be Ib Thompson, "a converted Dane" who was chief financial officer in England. But Pilliod also felt Thompson needed broadening, so he arranged intensive exposure to nearly everything. "Overnight," says Pilliod, "he became the highest paid 'trainee' in history. Under trucks inspecting tires, weekends in the factory—the works! After about three months he said to me, 'You remember saying I didn't really know what made the company tick? Well, you were right. And I don't think we should let anybody on the Policy Committee until they've had experience in other fields of the company.' "

An illuminating example of the advantages of broadening took place at an unaccustomed high level when the three executive VPs of Union Carbide—Warren Anderson, Douglas Freeman and Fred O'Mara—switched jobs in 1975.

Having spent their careers in one particular division, says Anderson, "we were two inches wide and forty-two feet deep—and that's *not* the kind of company we have. But at management committee meetings, if a subject came up like 'Should we spend three hundred million dollars to build an oliphants plant,' my fellows pushed me into the arena and said, 'Now you go sell that.' Well, I was talking to people who had not grown up in the chemical business and maybe didn't completely understand it."

And that's not all. "Before the switch," says Fred O'Mara, "you had logrolling going on. No one would really pitch against another guy's project unless we were just consumed with the feeling that this was not the right thing to do. Now, since the change—well, it's not nit-picking, but questions are raised."

In March 1975 an explosion in Belgium virtually wiped out Carbide's polyethylene-producing capability. The question was whether to rebuild or not. "Before the switch," says Anderson, "it would have been in my bailiwick because I had chemicals and Europe. I would have gotten together with our European and domestic people, tried to sort out what made best sense and presented it." But between the explosion and time for a decision, the job swap happened. O'Mara got Europe, and Freeman took over chemicals and plastics.

"Fred O'Mara had a chance to visit our facilities in Belgium, our polyethylene plants in Sweden and the U.K.," says Anderson, "to get a feel for the customers and competitors, so he began to have an opinion. Meanwhile, Doug Freeman was getting acquainted with the chemicals and plastics business, and he spent a lot of time on polyethylene. So when the subject came up in August and September, it was sort of difficult to get a word in edgewise. You began to have dialogues, not just advocates selling their positions.

"Now, there's free-flow discussion. It's turned this management committee into a much closer-knit group asking what's good for Union Carbide, not just this division or that division. Now there's much better understanding of what we do, why we do it, what the alternatives are. And when you have an understanding and acceptance, implementation is *so* much easier."

Obviously, broadening must be part of your positioning. There are just two caveats. First, you must undertake every broadening assignment wholeheartedly, not as some temporary aberration in your "real" career. You cannot hide behind what the president of Kaiser Industries calls "the cloak of professionalism." That is, you cannot go from engineering to sales with the attitude that in a pinch all will be forgiven because, gee, gang, I'm *really* an engineer. If you want to be an engineer, stay in engineering. "There are a number of people in the company," says Ford executive VP Donald Petersen, "who are somewhat in limbo because they started to wander from job to job and never really made a new commitment. As you shift into more general business positions, if you aren't able to produce well, you'd better get back into your discipline and ride it on up as far as you can."

Not that Petersen is against broadening. But it must be done right—and at the right time. The second thing to watch out for is making your move too soon.

"One thing we hear a lot when we're interviewing at schools is 'Are you interested in specialists or generalists?'" says Chrysler's Glenn White. "I think that point gets overplayed. You've got to have a specialty to reach a certain level within a company. *Then* you can think about becoming a generalist."

Still, if you want to be a boss, you must make the move in season. When you do, what sort of progression should it be? Even in a company committed to broadening, it is finally up to you, and no matter how interested they are in your success, their interest is not a patch on yours. What sort of positioning should you aim for? Analyze the broadening litany of someone who was thrust into successive new assignments by a company that is a convinced champion of programmed broadening.

"We believe in having a man responsible for a profit center at as low level as possible," says Claude Ramsey, chairman of Akzona, Inc., parent company of American Enka, among others. "This carries with it the obligation to see that young people get broad experience—in production, sales, finance, research and so forth—at a fairly young age.

"For example, we have a young fellow, thirty-four years old, running the largest division in our fiber company, doing maybe a hundred and fifty million dollars in sales this year. He worked for us one summer between college and graduate school in market research. When he finished graduate school we gave him a job as sales trainee in fibers. We put him in the New York market—the toughest. He did very well there for two or three years. We brought him to Akzona as an assistant treasurer and let him handle—completely, even including choice of the investment bankers—a sixty-million-dollar debenture issue. We let him put together the annual report that year. He did well. We had an opening for a chief financial officer in our chemical company in Chicago. Well, I'll put it another way: The chemical company president asked for him because he had been exposed to him. He ran that job for two years. Then we brought him back to fibers, made him an assistant general manager—until last year. Now he'd had experience in sales, production and finance, so at age thirty-three he was ready for this job, running a hundred-and-fifty-million-dollar business."

Maybe the details don't apply to you, but the rhythm of broadening and the general direction make sense for all people charting their own course. If your company wants to help, fine.

If the company blindly prizes the momentary efficiency of having, in place, people who "really know" their job (and know precious little else), do it anyway. It is essential. Because it puts you, all along the way, in the best position.

# III STANDING OUT—AT EVERY POINT IN YOUR CAREER

*You get to be a boss by standing out as a performer. But once you become even a first-level supervisor, your individual performance becomes less to the point; from then on you have to stand out as a boss. That is a lot harder because it turns more and more (as you get higher and higher) on the abilities of those who report to you. And they are not as good as you are—or they would be boss.*

*It is a cliché of management that superb performers sometimes fizzle as bosses because they cannot bear to let subordinates, who on their best days may not be fit to carry the boss's attaché case, do any significant portion of the group's work. Obviously such people cannot be elevated to lead bigger groups.*

*So the problem, right up the ladder, is to show how well you get things done, not as a performer but as a boss. That can be fearsomely hard to do, especially in a junior or mid-level post in a good-sized organization with little evident scope for individuality. There may be ironclad policies, rigid routines and exact Standard Operating Procedures (SOPs). What one department does may be nearly indistinguishable from what the next one does. And the results may range from ambiguous to impossible-to-measure.*

*That is not an atmosphere in which it is easy to shine, or even faintly glimmer. Yet that is increasingly the corporate atmosphere in which young executives find themselves, making it excruciatingly hard for management to tell who is the outstanding boss among a gathering of junior bosses.*

*Things you can do to make it easier, even inevitable, for them to spot your merits as a boss are the burden of the next two chapters.*

# 6 Operations: Running Your Group So You Stand Out as a Boss

Perhaps the hardest idea for bosses to get used to, as they rise, is the diminishing pertinence of their own performance. It counts for vanishingly little in how they stand out *as a boss,* and can even get in the way if they become preoccupied with performance because it is the area they know best. The danger is that they may concentrate exclusively on technical aspects of their subordinates' performance, closely monitoring and directing them, always with the lurking notion that in a pinch they can interpose their superior powers to bail them out and improve results.

The quality of performance is important, of course, and so is the boss's role as tutor. But only as background. What management looks for in a boss requires a shift in your concentration from performance to planning. Because *what* your subordinates do, even more than how they do it, is what makes you stand out as their boss.

There are three stages to your planning.

"First," says Kaiser Industries president William Roesch, "someone has to conceptualize. And you need input from people at as low a level in the organization as possible because they are most familiar with your assets, know the competitive world and see the opportunities."

Next you have to decide how to carry out the concept. You must formulate a plan of action "which," says Roesch, "you submit to rigorous analytic controls." At his level, that can mean computerized sensitivity studies and the like. But for basic analysis, common sense, a sharp pencil and long, hard thought can take the place of a computer. (Not vice versa, though. Garbage in, as they say, garbage out.)

"Finally," says Roesch, "you implement one hundred percent psychologically. Getting something *done*—getting people to cooperate, the right person to do the right thing, everybody in the right frame of mind—that's all psychological."

Let's see how each planning stage can help you run your group, at any level, so you stand out as a boss.

*"First, someone has to conceptualize."* What should your group be doing?

A group can stick to its nominal function: a bookkeeping group can keep books as assigned, an engineering design group can work on assigned projects and so on. The job being done is routine and the degree of excellence with which it is done involves only gradations of routine performance. If the books kept by group A are more accurate, neater, and more up-to-date than those of group B, boss A may be preferred over B, but he will not truly stand out and can expect promotion only for want of someone better.

Outstanding performance is on another plane. It is not routine response to tasks set by management but an aggressive and creative anticipation of needs. You must understand the company's goals, how divisional and departmental efforts fit into the overall scheme, how your group can better help achieve those efforts and those goals.

Why are you keeping the books? What do they contribute to the department's efforts and the company's goals? How could they be kept to make things easier for the people who get them after your group is done with them? Are there more useful ways of doing the job? Should some entries be added? Some deleted? The format changed?

You need help in conceptualizing your group's function. The "loneliness of command" talked about so much (especially on late-night war movies) refers to buck-stops-here responsibility for decisions; making these decisions should be a convention. At minimum, *every* sub-boss and key performer should participate; if its size is not too unwieldy, the whole group should have a say.

This approach pays off handsomely at every level. The larger the unit, the bigger the numbers and greater the leverage, the more visible the effect. The smaller the unit, the greater the novelty. Imagine the impact when it transpires that Jones, recently elevated to command of the supplies department, or Smith, head of the steno pool, have been holding seminars in how their respective services can add to the efficiency and profit of the rest of the company!

A vital ingredient in the group's conceptualizing should be priorities for the entire group and every member. "Some people," says John Bryan, Consolidated Foods chairman, "go through the day just doing their job, never realizing there are only two or three things that are *important* in this department, and they should do those first, and the very best they can. Getting them to realize that—*that's* running a department."

And if something is important, is the right person doing it? "My father," says Bryan, "once dropped by to see a competitor, the president of a meat-packing company doing something like fifty million a year in sales. One of the supervisors walked in and asked the president if he had ordered the supplies for tomorrow for his department. The president said, 'No, goddammit, I forgot about that!' and he was all mad at himself because the department couldn't work tomorrow." Of course he was right to be mad, but for another reason; that was no job for the president to assign himself. The more vital the job, the more vital that the right person has it.

Make sure that you and all your people agree on what they are supposed to be doing. Leonard Harris, director of special projects for *The New York Times,* suggests that everyone create and maintain a job-description manual. "Quite detailed," says Harris. "A person doing filing explains how he or she does that filing: under what circumstances, how often, using what systems, what kinds of headings, which of it is permanent, which is not, which is sent to corporate records, which is not. And so on."

Such manuals assure continuity through illness, vacation and job change. More important, they give both performer and boss a chance to ponder the priorities of every job in the group. "You have the opportunity," says Harris, "to look and say, 'Is it real work or make-work?' Over the years a large amount of inefficient, ineffective, uneconomical work becomes ritualized. And those people can be better utilized."

In determining priorities, keep referring to the company's goals in light of the role your group plays. Otherwise you can lavish endless time and effort on side issues, becoming engrossed in "interesting little problems."

An example of how to do it *right* is cited by Dick Jackson. Litton Microwave needed a new plant and turned main responsibility for site selection over to the director of business planning. There was a rich variety of ways to go wrong —plenty of fascinating issues that could have fogged the decision, each wonderfully distracting. What would freight costs be in various parts of the country? Labor costs? Efficiency? Start-up and training time? Learning periods? Without focus on the company's goal and his role therein, he might have endlessly submerged his group in each juicy issue. "You could get tied up in a six-month analysis of freight costs alone," says Jackson, "when all you need is to be close enough to make the right decision." (Or, as the chairman of First Boston Corporation puts it, "Any idiot can make a correct decision with *all* the facts.")

Most of the ancillary considerations argued for a site away from Litton Microwave's Minneapolis headquarters. The Atlanta area was often mentioned. Certainly the company wanted the best site possible. But the goal was not really to select a site or build a plant; it was to manufacture a product. And a major consideration had to be that it was a new and advanced product. "We'd never built it before," explains Jackson. "No one had; it was a new concept. And if the site is fifteen hundred miles away, how much time and attention are we going to be able to give it?"

By keeping the company's goal in mind, the young director of business planning could assign priorities for his study without getting bogged down in trivia. He would not spend six months on freight costs because freight costs were not the real issue. The plant was built in Minneapolis.

There is still another dimension to conceptualizing your group's role. To stand out, you should go beyond what management indicates it wants done. You need a sense of innovation. "Most managers come to a job, pick it up where it is and just keep going," says SEC chairman Roderick Hills. "They don't sit down and say to themselves, 'Here's a job. I know how my predecessor did it, but what is there about my environment, my responsibilities and the end result I am trying to achieve that suggests ways to do it better?' It is absolutely incumbent upon anyone who wants to do anything out of the ordinary to do that. Even if you're just running a maintenance crew sweeping out a building, you can do it. You can consider the procedures used to do the sweeping. Are they the most efficient? During what times of day is it best to sweep? In what area? Which people can do what functions the best? You can see if you have a good mix of people, whether they're overpaid or underpaid. You have to sit down and write out the things you think you can and should achieve."

Instead, most people take the group's mission as an immutable *given*. Management, they figure, *must* know what it wants. And surely management will *say* what it wants. To the letter.

"I was once in a plant engineering bull pen," says Louis Ross—at forty, the youngest VP at Ford (currently; Lee Iacocca made it slightly younger). The manager from Dearborn came out, and he went to the fellow in front of me and said, 'Jim, we've got a problem with accelerator pedal efforts. Go down to the line and measure a bunch of them and let me know.' Jim came back in an hour and told the big boss, "I measured ten, and the pedal efforts were two pounds each for eight of them and ten pounds for two."

"The boss said, 'Well, what was the matter with the two that had ten pounds?'

"Jim said, 'You didn't ask me that.' He was so impressed with the guy's authority, out from Dearborn, he did *exactly* what he was told to do.

"The boss said, 'My God, Jim! Go find those two cars and see what's wrong. *That's* the problem!' "

You wonder how he could miss only because it was a one-shot, individual assignment. In terms of an extended group project, it is a woefully recognizable situation. Groups drag on for years, doing exactly (and only) what they're told, the reward for which is to be told exactly what to do next time. That is also the penalty. You must jump the rut of responding dutifully to assignments and put your group aggressively in the way of what *should* be done to achieve the company's ends.

No one, certainly no book, can tell you how to innovate in your specific job. But we can isolate some general rules about how to look for opportunities and think about innovation, and then extrapolate from examples of other people's innovative operation.

The first rule is never to look at your group's operation as an activity designed simply to accomplish certain tasks. It is a service. Ask yourself what *use* what you do is, and to whom, and then how it could be more useful. Ask yourself and your group. And ask the recipients of your service.

One of the first assignments William Adams got at INA was to "update the planning manual," which was at that time studiously ignored by everyone anyway. "My approach," says Adams, "was to ask principal line managers what a planning system could do for them and then get them to help make the system useful—from *their* point of view." Suddenly the planning manual was being used. And Adams got some important attention.

"Look at any filing system," says SEC chairman Roderick Hills. "Why do people keep those papers? Generally it is only because someone told them to." While a student, Hills got a summer job as filing clerk in an aircraft plant personnel department. The system had been set up to make filing *all* information easy, with the predictable result that retrieving any of it was almost impossible. Hills determined which data would be useful in day-to-day management decisions and rearranged the system to make that *specific* information automatically retrievable. Suddenly the emphasis was no longer on storing but on using information: "To help the employment interviewers, for example," says Hills, "use the work experience in the plant to help them decide whom to hire." When Hills returned next summer, it was as assistant personnel manager.

The next rule is that innovation consists of anything at *all* better. It does not have to rival the invention of the wheel. Two examples:

Milton Glass, treasurer of Gillette, started as an assistant timekeeper and eked out his negligible salary with suggestion awards. For instance, wooden fire doors were constantly being replaced, ruined because people wheeling loads of material went through the swinging doors by pushing the heavy metal hand truck into them. His suggestion was to screw steel plates on the doors where the trucks hit them, which meant "a substantial cost saving," says Glass. "I got a nice big award for that."

When a cosmetics company needs a package for a new product, a new one is designed at great expense, then produced at even greater expense. Michel Bergerac, chairman of Revlon, is especially proud of one package that was not designed but innovated. A bottle was needed for "Jontue," and some innovator saw that if the "Charlie" bottle was turned around it looked like an entirely different package. Naturally the unit cost went way down because the same bottle was used.

The final rule is perhaps most important of all, because ignoring it scuttles any chance for innovation. You must never let "what everybody knows" stand in the way.

"When I was in product planning, I was on the Fairlane," says Louis Ross. "The issue was, should we have a two-door sedan or two different hardtop models? Two-door sedan sales were down, but nobody had ever dropped the two-door sedan. And everyone *knew* you don't have two hardtops in the same line! Well, we did a proposal for clearly different kinds of hardtops, appealing to different customers: one a fastback, the other a more formal stiff-back roof. Surveying these, sixty percent wanted the conventional model, thirty percent wanted the fastback and didn't want the other. So now we had vanilla and chocolate: a clear choice, because if they both appealed to the same market you would have sold the same number with one model. It was an unconventional idea, but we won!"

If innovation did not run counter to what everyone knows and the way things are *always* done, it would not, after all, be innovation. This does not mean that you listen to no one and ignore all advice or experience; it does mean that you question pat answers and never unquestioningly accept *any* procedure as sacrosanct. Look at everything, even while you follow SOP, and ask yourself, Is that really what we should do? Is that really the way to do it?

That is a good part of the fun and the challenge of running a group. And the opportunity—because when you innovate, by definition you have the field to yourself.

*"Next, you must formulate a plan of action which you submit to rigorous analytic controls."* This is the stage where you translate concept into a plan for action.

The idea is to avoid an activities trap, with everyone in your group busy as bees, accomplishing nothing. Back when he was an engineer at Ford, Louis Ross realized he was in that trap. An executive on an inspection tour asked him what he was doing, and Ross hauled out his list. "In that hectic plant environment," he says, "as problems came up you wrote them on a three-by-five card and started to work on them. I had maybe twelve items on the list. 'What have you done on Number One?' the guy asked. I had about thirty percent of it accomplished. He rattled off what I'd have to do to finish it. 'What about Number Two?' And when we got through I was embarrassed, because I had twelve problems I was working on, but *none* of them was I really putting to bed. I said to myself, The next time he sees me I can't be in that position. I've got twelve problems, but before I go home tonight I'm going to have problem Number One solved, no matter what happens! Because I found myself working on so many things I was becoming ineffective."

Even if you and your group do not work on problems that can be dispatched in a day, you must start with a definitive plan as to who works on what, in what order, and with what benchmarks and schedules for completion.

Once you are sure of the direction the group's efforts will take, you should have a personal and group checklist. It does not have to be elaborate. "A yellow pad's all I use," says John Bryan. When he was running Bryan Packing Company in West Point, Mississippi, he would plan the next day's activity every night. "If I was figuring out how to get the efficiency up in the slaughtering department, I'd jot down that I had to check this and that, and see about this, and so forth, so I didn't wander through the day. I still do that now with a list of what must be done tomorrow and another list of what I know I'm not going to do tomorrow but want to keep in mind. You have a new list every day."

Thomas Barnum, president of Sara Lee (one of Bryan's companies), is more precise about his checklist. Every day he draws a vertical line down the center of an 8 1/2-by-11-inch paper, then draws a horizontal line bisecting one of the halves. On the half-page he jots down the initials of everyone he wants to see, with a note reminding himself what he wants to see them about. In one of the small boxes he notes things to discuss with his secretary; in the other, phone calls to make and dictation to give.

Of course there are many interruptions. It is the nature of the boss to be interrupted, since, for the maximum amount of work to go forward, the boss must approve, direct, start, check or supervise the work of so many others. If everything had to wait until the boss was finished, the whole group might periodically be standing idle. Barnum estimates that 75 percent of his day is "responding to meetings and intrusions." That is the whole point of the list. In between times he knows what to do and in what order. It gives shape to his day and coherence to his activity. It assures that plans get carried out.

*"Finally, you implement one hundred percent psychologically."* You have to conceptualize, formulate plans and analyze them, but when you put them into action, William Roesch says, you can forget everything but the psychology of the people you must act through. Indeed, that is vital at every point.

Take the idea, discussed earlier in this chapter, of job-description manuals from each group member. To be of any value, they must be dead honest, which means that the people creating them must be sure they are not digging the graves of their own careers. The same goes for group participation in every phase of conceptualizing, innovating and planning. Why should people open up and go all out unless they can trust their boss to reward them, to protect and promote their interests? They would be foolish to expose themselves unless there is a complete sense of openness and trust. And yet the boss's ability to elicit ideas and effort is central to standing out. "When you deal with larger issues and organizations," says Ford's Donald Petersen, "there is no way one, two—or ten—people at the top are going to have all the creative ideas. So if I see people who are drawing out their organization in easy and open communication, that's the kind of people I think can move on because they're learning how to use a large organization."

Before you can expect much to happen—a flow of ideas, maximum effort and cooperation—you must create the right sort of atmosphere in your group. They *have* to trust you; there *must* be an atmosphere of openness. How do you bring it about?

First, you must be in literal contact with all members. And you must initiate the contact. "You may already have an open-door policy," says Loews Corporation president Robert Tisch, "but that isn't enough, because many people are afraid to come up to the executive floor. You must go out in the field to see them." It takes some time, especially when you have a sizable organization under your command. But the rewards are much greater than the effort. In one way you actually save time by popping into subordinates' offices. "I can courteously end the meeting just by leaving," says Akzona chairman Claude Ramsey. "Whereas if someone comes to my office, I can't just kick him out. Or if a division head comes here to Asheville, I'm going to have to spend time with him and entertain him when our business is through. I save a lot of time by going *there.*"

Just as you must initiate contact, you must initiate the spirit of open communication. If you expect your people to let you know what they are thinking, you must let them know what you are thinking and what's going on. The mock-entrepreneurial school insists people should be told only as much as they must know to do their jobs. But "their jobs" should be to contribute all they can to the group's direction, planning and performance. Some details may have to be classified, but you should reveal as much as you can about every phase of the group's operation to as many people as possible.

Certainly you should be immediately forthcoming about the outcome of what people do. They have a positive right to know that, and you should make regular progress reports— daily, if it is a project of peculiar interest or moment. Leonard Harris recalls a time when an idea for a new magazine had been worked on hard, well and enthusiastically by some of his peo-

ple, only to be dropped by *Times* management. He had to go
out of town for about five days just as the decision was made.
"I got back to some very upset people—upset because they had
never heard why the idea was dropped. Was it their fault? They
didn't know. I should have immediately made a few phone calls
saying, 'The idea isn't flying—but you did a marvelous job, Joe,
and you did a marvelous job, Sue.' "

It is also crucial that there be no tincture of fear in the
contact between you and your people, even when you are being
critical. You must criticize in a spirit of helpfulness, not chas-
tisement; improvement, not humiliation. "It's one thing to be
critical," says J. C. Penney chairman Donald Seibert, "and
another to supply instant answers. If you say, 'That's lousy;
here's what you ought to do,' next time the guy's going to ask
you first, 'What do you think I ought to do?' It's something else
to say, 'That doesn't do anything for me; what else do you think
you can do?' "

Your people should be able to answer that question—
or originate suggestions—equally fearlessly. All subordinates
should know that if they have given an issue honest thought and
effort, they will be all right, even if you reject their conclusions.
"Only the old, hard-shelled guys like me," says Union Carbide
executive VP Fred O'Mara, "can remember how it was where,
if you had an opinion, you had to have it brass-bound and
riveted because you couldn't afford to make a mistake. Today,
a guy feels free to sit with the management committee and say
his piece without getting all shook up and preparing for sixty
days. If he blows it, we don't kick him down the stairs; we pick
him up, dust him off and tell him to go back and do it over
again."

The final element in establishing the right atmosphere,
and the most convincing demonstration of your interest in your
people's best interest, is your eager dedication to pushing them
as far as possible: thrusting them into the limelight, giving them
all possible credit and exposure, promoting them—even if it

means spinning them off to other groups. It is also the best single thing you can do to stand out as a boss.

There is a paradox. Past rudimentary levels, the greater the credit for group results that goes to the boss for personal performance, the less likely that boss is to advance. Your technical competence is no longer the point once you take over a group. By putting you in charge, management says, in effect, We know how good a performer you are—now show us how good a boss you are. Suppose that through prodigies of effort virtually all your group's results came from your personal work. Because you're a whiz, the quality is superb. Even so, how can management decide if you can head a larger department? No one knows if you can produce results *through* others.

Strenuously push your people forward, taking every opportunity to thrust their accomplishments before management. "If you're looking for a way to be recognized," says Donald Seibert, "give credit to the people who are working for you. That shows you can get the results the company is looking for —but, more important, *you get them through people*. It shows you can manage."

And it is never hard for management to tell whether a boss is using his people. "It's quite revealing," says Ford's Donald Petersen, "when I go to a division for a four-hour operating review and only hear from the general manager and maybe one appointed spokesman. As contrasted to a meeting where the general manager speaks for fifteen minutes and then I hear from ten or twelve people."

The logic of the situation seems self-evident. But even at Ford, where management is not shy about saying what it wants, some people don't get the word. "I have a peer in engineering," says Stanley Kieller, "and we have been in several meetings together. When I go in, my people are present. I give the introduction, they present the facts, then I summarize. This other engineering supervisor has his people sit behind him. He presents the entire meeting. If a question arises, they do not speak. They either pass him a note with the answer or hand him the right document. I think visibility for my people pays off better. If they know I'm sincerely concerned about them getting ahead, they will make sure I get ahead."

They will also circulate the word that here is a boss worth rallying around, a message sure to attract the best subordinates. "You know how technicians talk among themselves?" says Litton Microwave's Rick Shriner. "It's like selling a product by word of mouth. You develop a reputation for how fair you've been with your people, how well you take care of them and reward them. Then you post a job and you get applicants from all over the company. Not because they want the job; they want to work for you—because, Gee! look at what happened to other people who worked for you. The word definitely goes around." The word also goes up.

So why doesn't every boss push his or her people forward? Mostly because of a fear that the group's results will suffer. Subordinates may not do as good a job as the boss would. And if some do, and are promoted out of the group, the boss may be left with people unable to produce further outstanding results.

These are not totally baseless fears. But they are offset by the advantages. Even if there is some diminution of efficiency and excellence, it will not be severe if the people you let do things are any good; and it is only temporary, until they get even better. What's more, the yeasty excitement generated by their spirit of accomplishment and reward may well make up for relative inexperience.

As for the fear that spinning off good people may cripple the group, that really should not happen. "With very rare exceptions, I don't think performance suffers," says McKinsey & Company director George Foote. "Because unless they spin these people off, there's no opportunity for the people below them to show what they can do. In fact, the people below may be less effective because they are locked behind someone who ought to move on to bigger things. So *not* spinning people off may actually work *against* the unit's performance. That's why the people who are great trainers also often seem to have the best performance, for 'some strange reason.' "

What a great parlay for standing out as a boss: turning in a great performance and turning out great performers!

# 7 *Relationships with Your Boss*

"To promote your boss is still the best philosophy in corporate life today," says American Airlines chairman Albert Casey. It also underscores the reciprocal nature of the proper relationship between any boss and a subordinate who hopes to stand out. "The people who make a manager stand out are the people who work for him," says U.S. Steel chairman Edgar Speer. *"They* promote him. All his boss does is recognize it." But you do want to make the recognition easy—indeed, inescapable.

Hook that up with the advantages of pushing your people, and you have the basis of the right relationship between you and your boss. You stand out as a boss because of your people; pushing your people and broadcasting their accomplishments celebrates your success as their boss. Just so, you are part of *your* boss's "people." You promote your boss the way your people promote you—by doing the sort of job he is eager to advertise to *his* boss. The right relationship lets him know you understand this interdependency and shows that you want to help promote him.

Start by actively seeking as much work and responsibility as possible. But it should be the right kind of work, the jobs that are hard to get done right. Until you show you can do those, your boss cannot rely on you for performance that will promote either of you. Cream puffs do not score many points for anyone. "In engineering," says Ford's Donald Petersen, "the one with the tough job is the one whose name is on the release of a new design. When you have to sign off, that's very . . . *real.* Contrast that with someone who has always done very well—but in 'development,' where you test the vehicle and improve the drive, or in writing up test specifications. Even if that person has done a beautiful job, it is not the same as someone who's gone from designing brakes to steering mechanisms to the chassis. You are bound to focus on anyone who's had to sign off and say, 'This is my work.' You find people you thought were going to be comers, but ten–twelve years later, they've still never taken on a design job. When the bullets were going by, they were always ducking."

The next step is to construct a reputation for always being right. The trick is never to make a flat statement unless you are positive. Distinguish between your opinion, however well considered, and your stark assertion of fact. Always preface the one with, "I think . . . in my opinion . . . I believe." Blazon the other with, "Now hear this!"

Of course you should virtually *always* be positive about the substance of your particular job. There will always be matters of opinion. But your boss should know that when you state facts about your group's activity, it is gospel. This means doing your homework, which should go without saying. But many high-level bosses insist that doing one's homework is by no means routine. "The risk some people run—especially MBAs just out of school," says Thomas Plaskett, senior VP at American Airlines, "is a tendency to shoot from the hip. They'll put together a plausible analysis, but when you start probing, the analysis crumbles because they haven't done more than collect data, throw in several nice tables and draw a few superficial conclusions."

Some of his people had just presented a tariff increase proposal for certain charter operations. Plaskett immediately questioned the validity of costs cited as justification for the increase. On probing, he discovered that they had asked finance for the cost of flying a plane from point A to point B. As usual, finance supplied fully allocated costs, where each plane bears a proportional share of corporate overhead. But charter operations are an "incremental utilization of the asset," Plaskett says. If the plane would otherwise be idle, the charter price can be low—indeed, must be, given competitive prices. Plaskett's people hadn't understood the figures they got; worse, they hadn't questioned them. "The data your people give you is generally accurate," Plaskett concludes, "but it's up to you to be sure that you've asked for the right data, and that you understand it." In short, you must do your homework and *know* you are right when you state facts.

The subsidiary lesson is that you must be totally forthright with your boss, as you want your subordinates to be with you. Bosses must never feel you are ever likely to snow them. "If I find any indirectness in a company president reporting to me," says Leisure Dynamics chairman Bo Polk, "there's no bonus for him. I mean if I have to find out things after the fact, or if I get a quick answer when he really didn't know. He shouldn't have a 'sales personality' with me. Keep it for the buyers."

Letting your boss know about your accomplishments is another matter. A little indirection is needed to avoid the more unattractive and counterproductive aspects of horn-blowing. Yet the issue of self-advertisement is critical, particularly at lower levels in large corporations where there may be considerable insulation between you and the boss whose recognition of your merits means most. There are four exceptionally effective techniques.

First, *selectively* send the right people copies of conclusive memos and correspondence. Restraint is everything. A blizzard of paper will soon be ignored, so you must save your shots, sending only those that signal particular triumph: superb test results, commendation from the outside, breakthroughs on a project of first importance. The test is whether intermediate bosses may want to brag about it to *their* bosses. If so, send the original with a simple, handwritten notation like, "Thought you'd want to know about this," in red ink.

Second—and more informally—keep the right people abreast of any project you know interests them by mentioning it in passing. "You catch them in the hallway," says Litton Microwave's Rick Shriner. "You know some people are pushing a project you're on, so you say, 'Hey! we made some good progress today!' And that afternoon they come down to actually *see* what you've done." That gives you immediate exposure at the best possible time, in the throes of success.

Third, increase your exposure and identification with good results by being circumspect about when, where, and with whom you share the fruits of your labors. Gary Tessitore, manager of operations cost and profit analysis in Louis Ross's group at Ford, knew there was going to be a presentation to executive VP Donald Petersen of some vital figures Tessitore's group had generated in conjunction with the finance staff. There was no argument about the figures or their implication. "This was a case where we all agreed," Tessitore says. "One of the finance staff was going to present it, or I was going to present it. And I wanted visibility with Petersen." So he arranged for it—by the simple expedient of not releasing the final figures to the finance staff ahead of time. The moral is to save your crowing for when it counts.

The fourth way of letting the boss know how well your group is doing, without seeming immodest, is something you should be doing anyway: lavishly praising the accomplishments of your subordinates. From your boss's viewpoint, "My guy, Joe, did a great job," means your group is producing good results, and since your group is your boss's group, it is welcome news. It also might be called socially acceptable personal horn-blowing, since your people's record is eventually your record. Your boss, in turn, can blow your horn a couple of levels up, thus (by the same indirection) blowing his own. Why deprive your boss of such generous pleasure? Praise your people for all that you—and they—are worth.

Another step toward convincing the boss that you are the one to rely on is to demonstrate what IBM's Edward Krieg calls "an interest in the process of management." Show concern beyond the immediate problems and results of your group. Be interested in the larger management issues that engage your boss. "For example," says Krieg, "at a sales meeting on how to attain the office's sales goals, an interested subordinate might say something like, 'I think we have too many people in this area, where the return on investment is poor; we might be better off risking some of the resource over here.' Or he says, 'I think we need more education in the new product, because I'm uncomfortable with it, and if you look at the quota board, its sales are not what they should be.' "

Most of all, display balanced executive thinking. Indefatigably search out ways to better your own group's results, but also remain alert to management implications of your efforts, to the fact that your group is not your boss's only concern.

"I've got a guy who works for me who's an excellent product manager," says M. E. ("Ted") Cushmore, marketing director of family cereal products at General Mills. "He'll always give me the recommendation best for his product. But he recognizes when what he recommends might not be optimum for my *group* of products. Something he might want to do for Cheerios might compromise the marketing plan. He'll say, 'I have some concerns about the impact on this or that brand, and if I had your job I might be a little cautious about making this move. But this has got to be my recommendation for *my* brand.' To me that shows an ability to think bigger than his current assignment. He's getting himself ready for my job."

Part of the process is seeing drawbacks in ideas that originate with the boss. You must be, on occasion, the loyal opposition. "You run a risk, as a manager, of coming off the wall, of making a decision too soon," says Thomas Plaskett. "You have to have somebody who will say, 'Now, goddammit, that's not right! You can't do that! And here's why.' You have to protect the boss from his own power. You have an obligation to keep him from making what you think is a wrong decision." It is especially important to question decisions if you essentially agree on most issues. The most dangerous yes-men are those who genuinely mean it, precluding closer examination, or reexamination, of policies and positions.

There should be a meshing of strengths between you and your boss. Just as, in your group, you orchestrate the varied strengths of your subordinates, you should figure out how your strengths can best complement your boss's.

"I worked for the president of this company for three or four years," says William George, himself now president of Litton Microwave. "And I felt one of my roles was to help make him more effective. He was an entrepreneur, a creative genius, the supersalesman. I was none of these. I was the businessman, the sound administrator, the person who could follow up on all the details and get things done. Bob was very good at getting things started, but he needed someone to follow through. If you have a weak spot and you're the boss, you want your subordinates to help you shore that up. That way you both look good!"

A final point about your boss's strengths: *Use* them! There is a natural, understandable—and disastrous—tendency to present only positive results and reports to the boss, hoping to eliminate any glitches before the quarterly report reveals them. But that effectively denies the boss timely participation and contribution; it wastes an important resource of expertise.

"I recall a district manager I had," says J. C. Penney chairman Donald Seibert. "When he came to look at my store, I knew he would be most interested in departments that were difficult to manage or had problems. If he was going to use his time effectively on a visit, he wanted to get into problem areas so he could contribute to a solution, not just look at everything that was working well. So instead of trying to think of every success story we had, I told him everything that was wrong in the store—where we had goofed or simply didn't have an answer."

Seibert remembers a lulu. His store carried heavy, fuzzy orange-colored work gloves, called "monkey-face gloves," used in nearby mills for handling hot or rough metal. A man might go through a pair a month, so they were a big seller. Unfortunately, Seibert once misread lot numbers and ordered forty-dozen boys' sizes. Penney policy was for store managers to eat their mistakes, so there were not many options. He could pray for sudden abolition of child-labor laws, hope no one noticed his peculiar enthusiasm for that item, or get help from the district manager—which he did. He is not positive who came up with the idea, but after brainstorming with the district manager, he put those gloves on sale in the women's department as "the lowest-priced garden gloves available." They sold out, and Seibert had to reorder.

"Looking back," he says, "I think what the district manager looked for was enough concern about the business to show that we were not afraid to be identified with problems as well as successes."

There is something else. Enlist a boss's participation in problems, and when they turn to successes, the boss will take a personal, keen pleasure in it and a more intimate interest in you—and your further success.

There is, though, one slight danger. In constructing the proper reciprocally helpful relationship with your boss, you may be stigmatized as the perfect sidekick. But there is an easy out. "I had made myself almost too good as Number Two," says William George, "and Tex Thornton tended to see me only as Bob Bruder's assistant. So, in effect, what I had to do to get promoted was to get my boss promoted. Which I would advise anyone. That may sound cynical, but if you want to get ahead, promote your boss."

Not cynical—just smart. It is the logical way to stand out.

# IV  STYLE

*When someone speaks of a boss's "management style," the term may mean anything from choice in neckties and office furniture to an entire business philosophy and world outlook. Cram enough meaning into a word and it becomes meaningless.*

*Yet this particular word is used so regularly (with what seems perfect assurance as to meaning) that it pays to take a look at what style really does mean, how it comes about, what its different uses are and what difference it makes—and especially how the development of a coherent style can help a boss run any size group better.*

*Quite often what is meant by "style" turns out to be a particular sort of behavior, whether the boss is generally reckoned to be a tough guy or a nice guy. Again, what do these styles mean, and what difference do they make in how a group is run?*

*Even within a commendably tight definition of style, it is a most elusive subject. No one can teach someone else style. Too much depends on totally idiosyncratic elements of personality. But by heeding what able practitioners of style have to say, and seeing how they constructed their own styles, you can get a better idea of what yours should be and how it can be molded.*

# 8 *What Is Style and How Does It Develop?*

Let's start by clearing up some of the more common misapprehensions. Style is not any one special way of dressing, speaking or behaving, or a function of any particular kind of personality. Style is not synonymous with flair or flamboyance, or a synonym for any special manner, demeanor or course of action. If you are haphazard about your person and how you go about your business, steered only by the moment's mood, style is not involved, no matter how notably gaudy your person and actions may sometimes be.

In short, most people do not have a style.

Style is an emphatic, coherent, consistent and, above all, conscious statement about yourself, the handle you offer the world; it is your trademark. In developing a style, you define the way the world should think about you and what it can expect from you.

Style must be planned or it cannot be consistent. Each aspect of appearance, speech, personality and action makes a specific contribution to the expectation you intend to arouse, so it follows that each must be calculated to enhance, not contradict or muddle, the message.

Take appearance. A man who wants his style to feature bold, dashing coups ought not to dress in dark blue serge with narrow lapels, four buttons, a Herbert Hoover collar and plain dark, narrow necktie, with his hair trimmed short; a flamboyant woman wouldn't wear bangs in front, a bun in back, with pleated skirts and white Peter Pan collars. However, those might be exactly the appearances to affect for people who decide their style should be one of stolid, almost crankily meticulous reliability.

That line of thought applies to every element of style, even the exceedingly subtle, because each does make a definite statement. The necktie a man wears says something about him, including the fact that he chose to wear one, since not wearing one also says something. A woman's hairdo—including whether or not she bothers having one—says worlds about her. How you smile, at what and when—or whether you smile at all —is an important element of style. Every choice should be conscious and considered, since neglect of any element can be just as eloquent as positive action.

"Managers consider how people take care of themselves as an indication of how they take care of clients or their work," says McKinsey & Company director George Foote. "Sometimes the two go hand in hand; sometimes they don't. Some great scientists were disheveled people." Also some of the great artists. But *none* of the great advertising account executives, bankers or brokers. It is a matter of expectation. Rationally, dress is no index of ability in any line—selling ad campaigns or bonds, painting pictures, writing sonnets or bowing fiddles. Yet we expect certain modes of dress from certain people. We might be leery of trusting our stock portfolio to a broker in scuffed shoes and frayed collar, or of trusting a portrait to a Brooks Brothers fashionplate, because with such determinedly different people we do not know what to expect.

That may be all right; cutting against the grain is dramatic and can be effective. But it is dangerous because it is apt to confuse. Unless they are part of a deliberate, all-of-a-piece style plan, the only thing exotic elements of appearance do is make the maverick stand out the wrong way—like a sore thumb.

Betty Musante is receptionist on the main executive floor of First Boston Corporation, a particularly starchy Establishment establishment. Not long ago, when visitors were trooping into a financial seminar, Musante's eyebrows went up as a young man in a maroon sport jacket passed by. When asked, she allowed that, yes, that style *was* unusual in those muted precincts. She doubted that the popinjay was of towering consequence in the local financial community—or soon would be.

By the same token, Kenneth Monfort says that if you simply do not feel comfortable out of your tweeds, vest and chaste tie, you probably are not going to like the rest of the atmosphere at Monfort of Colorado, either, and probably will not fit in.

Fitting in is the point, in the absence of a conscious decision to warn people to expect the unexpected. "If a person comes into my office these days with a brush haircut, I wonder what he's saying," says First Pennsylvania chairman John Bunting. "You immediately feel here's somebody who's angry with the way things are; he's almost overcoming me with his 'straightness.' "

Other places, other customs. William Spoor says that what hair is still evident at Pillsbury board meetings is worn pretty short, so he would presumably feel that a director with long hair was also trying to say something. In either case, the only bad effect would be if the message were inadvertent, a product of inattention to what various elements of style mean. You should mean what you say—and what everything about you says.

Furthermore, it should be a close approximation of the truth. All style does is dramatize those aspects of yourself you want to make memorable. The sum of the elements of your style is your image in the world's eye and, as John Bunting puts it, "image is the reflection of reality"—or should be. "The key is," says Gillette chairman Colman Mockler, "does a person try to be something other than what he is? Some people are naturally flamboyant, some naturally reticent. You don't hold either against them. But if people who are naturally reticent try to be flamboyant, it soon becomes apparent that they are trying to be other than they are. And there isn't much use in setting up the inner strain of constantly trying to be what you are not." So your style should be apposite to what you basically are, developing around the circumstances of your job, what you do, what your people do, how you intend to deal with them, direct and control them.

A jarring style—for example, breathless, dramatic strokes in a situation that routinely demands measured calm—will make you stand out the wrong way. It will also make you appear to be doing things the hard way. At the center of your style must be an air of easy excellence. That does not mean you must be excellent at everything you do (improbable for anyone), but that you should contrive to do mostly the things at which you *are* excellent. Your style should let you radiate assured confidence. As film director George Cukor says, "You have to know your limitations and not go into alien territory, embarking on projects that call for a style that isn't right for you. Don't compete at things where you're not sure of yourself."

John Bunting, for instance, is a master stylist. He runs to flamboyance, not avoiding publicity or controversy, an avid and accomplished public performer. But he is careful to pick his spots. "You can't be good at everything," he says, "so you have to decide what you're going to concentrate on. I don't mean you ignore everything else, but you should pay more attention to those things you do well. I continue making speeches because I am good at it and therefore it's something the institution can be proud of my doing. An institution *wants* to be proud of the person at the top. I can't make loans; I didn't come up that side of banking. If I started being a lender, I don't think they'd be proud of the loans I'd make."

The principle applies no matter what style is involved. Colman Mockler is the antithesis of Bunting, and his style matches his image of the precise, control-conscious, conservative financial man. He does not try, in fact or style, to be the soul of Gillette marketing. His institution is proud of their chairman's presence, his financial acumen, dignity, reserve and air of easy expertise; they might not be too wild about any Right Guard promotion schemes he hatched.

Having decided on an appropriate direction, sort through the various evidences of style, retaining the consistent, rejecting those that clash and confuse. All elements of appearance, manner, bearing, diction and the like should comport with whatever style you feel presents you to best advantage. For the flamboyant, there should be strokes of the unexpected; perhaps an aura of rush, pressure and excitement. Everything about you should contribute to that. For the solidly reliable, everything should bespeak reticence and reserve in the presentation, an aura of calm deliberation. It is not a question of artfully confecting false patterns of appearance and behavior, but only of emphasizing those elements that amplify what you are and what you do.

Examples abound of how the various elements blend and work; all you have to do is look for them. "Study style," says Mary Roebling, chairman of Trenton's National State Bank. "Study people you know and people on television, in movies, on the stage. Read books, periodicals. This aspect of style is like cooking. You need good and varied ingredients; then add seasoning, spice. The reach and color of your vocabulary, the clarity of your mind, the smile, the gestures, your clothes, all are factors in the effect you have on others."

She also says, "Have flair. Be excitable. Be exciting." That goes even for those whose essential style is one of solid reliability. You can make the humdrum seem an adventure to your people when your style is a perfect dramatization of your most exciting qualities. "Don't be a bore," George Cukor sums up. "You don't have to be funny; you don't have to sing and dance for everyone. Just don't be boring, don't be heavy-going." The drama of your personality, the excitement of how you feel about your work and the way you do things, these can shine through even routine and tedium; they can illuminate those around you. And that is the triumph of style.

# 9 *What Difference Does It Make?*

There are two reasons for cultivating style.

First is distinctiveness. You should develop a style for the same reason corporations spend millions to impress their trademarks on the public mind: easy and immediate recognition, memorability and differentiation. That is important at all levels. "When you're talking about people in an executive-training program," says John Bunting, "they are all about the same. But you do begin to perceive the person's total style; style has a great deal to do with it."

At the other end of the ladder, Bunting estimates that any of some four hundred First Pennsylvania executives have all the mental and professional equipment necessary to become the next chairman. "So the one who emerges," he says, "is going to emerge on the nuances." Which is another way of saying "style."

The distinctiveness of your style also helps program acceptance of your contributions, conditioning people to look to you for certain kinds of results. "One of our vice-chairmen," says Bunting, "has unusual ideas and an unusual style. His name is Nathaniel Bowditch, a Boston Bowditch, and he's the type that walks down the hall reading a book. The creative mystique he brings to a meeting creates an attentive audience for his ideas. Some people can't 'be creative' because they don't have the style that surrounds the creative person. 'They couldn't be creative,' you say; your mind just rejects the idea. Even if they 'stumble' on creative ideas, 'they're getting them somewhere.' A creative person has to have a creative style for you to accept it." When this happens, people automatically swivel around and look to that person whenever it's time for creativity.

There should be the same sort of effect with any other style—which points up why your image *must* be a reflection of reality. The last thing you want to do is excite expectations you will surely disappoint. But the right style makes your strengths more readily evident and gives you more frequent opportunities to show what indeed you can do.

The second reason to develop a style is even more important. It can influence the way your group goes about achieving its goals.

To begin with, a notable style becomes a promise. When Muhammad Ali, in his heyday, insistently proclaimed himself the greatest, his style committed him to performance beyond any that could be expected from someone with a less blatant style, someone whose modest and retiring image would allow him—maybe even induce him—to be a graceful loser (Floyd Patterson springs to mind). Ali had to go all out all the time. He could never even contemplate "honorable" defeat because his style asserted that for him there was no such thing.

Your style can do the same for you and your group. It can make failure, shortfall or dereliction so unthinkable that you and your people will flog yourselves to whatever degree of effort is needed to avoid them. Style, in effect, will keep you honest.

"A lot of people say I'm 'seeking publicity' when I say certain things," says John Bunting. "What I'm really doing is fixing myself so that I can't change." He has set up as a particular kind of person and has made his bank appear a particular kind of place. He is *the* heretic of American banking, leader of a liberal, socially conscious, open and heterodox corporation. He is stuck with a notable style—personal and corporate—which is exactly what he wants. It keeps them all to the mark.

"For instance," he says, "we've said a lot of things about what we're going to do in the black community. So if Bunting doesn't do these things, he *really* is a phony, and the whole world can see it. So I don't mind people who say they're going to do this and that; they're exposing themselves, putting themselves on the line."

It is not only a matter of the boss's personal commitment's being riveted by style. That style (especially if it is strong, clearly defined and emphatic) informs the doings and attitudes of the whole group. "A lot of people say, 'Nobody really runs a company,'" says David Fausch, Gillette's VP for corporate relations. "I thought that too, when I was still with *Business Week*. But I can see now, being on the inside, that people do indeed run companies. Mockler is running this company—by example, by directive, by communication." In short, by style. And if a boss can exert practical moral influence on a multinational corporation, it is surely possible on a more modest scale. In fact, the influence of the boss's style is curiously amplified by a sort of reverberation. Setting the group's tone by example, the boss helps mold the group's style; soon "that's the way we do things here." That group esprit affects all current members and attracts and instructs new members; it then may become emphatic enough to play back to the boss, reinforcing that personal style, shaping future actions and decisions, even dictating the style of any new leader.

As a boss, your style has a further effect. The more notable it is, and the more recognized you are for it, the better pleased your people are. It is an intracompany version of the psychological income one gets from working for a well-known company. Your celebrity fosters a coterie feeling among your subordinates. They are proud to work for you. Maybe they affect amusement at your style, especially if it is flamboyant— "Oh, the boss always carries on like that!"—but they're proud, nonetheless, because the boss is *known* and so, therefore, are they. Their pride and pleasure are functions of your style, of your doing the things you can do best and taking care to do them in as consistently dramatic and memorable a way as possible. When the boss on any level has style, that élan and spirit of bravura performance rub off on the least naturally inspired. There is engendered a feeling of self-expectation. "We are Joe's group, and we always do the best work on the floor." And, in general, "Our team is red hot!"—a self-fulfilling prophesy that ignites them into an elite group of voluble over-achievers.

One of the most general and worrisome questions of style can be summed up as "tough guy versus nice guy." One or the other is superimposed on whatever other style a boss adopts, and the vexation comes because the words "tough" and "nice" are popularly used as though they were polar and mutu-ally exclusive quantities and as though a choice automatically has to be made to be one or the other.

As a result, each word has developed two distinct mean-ings, one pejorative and one favorable. Which definition you get in an impromptu word-association quiz depends on the particu-lar boss's self-image. Those who instinctively consider them-selves tough immediately take "nice" to mean soft, a pushover, a courter of popularity—not widely admired attributes.

Ralph Anspach is a professor of economics at San Fran-cisco State University. He constructed a board game, a parody of "Monopoly" he called "Anti-Monopoly," which soon be-came a modest underground sensation. He and his wife, Ruth, formed a corporation to make and market the game, the officers being friends and associates. Within a few months a couple of "friends" tried to gain control of the corporation and push Anspach out. Up to then Anspach had run the company as a total participatory democracy, in the collegial style of manage-ment. Afterward he developed a different management theory. "First," he says, "you establish your authority, *then* be a nice guy." Ruth Anspach adds, "They thought Ralph was such a nice guy they might as well take over the business!"

Of course, that sort of thing is not really niceness. It is weakness, a disinclination to step in and assert oneself. Sometimes it results from lack of confidence; sometimes (as in Anspach's case) from a mistaken notion that a boss must never impose in any way lest subordinates be stifled. But it does subordinates no favor to let them go undirected. "The nice-guy boss doesn't want to get involved with problems," says Stanley Gondek, controller of Sara Lee. "That's the 'anything-you-want-to-do-go-right-ahead' type who wants to be a nice guy and say, 'You handle it; anything you do is OK with me.' That's not being fair to people. You've got to give them direction."

Gondek once saw the results of the wrong kind of niceness in his own company. The manager of new-product development was supposed to direct the confection of items to maintain Sara Lee's leadership. But according to Gondek, "He completely let his staff go, letting them 'be creative.' " Without direction, the staff's creativity did not flow in useful channels or contemplate the realities of commercial production. If there was time free on machinery suited only to producing coffee cakes, sure as little green apple tarts the staff developed a new dessert cake. It might be sensational, a creative triumph, but it was unproducible. The manager soon had to leave. That permissive sort of nice-guyism is an inevitable disaster, which is why Gondek concludes, "I think the 'nice guy' just doesn't get involved in his responsibilities."

But "nice" can have another meaning. It can involve what most bosses call "people skills"—being sensitive and respecting one's subordinates, their wants, needs, goals and ambitions. Once it is clear that this second, favorable definition is meant, even those bosses who had instantly assumed that "nice" means "weak" freely admit the other sort of niceness is essential.

There are also two distinct meanings for "tough." Those with a more elaborate concern for people skills assume, when asked if they are tough bosses, that you mean being feared, domineering and harsh, exacting performance through intimidation. They instantly deny what they consider an accusation. At the same time they tell you that, unlike the pejorative kind of niceness, the intimidating kind of toughness can work. "You can be a boss by fear," says William Bernbach, founder of Doyle Dane Bernbach. "You *can* be effective by purveying fear because a worker has a family to feed and to survive he has to take a lot of things he hates taking. But another kind of boss says, 'I don't want my people to do things out of fear of me; I want them to do things because I've inspired them and because they understand.' Well, both kinds of boss may get the job done."

True. But the consensus is that the harsh, grinding kind of toughness does not work as well or as long—for perfectly sensible reasons. If people perform mostly because they are terrified by the consequences of not performing, whether these be dismissal or vicious hectoring from the boss, the most they can be expected to deliver is whatever minimum is enough to escape the boss's wrath. It is not the ideal atmosphere for advanced performance, because as the pressure of fear diminishes, so will effort. And it is not only that when the cat's away the mice play; even under direct, baleful glare they probably do not work as well as they might. "People don't function well when they run scared," says Goodyear chairman Charles Pilliod. "You don't get the best out of them. You can needle them, you can push them, but you don't threaten. I know it's done by some of our people, but I don't go for it. If people are running scared, they're not going to make the right decisions. They'll make decisions to please the boss rather than recommend what has to be done."

Given a chance, employees will not put up with such an atmosphere. And corporate management knows it. "That kind of harsh toughness," says General Motors public relations man

James Williams, "seems to be a thing that's going away in GM."

"I think it's going away in *all* business," says Chevrolet general manager Robert Lund. "I don't think there's a place for that kind of toughness. I'll tell you: That's one of the things that brought about unions. People used to say, 'Goddammit! Do it because I say so, period!' That's an old-fashioned, outmoded approach to getting things done."

Chronic employee fear has another drawback. The harshness that produces it contains a built-in, self-defeating, desensitizing factor. After acute terror passes, people register only a debilitating ache of resentment and humiliation. They no longer really hear the screaming, which makes it tough to get their attention when the boss is truly and justly exercised. "I worked for Attila the Hun once," says Thomas Plaskett of American Airlines. "If he didn't fire you twice a day you thought something was wrong; he didn't love you any more. Well, that constant hammering and badgering, the dogmatic, traumatic tirades lost their effectiveness. You never really knew if the guy meant it or not. It is much more effective to save anger."

Much more. Carefully husbanded anger is awesome and explosive when it does erupt, expressly because it is a rare commodity. For instance, Consolidated Foods chairman John Bryan has a soft voice, mellifluous southern accent and virtually no temper. "If I let out with some expletives and screamed at people," he says, "they'd faint." But when they came to, they'd hop!

So not even on the count of effectiveness is harsh toughness a useful style. But remember that "tough" can mean something other than harsh. It can apply to the boss who is stern, even very demanding, but fair. And the fact is that no one outside of a family business will go beyond the first few levels of authority without that kind of toughness. It means being implacable in your demand for excellence, in setting and attaining goals, while adamantly refusing to brook the slightest lapse from honest effort.

Nothing in that definition argues harshness. There is no necessity even in the most resolute and demanding kind of toughness for doomsday threats, nastiness or fear, nothing to occasion that breeder of emotional sabotage, resentment. Your tough-minded demand that everyone in your group strive for the best possible performance and results, should be coupled with a sharp concern and respect for their dignity, human failings and human feelings. They can feel good about coming to work and about their day-to-day contact with you, yet at the same time know that under no circumstances will you accept less from them than their best and that if they give you cause you can be the wrath of God.

With the right kind of people-sensitive niceness, the outward manifestations of toughness do not matter much. What counts is the level of sensitivity, not the decibels. "I'm a hollerer and a screamer," admits Savin Business Machines chairman Paul Charlap. "I'll say, 'Goddammit, Max'—and pound the table—'how can you be so dumb! You didn't get that done. How in the hell!' But he knows I love him. That's the difference; they all know I love them."

Of course, as an entrepreneurial and charismatic type, Charlap has more leeway than most corporate managers. But for all the hollering and table-pounding that are an inextricable part of his style, he firmly believes in blending sensitivity with toughness.

"We all have to get our jobs done right," he says. "If that's being a tough boss, then I'm a tough boss. There is no excuse for being mean, unpleasant, or making people feel demeaned. But that doesn't mean I don't want performance from them. I have a level of expectation, and I expect everybody around me to perform at that level. Nice guy? Hey! Everybody's a nice guy to the people who perform. And the ones who don't perform, and give you excuses . . ." He gives a small shrug of dismissal.

The essence of style is having people know what to expect from you, and letting them know what you expect from them.

# V HANDLING THE COMPETITION

*That does not mean the company's competition, but yours.*

*In a sense, of course, it is what this entire book is about. You want to be the kind of better boss who gets to be a bigger boss, and everything you do to become better affects your competitive position; it is all "handling the competition." But indirectly. There is a much more blatant, head-to-head interplay between you and others bucking for, roughly, the same promotions. What should your attitude be toward them?*

*Certainly the more obvious kind of backstabbing is today considered infra dig—also downright dangerous. Management does not like it, and neither do competitors, who are apt to stab back.*

*So you must find ways to handle your competitors that they will approve of—and yet, at the same time, will convince management that you, and not they, are the one.*

# 10 *With Enemies Like This, Who Needs Friends?*

It is no surprise that competition gets stiffer as you go up the ladder; the news is that it is getting tough at descendingly lower levels.

The post–World War II baby boom is now stuffed into companies at an age to compete for important posts. And that is counting just WASP males. Add minorities and women, both newly qualified in significant numbers as competition, and you have the makings of a downright fearsome competitive situation. We are already to the point where an MBA is nearly an essential ticket for the fast track.

All of which helps explain why "the Competition" is the only subject that finds people at the top less than immediately candid and forthcoming. You have to probe and press for them to admit that anyone ever thinks about it in their organizations. They routinely dismiss its importance, perhaps figuring that if no one talks about it, it will go away, and they assure us that it really is not *worth* thinking about. Just do your job, they say, and don't worry about the competition.

Fat chance. You cannot blink the fact of competition or ignore its relevance to your progress. Nor is there any reason you should try. The only thing that makes top bosses nervous is the vision of competition run amok, with people dwelling not on doing their jobs but on *doing* their competitors. But nothing in the idea of competition compels or even implies such behavior.

What triggers management fears and has given competition a bad name is the large and ever-growing body of literature on the how-to-succeed theme—some pretending to seriousness, others more frankly light entertainment, but all celebrating silly gamesmanship, power ploys, Byzantine cabals and intrigues as being what competition is all about.

It is not. Forget morality; in the real world, the kind of competitiveness that features anything from strategic noncooperation to active backstabbing simply does not work. Whoever attempts it must assume that the people watching and judging competitors are credulous fools who will not notice what is going on—or, noticing, will anyway elevate someone who has proven to be ruthless, untrustworthy and, maybe worst of all, heedless of the group's results. Because remember that if A sabotages B's work, the record of their mutual boss also suffers, since it is the sum of A's *and* B's work.

Furthermore, the gambits of destructive competition are so obvious, in all the worse senses of the word, that no one is fooled. For instance, a paramount feature of the sillier how-to-succeed literature is "advice" on how to assume the trappings of power—the slightly bigger office, the better location, the extra stick of furniture—with the thought that Mr. Big will be impressed and give the usurper that power whose accountrements are merely being affected. Nonsense. "People play tricks on themselves," says Herbert Patterson. "I remember in the Chase Bank training program there was one telephone for two desks, carefully placed with two legs on one desk and two on the other. There were always some people who would pull the telephone over on *their* desk, as if they had their own telephone. Those people never really succeed because they delude themselves that the appearance of superiority means something, that status can be achieved by moving a telephone six inches. That kind of thinking ruins you, God knows, with your competitors but also with the bosses because it's a pettiness they won't put up with."

Of course not. It is only in fiction (of one sort or another) that such foolishness works. No one whose opinion counts will be awed because someone has euchred the office manager out of an extra chair or a slightly wider bookcase. They *know* an individual's status because they review that individual's results.

So management ill ease with the notion of competition is a triumph of myth over reality. The trouble is that enough has been written and said about how-to-succeed so that the more impressionable are tempted to try such shenanigans. It does not do them any good, but it has soured management on letting people even being aware of competition as a fact of life. Too bad. Because, as we'll see, the right way to handle the competition helps get the job done *better.* And true competition is a positive good. "I think a certain amount of competitiveness at all levels brings out the best in people," says Herbert Patterson, whose disdain is only for the gimmicky sort. In his own career he emerged as president of the Chase Manhattan Bank from a top-level competition with two other candidates. "In a training program, or up the ladder," he says, "a little competition, at least knowing you have competition, is a very healthy thing. It's only when you *concentrate* on the competition that your efforts suffer."

By "concentrate," Patterson means worry over how well someone else is doing the job compared to you, concentration on the processes of promotion rather than the job itself. That is the sort of thing that induces one to fight the competition, which is exactly the wrong thing to do.

The right thing is to cooperate with the competition. In fact, to co-opt competitors!

"My handling of the competition," says Litton Microwave's William George, "was always to marry them, to work with them and to cooperate. If you support me and I support you, we'll both get our jobs done a lot better. If I'm trying to make you look bad, inevitably I'm going to look bad too because the company will suffer."

Whenever possible, go beyond mere cooperation. Handling the competition also means aggressively bringing into the planning and execution of your group's most important projects whomever you peg as your most formidable competition. If they're that good, why not get them working *for* you?

It's a hard sell. There is something unsettling in the idea of asking one's toughest competitor to contribute to pet projects. It seems like asking for help—and polishing his halo. Still, it is best. "You certainly think about the fact that one of your competition has done a bang-up job," says Ford's Stanley Kieller. "But your task is to get the job done, and if it takes going to that fellow, why not use him? If he has some super-magic, I want to know what it is."

Using competing superstars does a number of things. With such superior help, your projects flourish, showing that you can enlist and coordinate the best talents available. The chairman cannot claim more. In addition, you are associated in everyone's mind with the superstars, including their minds. Soon you are identified as part of what's known as the "power coalition," the people with real clout at every level in an organization. And your access to the power coalition is the surest road to shining results for any project.

"When we introduced the Trac II razor," says Gillette's Donald Port, "we had to get the cost as low as possible. That was my assignment, specifically, so I put together a committee. We entertained all ideas for reducing costs, then identified a person responsible for investigating and reporting results on each." Port knew he would have to rely on peers whose compliance he could not command, and on people in other groups with whom he would not even be in touch.

"That's why," he says, "I had a representative with what I considered sufficient horsepower from each of the organizations involved: R and D, corporate engineering, manufacturing and marketing. I pulled the committee together at least quarterly to review progress and, on occasion, rather pointedly suggest that 'there are some things we're waiting for from your organization which haven't materialized yet.' A little peer pressure worked quite well!"

The program was a stunning success—a success Port necessarily shared with his competition, but as their ad hoc leader. And it was a degree of success he could not have thought to attain alone or by diktat, even if he'd had more paper authority. He handled the competition by helping them help him look good, a strategy that propelled him into the chairman's office as project manager.

Despite the spirit of cooperation and co-option of the competition that should prevail, there are some areas in which you should act on your own, to your own ends and for your own benefit.

It is not a matter of hostility or sabotage. But some successes need not and should not be shared. Recall the young manager at Ford, Gary Tessitore, who in chapter 7 explained the timing and reasoning of his decision to withhold the results of his group's efforts in order to assure his role in an important meeting. That is an example of perfectly legitimate suspension of total, all-out cooperation. Cooperation does not mean, ever, that you have to give away the store. But there is a right and a wrong kind of noncooperation, with often a thin line between them.

The *wrong* kind is epitomized by the dread word "politics," which instantly sets management teeth on edge. "The boss should make it clear that almost anything—other than dishonesty, of course—will be tolerated except office politics," says Akzona chairman Claude Ramsey. "If this becomes known in the organization, then those who might be inclined toward being political may not develop that way. If a young man shows that first bit of flair for being a politician, and if he's slapped down very hard, he gets the message."

The reason for Ramsey's vehemence is that politics embodies the worst aspect of competition, with total concentration on the processes of promotion (or, more often, blocking another's promotion) rather than the job at hand.

For example, three group heads, Tom, Dick and Harriet, meet with the department head to decide on a plan of action. Harriet makes a proposal. Instantly, Tom criticizes the plan—not on its merits, but because he knows the boss hates Harriet's guts. Dick, on the other hand, immediately springs to the defense of Harriet's plan. He gives its merits no more thought than does Tom. But Dick figures Tom is his real competition, whereas Harriet is not in the running, so it is safe to support her plan and may cause Tom to lose a round.

That's politics.

So are logrolling (I'll support your pet project if you'll support mine; I'll talk up your department if you'll talk up mine), combinations to stop a front-runner, automatically siding with friends and against enemies, decision by cabal, promotion by personality, backbiting a competitor—and lamentably many other permutations. All reduce to a subordination of the job to whatever are apprehended as the "smart" steps to promotion.

If you are the object or victim of politics, confront the politickers and see what can be worked out. If they won't listen to reason, appeal the issues to management in terms of the effect politics is having on the quality of the job. Not, notice, "They're ganging up on me"; nobody likes even a justified whiner. If your concentration is obviously on the job, and your dismay is not at your personal disadvantage but at the adverse effect politics may have on results, your complaint will do you credit—and do the politickers in.

Naturally, you should avoid politics yourself. But that does not mean you must automatically avoid all combinations and alliances under all circumstances. Some alliances may even be essential, the only likely measures against depredations of a competitor who is the overenthusiastic partisan of his own interests.

"It's teaming up with a couple of other managers because we don't like something the guy over there's doing," says Litton Microwave's Rick Shriner. "A for-instance, recently, was over facilities. We're building a new one, and one fellow was trying to grab more than his share of the new labs. Well, the other two department heads and I said, 'Hey! We just can't let him do that!' So we started in on him. It was one of those things: a little jockeying for space. You can justify it because you're trying to do the best for your people."

Notice, it was *not* a cabal to ruin some fast-comer whose performance looked otherwise unstoppable; it had nothing to do with performance or promotion. The alliance was only to stop someone from getting more than a fair share, to stop an act, not a person.

Other alliances may have the color of politics, but really are not political in any pejorative sense. "Sometimes you hear that certain people have cliques they pull along with them," says Ford VP Louis Ross. "Another view might be that they have found two or three key performers and they naturally bring them along. You could view that as politics. On the other hand, you could view it as senior executives wanting to use proven expertise."

In the New York Police Department, we are reminded by American Airlines senior VP Robert Crandall, that kind of thing is called "the rabbi system." Every promising young cop hopes to find a superior officer who will appreciate his work and be his "rabbi"—his confessor, protector, press agent, looker-out-for, general support, guide and (in some sense) promoter. If the relationship is based on something other than performance, it is political and pernicious. But if a higher-up is impressed with your performance and potential, is interested in your future and makes you a protégé, it is simply an interlevel version of the power coalition. People *should* rely on people they know are competent.

John Knutson, for instance, is back in Detroit after five successful years at a Chrysler facility in Mexico. A number of his superiors in Mexico are also back in Detroit and are in quite high positions in the company. He had a chance to work with those people on a much more intimate basis in Mexico because the size of the operation was so much smaller. "I haven't gone around asking these people," Knutson says, "but they've seen what I've done and presumably have an evaluation. So if I do have promotion possibility, they can put in a good word. You can't do much about it, except do what you're doing as well as possible so you don't trip yourself up." Or let down your rabbi.

In other words, no star will let you hitch your wagon on if you're a drag. That applies equally to superiors and to peers, your fellow members of the power coalition. But if you are doing a good job you are a welcome addition, a consort and ally. You handle the competition best the same way you handle superiors best: by a mutual interdependence that invites and rewards them for helping you look good. It follows that your most valuable ally is your toughest competitor. Hence the title of this chapter.

# VI CONTROL

*When you were an individual performer it was easy. You kept on top of your work, and as soon as you spotted something going wrong, you fixed it. Control is the method used to end up with good results despite Murphy's Law. The trick is to spot glitches before they cause real trouble.*

*As soon as you become a boss, you start to lose control. You are necessarily at a remove from where trouble must be spotted. The bigger the boss, the greater the remove. And so you must institute some systematic way to be sure that you will be aware of things going wrong in time to do something about it.*

*The question is what sort of control you should exercise. Should it be loose control or tight control? What's the difference between them in effectiveness, both in attaining the results you want and in the effect on subordinates? How can you tell what kind of results to expect, and how can you measure the people who are getting the results for you?*

*A classic problem for any boss is "letting go"— allowing subordinates who cannot do the job as well to go ahead and do it anyway. Yet, as we've seen, being able to let go is an absolute requirement for rising as a boss.*

*In the next three chapters we'll see how control lets you eat your cake and have it, too—letting go of means while still shaping ends.*

## 11 *The Whats, Hows, Whys and Whens of Tight vs. Loose Control*

"First of all," says Edgar Speer when asked how anyone can control an outfit the size of U.S. Steel, "you don't even try to control how people do their jobs. There's no way to do that, furthermore no purpose. Everyone does the job a different way, and they all want to show how well they can do it their way. The function of a supervisor is to analyze results, rather than try to control how the job is done."

As boss, you can urge upon subordinates what you consider better ways of doing things; you can help sub-bosses plan and supervise their own subordinates' performance. But finally you must let individuals do what they do the best way they can. Nothing else makes sense. "Even if you start out with all good people," says Loews Corporation president Robert Tisch, "unless a company head—or a section head—lets them 'do their own thing,' use their own minds, he's not going to get the most out of them." Nor out of himself, since when he ties them down to doing things his way, he ties himself up making sure it *is* his way.

That sort of trouble can develop when a boss confuses ends with means. "Differentiate in your own mind," advises National State Bank chairman Mary Roebling, "between basic policy—key directives—and detailed statements which amplify basic policy. If you design policy in great detail and forbid your employees to tamper with your pronouncements, then your company will not have nearly the range of brainpower, creativity, energy and spirit needed to breathe life into basic policy."

Still, there is a choice between tight and loose control.

And there are some questions. Under what circumstances is each better? How do you effect whichever kind of control you elect? To start with, what is the difference between tight and loose control?

"Tight control," says Gillette treasurer Milton Glass, "is where my boss says to me, 'Let's review what you have to do in order to perform your function, and decide what's required in the way of staffing, support services and so forth. Then you'll implement that.' That's a system of direct, tight control: supervisor to employee to sub-employees."

How the job is done is still left up to the individual, but at each stage there is detailed supervisory agreement on what elements will be involved in doing the job. The overall goal is fragmented into a congeries of way-station goals, making the later control stages of monitoring and rating progress both easier and more detailed.

"The other system," says Glass, "is to say to me, 'The company has certain goals toward which your function is expected to contribute. I am going to impose a budgetary control over your costs, and you must decide how to spend that money to achieve the stated goals.' "

Cost is not the only key. The "budget" can be anything —time, personnel, resources—or it can simply be an inflexible goal. In any case, the mix of resources to achieve the goal is totally up to the individual with line responsibility. Since there is no supervision or prior agreement on intermediate steps, loose control can work only under some compulsion. It need not be Draconian: "Meet the goal or you're fired." It can be as mild as "Meet the goal or we'll institute tighter control."

Now, which system is better, and when?

"Tight control," points out Leisure Dynamics chairman Bo Polk (who favors the other system whenever possible), "makes up for deficiencies in people." Since sub-bosses and workers under loose control have greater autonomy in selecting steps toward goals, they must be of a high mental and technical caliber. Otherwise, the boss does well to keep a tighter rein on planning and establish more checkpoints for keeping tabs on progress.

The same is true in situations where imagination and initiative are positive drawbacks. "With tight control," Bo Polk continues, "there's never confusion about orders or authority. And where the environment doesn't change much, tight control is very efficient because you don't have the guy sitting there thinking, Should I do this, this, or that? You know you want him to do *that.*"

An offshoot of efficiency—reassurance—is also maximum with tight control and is called for when people are undertaking new kinds of jobs, when they are under exemplary pressure because a project is crucial, or when things are going wrong. "At those times some people very much *seek* tight control while they're trying to work out the problem," says Leonard Harris, special projects director of *The New York Times,* who also prefers loose control but recognizes the occasions and need for the other. "They give you signals as to the amount of input and guidance they require from you by posing all the different ways they might go, by questioning decisions or being unable to make decisions, and by the way they keep you overinformed and overinvolved."

The advantages of loose control are reciprocal to those of tight control. Just as tight control makes up for the deficiencies of your people, loose control exercises and develops their strengths. The looser the control, the more room for development. The need to meet a firm goal while under strict budgetary control of some sort ("You have only two weeks"; "You can use only people in your immediate section"; "You can use all the people and resources you want—as long as the time charges don't exceed x dollars," etc.), and to meet the goal, within budget, with methods of their own devising—all that is wonderfully stimulating for your subordinates' ingenuity, imagination and *self*-development.

At the same time it frees you, as boss, for personal development and the exercise of ingenuity. It lets you make the most of your own time and talents. If you are intimately involved with the minutia of your subordinates' decision-making, if you have to stay on top of the situation and monitor progress day to day, it follows that you can do less yourself and supervise fewer people. "Whereas with the other system," says Milton Glass, "you can have more people reporting to you because once you've identified goals, you can work independently of your people." In fact, everyone involved can get more done, in some rather surprising ways.

When Michel Bergerac was lured away from ITT–Europe to take over at Revlon, *Fortune* reported some apprehensions. Bergerac was widely considered a charming, friendly and immensely popular man; even so . . . tight ITT controls! What a blow to a freewheeling, creative marketing organization! The people at Revlon were said to be trembling.

A few months later *Fortune* sounded the all clear. Bergerac was quoted as saying, "You can improve a company to death," and he intended not to have that happen at Revlon. Sighs of relief were said to echo the flouncy French Regency halls.

Only one thing wrong: The report was based on a totally erroneous notion. In fact, the first thing Bergerac did when he took over from Charles Revson was to abandon the *truly* tight, autocratic control of the entrepreneur who has a finger in every pie, and institute—surprise!—ITT-type budgetary controls. The difference was that they were minus Harold Geneen's peculiarly sour abrasiveness. It was simply a difference in style, Bergerac's being light, Gallic and charming. But all the control elements were there.

They included, says Bergerac, "good solid accounting practices that gave us an accurate idea of our money position," And "the ratio between people, materials and sales volume, starting with an accurate census of how many people were employed and where they were." ("It is amazing," Bergerac says with disgusted awe, "how many companies actually do not know how many people work for them!") Suddenly, every department head knew how much it cost to add one person—and, significantly, how much it saved to subtract one.

Almost immediately Bergerac established the first budgetary control. He gathered his manufacturing people and decreed an across-the-board 5 percent cut of inventories. "When they stopped fainting," he says, "they found it was perfectly possible." Overnight, department heads found themselves registering 5-to-6-percent windfall profit increases on financial controls alone.

The same principles of control were carried over from finance to operations: Set a goal and let people attain it without hovering over them, keeping secrets from them or stifling them.

The result was that profits at Revlon soared while, as Bergerac says with pardonable overstatement, "the other cosmetic firms would be broke except for being purchased by the big drug companies."

The surprising lesson about such loose budgetary control is how it serves operational freedom, even creativity, a point routinely overlooked. When Revlon introduced "Jontue," a cologne with atomizer attachment, they spent some $2.5 million on promotion. In the old days a tenth of that would have been thought generous. "But when you have a sound financial structure," says Bergerac, "you can afford more money and to take more risk without going bust if it does not work out. You can have a group of people playing around with innovative ideas, and if they do not come up with anything, it won't hurt you."

It is the same at all levels. Fiscal health of the entire organization allows flexibility in programs, venturesome attempts to use people to better advantage, imaginative and far-seeing excursions from the daily churning-out and hawking of the main-line product. You can take chances with people and treasure only if you are secure. That goes for the conditions of work, too, as well as finances. Once any group's goals are firmly understood and on the way to accomplishment, once the basic mission is well in hand, supervisors at each level have time and talent left over for development of people, for innovation, for experimentation in technique and even for new kinds of goal-setting. With tight, rigid, step-by-step control no one has any time left for anything.

Of course, this discussion of the relative merits of tight versus loose control has assumed pure states of circumstance and personnel that plainly call for one or the other system. That is hardly ever the case. You will more likely merely *tend* toward one or the other, exerting now more control, now less, depending on how things are going and how your people are reacting to a given degree of control.

In any case, the steps you go through to institute either sort of control are identical. First, there is the setting of goals ("objectives" in current jargon), which includes input from subordinates and the mechanics of decision; then communication downward, to be sure everyone understands the agreed-upon goals; next, monitoring of progress toward the goals and of results in general; and, finally, rating of performance to upgrade the organization's quality. These steps are the substance of control and are the subject of the next two chapters.

## 12 Deciding on Goals: Communication Up, Down and Sideways

There is reason to speak of goals and not objectives. Goals are what you strive to reach eventually; objectives are intermediate points in your campaign to reach those goals. The distinction is important: in management by objectives, "management," not "objectives," is the key word.

Unfortunately, down in the trenches "going on objectives" itself often *becomes* the goal, with the result that announced individual and group "objectives" often make only a coincidental contribution to the company's goals. That happens for one of two reasons.

First, some jobs seem so intrinsically unmeasurable that the boss takes the easy way out. "It's easy to adopt the buzz words and jargon," says INA VP Harold Johnson, "so people will tell you they're on objectives but really aren't. Their objectives turn out to be 'I will do a better job doing so-and-so' or 'I will make every effort to bring in new business.' They aren't quantifiable and have no target dates." This is most often the case in such seemingly amorphous areas as design or in those, like public relations, where there is no directly attributable and readily discernible result of effort.

Second, many jobs call for specific, often repetitive, activities that seem to have no bearing on any conceivable goals. Bosses who want to go on objectives (or are told they must) then take workaday activities and declare them objectives. A secretary's instant objective is writing the usual twenty letters a day, with no more than the usual five typos, filing fifty forms, having coffee perking by nine fifteen and, maybe, smiling a lot. A sub-boss has an objective of producing two work-flow charts a week and writing fifteen job descriptions for personnel each month. And "general supervision." And so on.

For control to mean anything, it must be based on goals that make a difference to the unit's contribution to corporate goals.

Take public relations, for example. "Too often," says Chevrolet general manager Robert Lund, "public relations departments are only reporters, and to me that should be a very minor part of their function. They should be very productive, aggressive; their job is to *create* good public relations, not just report on good things that have happened to a company. You can measure what they do in terms of the impact they make on the American public or community or whatever you're working with."

But how, with impact seldom accurately measurable or attributable to specific PR activity? The temptation is to settle for "objectives" on the order of either "I will improve the company's image" or "I will turn out eighteen press releases a week."

It does not have to be that way. Perhaps effects are not always traceable, but they can always be inferred from the greater or less evident suitability of the actions taken to bring them about. If the boss of a PR department has given real thought to the contribution the group can make to company goals, the goal set for each subordinate easily falls in line. It will be not to churn out "so many press releases" but to create an appropriate kind of promotional material, featuring a relevant kind of information.

Another kind of goal might be PR activity calculated to produce effects in line with company goals. "I remember one company in Indiana," says McKinsey's George Foote, "where the public relations department had as objectives for the year that they would arrange two sit-down dinners with the CEO and each of the two senators from the state, plus similar affairs with the congressmen and the governor: small gatherings, informal settings, and so forth."

Such events might not advance the company's PR cause, but they gave it a good shot. They were also measurable goals: the dinners either did or did not happen within the year. They were the sort of goals comprehended by the original concept of "objectives." And exactly that sort of constructive goal-setting is possible for the most amorphous function (QED, since PR is no worse than first among equals when it comes to amorphousness).

The same is true at the other end of the scale, where duties seem to be too concrete—and inconsequential—to bear any objectifiable relation to goals.

Consider goals for secretaries. "I've seen it work very effectively for secretaries," says George Foote. "You sit down and say, 'What are your major responsibilities? What should they be? What's going to be the measure of performance?' One responsibility, say, is to keep the files. So you might say, 'My files are bad, I never can find anything, so one of your objectives in the next six months is to develop a filing system we can *use*. Now think about what you want me to do to help.' " In this case it does not matter what the group's goals are; your secretary's goal *must* reduce confusion and free time for everyone using the files, as well as enriching the secretary's own job by increasing responsibility and a sense of participation, since restructuring the filing system can make a huge operative contribution to the group's goals, as Roderick Hills suggested in chapter 6.

"Not," says Gillette chairman Colman Mockler, "that there's a goal written on a piece of paper and everybody says yes and goes their merry way. Part of the goal-establishment process is input from people as to what they feel is a reasonable and proper goal. It may not always be exactly as they would like to see it come out, but it should be something to which they contributed."

"Because," adds Texas Instruments founder Erik Jonsson, "nobody knows more about a job than the person who does it every day. Somebody else might have a bright idea that affects that job, but it's essential to talk to the person doing it before making drastic changes." Especially to get wholehearted cooperation.

Actually, the indicated method for deciding on goals is no different from the best process for making *any* sort of decision. It is true, as First Boston Corporation chairman George Shinn says, that "any idiot can make a correct decision with *all* the facts." But it would be equally idiotic to force a decision until one had assembled as many facts as possible in a reasonable amount of time.

"My greatest consideration in reaching decisions," says General Mills chairman James McFarland, "is marshaling facts. I'm uncomfortable feeling that something hasn't come to my attention that should be in the equation, and I have always resisted making the decision when I've had this feeling of discomfort. That doesn't mean you wait forever; I'm not talking about procrastination. But you should marshal the facts, using all major sources of input on the decision."

Plainly, the people who will carry out a decision about anything, especially their own goals, should be encouraged to contribute their input. You must be endlessly receptive to subordinates' ideas, creating an atmosphere in which they do not consider it a risk to expose their thinking to you. Ann Bontempo, PR director at Loews, says the most important aspect of communication is that "if you have an idea you want to present, it doesn't get lost; it works its way up here. If it's not acceptable, you'll be told why it's not within policy or the budget or whatever. But you're not sat on; you're not rejected in such a way that you will not try again next week."

How the boss rejects ideas is all-important. Even if the present idea is rubbish—unless you are convinced that its champion is the author of nothing, ever, but rubbish—you must patiently hear it out and then explain why and where the thinking is faulty. "You have to be willing sometimes," says Consolidated Foods chairman John Bryan, "to listen to some remarkably bad opinion. Because if you say to someone, 'That's the silliest thing I ever heard; get on out of here!'—then you'll never get anything out of that person again, and you might as well have a puppet on a string or a robot."

It is a good idea to institutionalize freedom of expression. William Spoor, for instance, holds a regular Monday morning meeting for Pillsbury general managers to "give them a forum to be heard, where they can each say what they want to about their business." As a concrete symbol that people can fearlessly tell him what they think, he has set aside what is known at Pillsbury as the "chart room," where, Spoor says, "Everyone's entitled, regardless of rank, to say whatever they want. We deal with the major issues in that room. We get very aggressive—and it's marvelous what comes out." Each participant must know there will—guaranteed!—be no comeback or reprisal for anything said in the privileged room.

Whether or not you set up a specific forum, you must discover where in your group usable ideas and opinions are most often expressed, by whom and in what form; then you must contrive to plug into the flow. Francis J. Sweeney, VP for health services and hospital director of Philadelphia's Thomas Jefferson University, one of the country's top medical schools and teaching hospitals, says, "I try to read the minutes of all the departmental staff meetings, because I find *that's* where ideas are generated and where controversy surfaces. That's where you see Jones saying to Smith, 'You don't know what you're talking about; the way to take care of those patients is . . .' You excerpt this out. You begin to get ideas this way."

Even if you cannot isolate such a clear-cut locale for the generation of ideas in your group, a thoughtful survey should identify which sorts of memos, studies and contact reports— even which lunch groups—are the most fertile sources. Then you must insert yourself into the stream. You should spot ideas and solutions where participants see only problems or contention.

That underscores the boss's best role in decision-making. If possible, you should stay moderator, arbitrator, referee and, finally, scorer rather than promulgator or dictator. You certainly retain the right to edit decisions about goals (or anything else) to make them conform with the group's mission and company's goals. But, where possible, let your subordinates' judgment prevail. "I try not to make decisions for them," says General Mills' Ted Cushmore, "and try not to override decisions. It depends on how much I disagree, and also on what the impact of a bad decision would be. If I disagree about fifty percent, but it's not going to make much difference, I'll let it go and see how it comes out. If I disagree more, or if it would be a big deal, I change it."

You have two major roles in the decision-making. The first comes when factions in your group are in conflict. In any clash of opinion or priorities you must be seen as a nonpartisan arbitrator.

Part of that role is to assure that sub-bosses are playing fair with their subordinates' point of view and that direct subordinates with competing views are both playing fair with you in the full presentation of facts that can influence decision. Insist that all alternative viewpoints surface. Only then can all parties to a dispute accede to any decision without grievance. "I first ran into a fundamental disagreement with my boss when I worked for Tom Feeney," says Ford VP Louis Ross. "It was a subjective issue, because in product planning there is no clearly right or wrong answer. So we agreed that in such situations we'd always present both views to the general manager. The recommendation would be Feeney's view. But we'd say, 'We recommend A, with the alternative of B, and here are the advantages of both. . . .' As long as my case for B was adequately expressed, that was fair enough."

Next, you must decide when the time has come to decide, when to end debate. Otherwise, the machinery of decision can grow so ponderous that when decision finally comes it may be too late to affect events. As liberally as you elicit input, you should ruthlessly limit the duration and vehemence of advocacy. "The people who succeed in this company," says Gillette VP Robert Hinman, "are those who fight hard for what they believe and then, once the decision has been made, join the team and play along without grousing."

One trouble is that people are often beglimmered by the persuasiveness of various arguments. Truly meritorious debate can go on forever. But the saving truth is that where reasonable people advance well-considered views, *any* decision is apt to be all right. What is not all right is endlessly striving for *the* decision while failing to make any.

When Ralph Anspach put down the corporate putsch described in chapter 9, the instance of the attempted takeover was a vacuum created by lack of decision. The young corporation had to decide whether the cost advantages of having their "Anti-Monopoly" games made by one manufacturer were outweighed by the danger of having a single supplier for their only line. It was not just a two-sided debate either; some of the group took positions in between. Everyone mustered telling arguments, each a miracle of persuasion, and the debate raged. Meanwhile, no games were being produced, no orders filled, and the company was headed for early extinction. That was when the dissidents made their move.

After disposing of them, Anspach made *his* move: He invoked cloture on the debate and made the decision. Any was better than none. And most decisions are like that, especially those about what goals should be set.

Once a decision is made, the next step in proper control is to be sure people who must implement the decision know exactly what is expected of them and why. "The biggest element in control," says American Airlines assistant VP Robert Baker, "is that the people who work for you understand why you want something." For example, he had asked one of his people for a list detailing six-month commitments of seven airplanes Baker used for charters; he was contemplating their use on domestic runs if the scheduling could be worked out.

"Now if I just said, 'Gimme a list of your commitments,' I'd get back a list which is no good to me," says Baker. "But I had explained that we wanted to fit these other operations into the fleet. So he brought back a spread sheet for six months that showed each airplane, because he understood why I needed the information and what I was going to do with it."

That sort of understanding is essential to the best sort of performance. It may even pay you to appoint someone near you—a secretary, perhaps—as official nag to keep reminding you, "Have you told so-and-so about such-and-such?"

Even if you remember to tell people what decisions have been made and what's needed, there is some question about how clear the message always is. "Somebody did some research," says INA VP Harold Johnson, "to show that most managers and their subordinates are off about twenty percent of the time in terms of what those subordinates understand the boss wants them to do. And when you multiply that, three or four levels down, you can find somebody working maybe totally opposite to what the organization thinks is important." It is a corporate version of that kid's game, Whispering Down the Lane, and there are ways to avoid playing.

First, remember that if everything is important, nothing is, because you have overloaded the circuits. Limit your communications and tag the ones that are of primary importance, the operational decisions. Put them on special paper, of a special color, with special mark or heading. And do not cheat; keep the distinctive format strictly for messages of moment.

Better still, make it face to face whenever possible. Not that verbal instructions or agreements are better understood (they should be followed by a written summary of agreement), but they allow real-time give and take so you can make sure that the people involved have understood. "If it's something complex," says Redactron president Evelyn Berezin, "or I'm worried about whether he understood me or not—I've had situations where I *know* a particular person has difficulty reading me —then I finish by saying, 'Now let's summarize this and see if we're all on the same wavelength.' And I let him summarize to be sure he's gotten the idea."

The process can be even more formal. Berezin gives us a perfect example of the whole range of decision-making, from solicitation of input to making sure goals are completely clear and understood. The issue was how to cut telephone costs. Before the key meeting some participants were assigned to come up with proposals.

"Then, at the meeting," she says, "there was a presentation made, and we discussed three or four ways. The plan came out of the discussion. I didn't say, 'You do this; you do something else.' You want to get the most out of those people. Therefore, it's in your best interest to try to bring out of them all the ideas and approaches they've been thinking of, and get them so they're constantly looking for ways of dealing with problems. But one thing you must do as a boss is *focus* on something. We didn't just have a vague discussion. What are we going to *do?* Is there any other information we have to get? What has to be done? And at the end I said, 'OK, let's summarize; what's the plan? Write me a memo—one page, no more, very short; just itemize what you're planning to do.' "

The goals have been set after enough input and discussion so that all the people involved can enthusiastically consider them *their* goals; they know what they are and what they must do to achieve them. All that's left is to make sure they are achieved and to determine how well.

# 13 *Monitoring and Rating: On Target or Better—or Else!*

Everything up to now is essential for exercising the best and most constructive sort of control over your group's results. Nevertheless, it brings you only to the threshold of what the uninstructed often mistake for the sum of control: arranging to know what's happening with enough detail and timeliness so you can do something about it if it is not happening right.

The mechanics of control should start with your unclogging the channels of communication upward so the important messages command your maximum attention. That means reporting by exceptions.

"The rule of exception is," says Kaiser Industries president William Roesch, "that I take to my boss, for decision, things that are different from anything I ever did before—and things of such magnitude they are obviously exceptional cases."

The corollary is that subordinates do everything else without disturbing their boss. So everything is disposed of at as low a level as possible, with minimum drain on the time and attention of higher authority at every level. Each boss and subordinate can easily agree what is exceptional and what is routine for maybe 95 percent of the subordinate's activity. For the rest, the boss sets categoric limits that can expand: "Come to me with anything involving sums over a hundred dollars" is how it starts; after a year the limit may be up to a thousand.

The principle is the same for reporting progress toward agreed-upon goals, except that here *any* shortfall in quantity, quality or schedule is defined as an exception, immediately reportable. The good news can wait. "If your people report all the good things that happen each month," says Gillette's Colman Mockler, "all the goals met or exceeded, you take up seventy-five percent of your time with good things. I'd rather take up seventy-five percent of my time on the exceptions." Because, of course, they are the things that need special attention.

Michel Bergerac established at Revlon a reporting procedure he calls "the dirty double-dozen"—the twenty-four most aged receivables, which would then be specially assigned for extraordinary collection efforts. It is a variation on exceptions reporting that can be used to clean up any area of deficiency, flagging trouble spots for the attention of your group's most able people. There is only one hitch. "You can have a man who's willing to go along with reporting by exception in just about everything," says U.S. Steel vice-chairman Heath Larry, "*except* what used to be his baby. Then there aren't any exceptions; he'll want to know everything that happens in that area." It is a natural and human tendency. It is also subversive of any exceptions-reporting system. You must make it clear to sub-bosses that they *may not* make exceptions of what should be routine transactions in their pet projects or areas that used to be their specialties. And you must rigorously ignore your own hankering after the days when you could roll up your sleeves and wrestle with some interesting little problem—that now should occupy your subordinates. It is, perhaps, a penalty of being boss that you must jealously reserve your time for doing what only the boss can do.

One of those things is a form of monitoring more searching and active than even the best exceptions-reporting system. It is not that you do not trust subordinates to report exceptions, but your perception of requirements and standards is bound to differ from theirs. What's more, exceptions are at least to some extent admissions of failure, and it is easy for the best intentioned subordinates to shade those in their own favor. So you must keep things on schedule by active monitoring.

"People are expected to minimize variances from budget," says Gillette senior financial analyst Edward Stanger, "but you can't just have a set of objectives and let them run by themselves. You require periodic reporting on progress—what variances were experienced and some explanation as to why they occurred. You keep *close* tabs on the really critical variables that would impinge on meeting objectives." That means you must figure out what possibly variable elements of your subordinates' jobs are most likely to have a decisive effect, determining what could become reportable exceptions beforehand and keeping on top of them.

Your basic tool for that is some sort of tickler file. Depending on your needs, it can be quite formal: a calendarized Rolodex with a separate card for every project, dated for action at a specific time (remember to build in enough lead time for inquiries so you can do something about shortfalls; there is not much point asking about the progress of Project X, which plainly will take at least three days to complete, the day before it is due for review upstairs). Or it may take the form of periodic review, where the first Monday of every month you go over Tom's projects; Tuesday, Dick's; Wednesday, Mary's and so on.

With long-term goals and projects, and to make sure sub-bosses are keeping on top of their subordinates' progress, your monitoring can be less structured yet no less attentive. "Around here my system is affectionately referred to as 'the piles,' " says American Airlines senior VP Thomas Plaskett. "Whenever I send any correspondence to anyone, with a question or asking them to do something, my secretary makes a copy of it. It doesn't have to be the whole thing if it's long, just enough to trigger my memory. It's dated and goes into a folder in my desk, by name, and when the opportunity presents itself —say, when we're in here of an evening—I'll say, 'let's have a look at your piles.'

"It's not intended to badger; it's to help individuals keep their hands around things. I'll ask, 'Where are you on this? When will it be done? What progress? Any problems? Anything I can do to help?' I make notes on my copy, and it stays in the folder until I'm satisfied that it's finished. Then I just throw my trigger copy away.

"We go through the piles every couple of weeks, depending on the intensity and volume of projects. I do it with the five who report directly to me. If they, in turn, have given the job to somebody in their organization, it means they have to have some system that flows up to keep them informed as to its status—because one way I judge them is how up they are on what's happening.

"Without this system, they might shuffle a job off to one of their managers or somebody on staff and lose track of it. I don't beat them up about it, but they get the message that they had better know what's going on and not just rely on one of their analysts or directors to do a job and pass information up the pipeline.

"It's a simple system, but it works. And with fifty or sixty issues going on at the same time, it's the only way I can keep track of them."

But we must not get carried away by technique. In discussing the mechanics of goal-setting and monitoring, it is important not to forget that the *reason* for control is to produce better results. You do that by getting people to do a better job or getting better people—preferably both. But to do either, you have to be able to gauge accurately the current quality of your people and the job they are doing. That calls for the establishment and application of a good rating system. Managing by objectives is a start because it gives bosses an unarguable handle on performance: a subordinate either did or did not meet the goals. Taken with loose budgetary control, going on objectives eliminates many of the less imaginative excuses such as "I didn't have enough people" and "We didn't get the support we needed." So you begin by noting how close any individual comes to accomplishing goals. But you must immediately go beyond. To improve performance and people, you need comparative benchmarks. The quality of the job, independent of its state of completion, is an essential component of rating. If Joe and Joan both met all their goals, which one did it more impressively? You must make this less precise aspect of rating as nearly objective as you can.

McKinsey & Company have an especially elaborate rating system, using a special form. They require performance evaluation after every project. Only one of four ratings is permitted: outstanding, above standard, standard, and below standard, entered as 3, 2, 1, or 0; no pluses or minuses allowed.

Five performance areas are evaluated: problem solving, client relations, managerial, communications and client development, and technical (the rater has to detail the technical skills being examined). Each of these areas is broken down into its logical elements. For example, "problem solving" requires ratings for fact-gathering and interviewing, identification and analysis of issues, and developing recommendations.

Next, the more subjective areas are rated: judgment and maturity, attitude, imagination and resourcefulness, innovativeness, and staff work. There is also a column for "other" in case the rater can think of something else. Finally there is an "overall study performance rating."

So much for the particulars. Next the rater is required to make some comprehensive conclusions, with comments to amplify and flesh out the raw rating. Raters are expected to identify "performance strengths" with suggestions for "development needs and suggested action." They are also supposed to indicate whether or not *on the basis of this particular project,* the individual has much of a future with McKinsey.

With modest adjustments you should be able to adapt such a rating sheet format to your own purposes. You can eliminate such items, if irrelevant, as "client development," adding whatever performance criteria you need: "promptness," "use of support services," "cooperation with other departments" and such like. You would then have a standardized format for your own use and that of your sub-bosses, so that everyone in the group would proceed from the same assumptions about what should be rated and everyone would be forced to evaluate essentials. Naturally, some areas are weightier than others in determining overall merit. But at least everything you feel relevant to a fair rating would be considered and accounted for.

Not that a set, formal rating sheet is an absolute must. Gordon Crosby, chairman of USLIFE, prefers to have subordinates establish the criteria for their own rating. "I would ask you," he says, "to appraise the requirements for your position. Then I'd get you to grade yourself on a scale of ten and tell me how you think you rank in each of those elements. After some discussion as to why you've graded yourself 'eight' instead of 'six,' or 'four' instead of 'seven,' I'd go through and tell you how I would grade you. This starts more discussion."

Which is the whole point. It is arguably better to arrange a standard rating format to diminish the effect of discrepancies in rating skills among sub-bosses. But what form rating takes is a negligible consideration compared to how any rating, once accomplished, is then used. The task of upgrading performance and people starts when you tell them what kind of job they're doing.

If it is anywhere from only mildly satisfactory down to awful, that is not an easy task. "Regardless of the system," says Ford's Gary Tessitore, "it comes back to the rater being able to stand up to a subordinate and say, 'I'm not satisfied with your performance.' That is an extremely uncomfortable situation, and people like to avoid it. I have given performance reviews to employees who did a poor job, and I really had to psyche myself up to do it."

Of course. Most people dislike such unpleasant confrontations, hate being the bad guy. But you must stifle your own distaste and see to it that sub-bosses are not allowed to shirk the hard yet necessary duty. Good or bad, subordinates have to be told what their rating is and why.

They also have to be told often. "There's nothing worse," says George Foote, "than telling people, 'I don't think you're doing very well.' And they say, 'Give me some examples.' And the examples have fled your mind because it's been so long ago. Or, just as bad, giving a yearly rating that's really based only on the last thirty days. Evaluations like that are not very helpful. It's much more helpful to evaluate as you go along; then someone can say, 'Yes, I can see that I did this wrong' or, 'Yes, I did that great and I'm going to do it great again, now that I understand what's wanted.' " Another part of the upgrading is to tell subordinates how high (or low) on the list they stand—by number, not name. That is, Pete is told he ranks sixteenth out of twenty-two people with comparable jobs in the department but is not told he ranks above Sam but below Susan. That eliminates the problem of personal jealousies yet is a spur to those who never before realized how slightly they are prized.

Even with larger groups, such forced ranking on a curve is possible with remarkable accuracy. Two techniques are especially useful. The first is to break up the large group into handier units of comparison (naturally you compare only like functions). "I once tried something as an experiment in Midland, Texas," says Exxon's coordinator of compensation, organization and development, Frank Gaines. "I told the chief engineer, 'Let's try ranking all your engineers out here.' He had sixty or so on his staff. So first we grouped them in five-year age brackets. Then he took the first group and I said, " 'Which one of these fellows is going the farthest?' 'That one.' 'Which isn't going to make it?' 'That one.' In about fifteen minutes, group by group, we ranked all his talent."

There is another way, equally useful for stimulating your own thinking and for forcing reluctant sub-bosses to rank their people. "At first they tell you all their people are great," says Erik Jonsson. "So you say, 'Look here, if things get tight, you'll have to make a tough decision, and I'm going to ask you to make it now. Rate your people in the order you'd lay them off if tomorrow morning you have to start laying off.' Don't worry; they'll keep their best people."

When performance has been rated and performers ranked, you are ready to do something about it. The technique to use is a personnel version of exceptions reporting. Having identified your exceptional performers, good and bad, you know where to concentrate effort to upgrade overall group performance.

Start at the bottom end.

"I call it the 'weak-link theory,' " says Thomas Plaskett.

"The manager should always be looking for the weakest individual in the group. You help him, train him, develop him, give him additional skills—all the good things. At the same time, you continue honest performance evaluations. That weak link improves—and is no longer the weak link—or you get rid of him. That process brings about an overall upgrading because there will always be a weak link." It can, in theory, continue until the surviving "weak link" is merely the least sparkling of an extraordinarily fine group.

At the other end of the scale, you can expect your special attention to the exceptionally talented to pay disproportionately handsome dividends. They will reward every bit of extra effort. "That doesn't leave too much time to worry about the people in the center," observes George Foote. "But if you really manage your exceptions—weed out your below-average and encourage your above-average—you've made a lot better use of your time than worrying too much about the people in the middle."

You do not abandon them, of course. But as we'll see in succeeding chapters, handling them involves established, ongoing programs, with little need for special attention.

There is a last point about control. Those "weak links" whom the rating system exposes as chronically and irremediably wanting, who defy all help and instruction, must be fired.

It should be done the right way. Because it is so distasteful a task, bosses often delay it, carrying incompetents until the day they can whip themselves into a state of indignation over the wretch's derelictions and do in heat, cruelly, what they should have done in cool consideration long before. Doing it right is kinder *and* more efficient. Even more important, doing it right has a positive effect on everyone else in the group. It underscores a spirit of fairness and humane concern for them, their problems and welfare.

The primary consideration in firing someone is how hard you have tried to avoid having to do it. Over a suitably long period, ratings and face-to-face evaluations should have left the person in no possible doubt, in the early stages, about your dissatisfaction and, in the later stages, about his or her imminent peril. It is wrong to use the threat of firing as a commonplace of discipline, but it is only fair to warn people when, in fact, they really are close to the ax. "If it comes as a surprise," says Thomas Plaskett, "I blame the supervisor more than I do the employee; the supervisor simply has not been honest with the employee." In fact, says George Foote, "One way to tell you're going to be fired is when your boss doesn't talk to you about your performance any more. That means he or she has given up on you."

When you do, finally, give up on someone, you should act at once. "If you think a guy is not doing a job," says Evelyn Berezin, "you don't crap around, you fire him fast. Really fast. You get him in your office, close the door and tell him why, eyeball to eyeball, and you don't mince words. If you're going to fire a person, you owe it to him to let him *really* know why." It is no favor to anyone to drag it out. The company is being shortchanged, and so are the others in the group who must take up the slack. Certainly the person being fired is better off the sooner it is over with; for employees who simply cannot cope, it will be a distinct relief. The struggle is over and they can get on to something new. "I'm sure," says J. C. Penney chairman Donald Seibert, "that everybody who's finally lost a job because of being 'in the wrong business' or just not performing well would have felt a lot better about it if somebody had recognized it three years earlier so they could have had a three-year start in some other career. Sometimes we're compassionate and 'don't want to hurt people'—and we end up doing them more harm than good."

Act fast and act with consideration. Do everything you can within company policy (and bounds of honesty) to make it easy for people being fired. If possible, leave them the choice as to whether they would like the use of the office, some period of notice, or pay in lieu of notice. Find out what they want others in the group told. In general, treat them as well as you can.

"Give them a little time to pick up the pieces of their lives," says Herbert Patterson. "Let them try to work it out—including the economics. Business can be inhuman enough in the demands it makes on you and your family without being inhuman in the way they get rid of you."

The best control of results is ultimately the constructive eagerness of your people to do their best. And the example of how you treat the worst of them well and thoughtfully cannot fail to encourage the good and the best.

# VII  *MOTIVATION*

*There are two basic questions about motivation. First, what do you want to have happen as a result of your efforts in the area of motivation? Surely you want your people to do the best job they can and stay alert for ways to do it even better. That means they have to* want *to do their best. You can set any standard you like and coerce performance up to that minimum, but you cannot make subordinates do more, let alone their best, unless they want to.*

*Which brings up the second basic question about people doing their best. Why should they? As a boss, you must keep this question in mind when you contemplate the motivation of people working for you. What do they want that they might reasonably expect to get by doing their jobs the best they can? And what can you do to make their jobs the kind that will deliver what they want if they do perform up to their peak?*

*Hairsplitters point out that since motivation is internal, the boss cannot motivate subordinates. Maybe not. But you can arrange their jobs so that they motivate themselves—* drive *themselves—to do the best they can. In fact, that* is *the job of a boss.*

*It is your job. And the starting place is what you already know people want.*

# 14 *The Paraboss Program*

Start with the few easy cases in your group, the ambitious ones who are already ideally motivated. What you know about their motivation and its consequences points toward the most effective strategy for dealing with the rest of your group.

What ambitious people want is to get ahead, which means they would do their best even at jobs they loathed. Yet the ambitious typically revel in their work and always seem to have the most interesting jobs their groups offer. It figures. They dispatch rote assignments with such vigor and careful attention that their bosses naturally give them new and harder tasks, with the built-in interest of novelty and more challenging complexity. The ambitious are sometimes overwhelmed but seldom bored. Furthermore, they know they are not cheese champions. The increasingly tougher jobs they master signal their growing powers and importance. Soon they discover a reason for doing their best beyond advancement: because it feels good.

As boss, about all you need to do to keep this natural progression going is to fuel their conviction that the way to get ahead is to continue doing their best. You thrust them forward and push them ahead as fast as you can, even spinning off excess stars to other groups if necessary—anything to promote the worthy. Such a policy is tonic to the ambitious. And, as we'll soon see, it plays a catalytic role in your program for the others.

How about those others? Ninety percent (or is it 99 percent?) of your group evidence little ambition. Why should they want to work any harder than necessary to get by? And what can you do about it?

Since 1960 there has been available a pat set of answers

summed up by the catchphrase "Theory Y." In *The Human Side of Enterprise,* Douglas McGregor, an MIT professor and business consultant, offered some assumptions about what people want and why they might do better. They boil down to three. First—unlike the old view, which McGregor called "Theory X"—most people do *not* hate work. In fact, they need work to satisfy their egos, to feel useful, creative and psychically fulfilled. Second (indisputable observation), people will do their best to achieve objectives to which they feel committed.

So far, so good. It is an appealingly humanistic view of people that fits comfortably with the enlightened policies of today's better educated and more psychologically attuned breed of manager. But then McGregor blew it.

The operative assumption of "Theory Y" is that a usefully large portion of the population can be convinced to make the company's objectives their own. McGregor never specified how this would come about, and it is at this point that even perfervid Theory Y fans either develop laryngitis or substitute rhapsodic visions for practical details. The assumption suggests dialogue that would strain belief coming from even the young Andrew Carnegie:

"And what are your personal goals?"

"Please, sir, I'd like our P and E to crack twelve next quarter and our market share to realize a five and seven-tenths percent increase, annualized."

"Good lad."

Maybe at the very top. But you do not have to shinny far down any totem pole to encounter yawning indifference to the organization's goals. "I am continually perturbed at how our division managers don't give a damn about the whole corporation," says Wilfred Corrigan, chairman of Fairchild Camera and Instrument. "Yet when I was in the same position, I didn't give a damn about the corporation either. I can remember, at Motorola, going to meetings where the president would introduce the new lines and I would sit there twiddling my thumbs, thinking, What's that got to do with me?"

Not much. Corrigan was, in fact, fiercely motivated to achieve the goals of his semiconductor division. If he had not been head of the division, or near the top, even those goals might have been too remote to enlist his interest or effort.

Today's successful bosses realize all this instinctively. They adopt, wholesale, Theory Y's cheerful assumptions about people and simply ignore the nonsense about people committing themselves to corporate (or even departmental) goals. (We are examining here, notice, long-term personal goals, not the sort of work-related goals discussed in the previous section.) Instead, bosses concentrate on their people's own goals, on what they know people want.

People want to do what interests them and feel they are growing, useful and, if possible, important. Trouble is, the unambitious do not think of those as realistic goals for themselves or of work as a likely source for their realization. They are prisoners of a negligible self-image that seems to preclude the possibility of change. But being able to look forward to interesting new things is one of the most powerful motivations. "I'm fifty-three and I feel I've got room for at least one more career, maybe more," says First Boston chairman George Shinn. "It's important to have expectations that are interesting." That is true even for the unambitious, and it is up to you to trigger their expectations.

In the absence of an inner drive for the growth of advancement, you must institute for your people a program of growth in place. You must force them through the steps of expanding interest and pride in their work, requiring them to go through the motions, like artificial respiration. You must lead them to what the ambitious find for themselves.

All this talk of "force" and "must" may sound sinister and manipulative. But it is not a matter of dragging your people kicking and screaming into something they really do not want to do. Quite the contrary. The reason this motivational strategy works so well is that it is rooted in the almost simpleminded observation that people want to do things they find interesting as opposed to things they do not find interesting. They simply are not accustomed to think of work as interesting until you restructure their jobs to include novel and stretching tasks.

How do you do it? That is reasonably simple, too.

Look at the paramedical and paralegal programs. They were winners from the start because everyone comes out ahead. Professionals are relieved of tasks they consider deadening routine, but ones that the paraprofessionals find interesting and challenging. So the level of performance in the entire unit is raised (delighting clients, saving patients' lives). The professionals have more time for tougher jobs, while the paraprofessionals give their all to work that had once been done perfunctorily as boring chores. It amounts to an axiom. Says SEC chairman Roderick Hills, "There are very few lawyers, accountants, doctors, engineers—professionals at any level—who don't find a great part of their work to be below the level of their education, capacity and skill. And in almost all their organizations you have subordinates who find their work equally tedious. If the parts of the job that could be discarded by the professional could be made available to the lower-level person, you'd make them both happier."

Why limit it to professionals? The same goes for people in every discipline, at every level, within every company. At least part of what every boss considers routine would be an interesting challenge for subordinates. Making it so is "the paraboss program." It is the heart of motivation.

The program will work only from the top down. First, you have to turn your immediate subordinates (those not animated by ambition) into practicing parabosses. Then the program filters down to their subordinates. Of course, your ambitious subordinates can immediately begin turning paraboss duties over to their own subordinates.

What is a suitable paraboss duty? "Routine" is a handy

tag to describe it, but it must not be something that always was mere drudgery. Even if repetition has made it for you a matter of spiritless reflex, it should have encompassed interest before you mastered it, just as a doctor, when an intern, was challenged by tasks he now turns over to a paramedic. That is the perfect kind of paraboss job, and it should be the specification clear down the line.

As the program matures, there are two other likely types. The first is any project that has been sitting, stone cold, on the back burner of your mind, the one you "mean to get around to someday" but somehow know you will never find time for. The second involves job swaps among subordinates. There are bound to be interest and excitement for one in what used to turn on another. Your subordinates may have their own notions of advantageous job swaps and promising projects, and they should be consulted.

In time, subordinates should have to explain why they have not passed on to a paraboss any duty they retain that manifestly engages less than their full talent. An acceptable justification would be that they enjoy some particular routine. You would not want to deprive them of that, or end all routine even if you could, since even the eagerest beaver craves spells of it—to measure the high spots, for one thing, and because no one can operate always on the farther edge of nerves and ability. But no fear: There is always enough routine to go around (recall that the chairman of Gillette said 70 percent of even an *engrossing* job is less than thrilling). Only now routine is enlivened. All employees experience the joy of being interested in at least some of their work, even those who never before realized they wanted to be.

When they find out they do, what can you expect?

A number will catch fire. Their interest and pride in doing a tougher job well will reach critical mass and become self-sustaining. They will begin to see possibilities. They will discover ambition. And it is here that your promotion policy pays off, since you have already created the air of dynamic expectation and promise that can sustain the fire.

You will not get this best result, of course, with everyone in your group or even with most. But the least you can expect is a generally heightened level of interest from parabosses, certainly on their new tasks, and it is not too much to hope that many will plow more diligently through the ham-and-egg parts of their jobs to get to the jam. In any case, it means that a sizable portion of the group's work will be done with more energizing pleasure, imagination, dedication and zeal than when it was the dreariest part of a superior's job load. It will raise the overall level of your group's performance.

Even the flat failures are a plus. If some in your group display invincible indifference to your best paraboss efforts, it should be a conclusive addition to the kind of weeding-out evaluation discussed in the preceding chapter.

That is not the end of what you can do about motivation in your group. Remember that people also want to feel useful and important. If the climactic vision of Theory Y were accurate, there would be no problem. Since it is not, things like formal job-enlargement and job-enrichment programs have routinely produced disappointing results and been phased out. The notion seemed promising in the flush of Theory Y enthusiasm. It was argued that by having people work on whole components, products or projects, instead of discrete parts, by bringing them in on such matters as testing, deadlines, costs and customer relations, they would quicken with managerial concern for corporate goals, would find the job more important, and so more worth their best effort. A pretty thought, but impractical for three reasons.

First, it costs an arm and a leg. Motorola, for example, found they needed 25 percent more people when they lost the efficiencies of the assembly line.

Second, the nature of work is such that formal job enrichment never could mean much except on the production line; office workers probably already have a "broader view" but cannot perform other departments' functions anyway. (Marketing is already aware of cost accounting but simply is not trained to keep the books, and vice versa—whereas wiring is wiring, and welding is welding, whether on part or component, without drastic retraining.)

The third and finally crippling demerit is that trying to make people feel the job is important because of its contribution to the whole (to which they may be indifferent anyway) is doomed. Would you feel more at one with the bakery just because they let you confect a pie instead of only pitting the cherries?

Successful bosses ignore teleology. They concentrate on making the job important for itself, not for its contribution to a "greater" cause.

The paraboss program begins the process by investing each subordinate's job with, literally, a new importance (since it now contains duties once discharged at a higher level). Then the two most important elements in heightening each subordinate's conception of the job's importance are your attitude— showing by word and deed that you consider what he or she does worth doing—and the generous speed with which you recognize and signalize accomplishments.

The most telling factor is the sense of urgency with which you treat each person's work. "I have a two-day rule," says SEC's Wallace Timmeny. "If something hits my desk that I've got to approve, and I can't act on it within two days, I get the guy in and tell him why. You sit on someone's memos, and you're giving the guy a message that what he's doing isn't worth a damn."

Such messages are usually broadcast unthinkingly, which guarantees repetition. The only cure is unceasing awareness of implications. Take what is often the unfortunate upshot of an otherwise laudable open-door policy. The boss reassures the troops about being always accessible. And remember, guys, no ceremony on our team; just barge right in. Some credulous helot does, and what happens? The boss holds up an imperious hand to warn against interrupting whatever profound reading, writing or figuring is going on, signaling unmistakably that nothing the subordinate has to do or say could possibly be important enough to risk dispelling the boss's train of thought. (It also lets the cat out of the bag about the boss's less than impressive powers of concentration.)

The most convincing demonstration that you consider people's work important is to do everything you can to let them get on with it. That is why many bosses insist the biggest motivational block in any group is the "bottleneck," which means any snag that makes individuals realize they cannot do the job right even if they want to.

Bottlenecks are not only physical. In fact, outside the production department they are more likely to be matters of policy. Or the boss's attitude—often the biggest bottleneck of all. If a couple of subordinates are doing an analysis and have to wait for figures that should have been up from finance last Monday, you, as boss, should be down in finance hollering because someone dares impede the work of your people. If, instead, you shrug and set them doing another project that is "just as important," you announce not that everything they do is of equal importance but of equal inconsequence. If you do not actively encourage them to get on with their jobs *now,* the inescapable conclusion is that you do not really care how (maybe whether) they perform.

All around him, in Washington, SEC director of enforcement Stanley Sporkin sees this chilling effect on the motivation of even highly trained professionals. Only worse. "I get the same question all the time from people in our sister agencies," Sporkin says. "I just got it from a guy over at Banking: 'Stan, how do you get your guys to put in twenty-hour days? After five o'clock I can't get anyone to do anything; they've all gone home.'

"I said, 'It's very simple. As soon as one of your people goes out, investigates and finds there's a bank that's behaving badly, he's considered the sort who rocks the boat and he doesn't get ahead. The guy who gets ahead is the one who finds no problems, raises no questions, causes no stir—and he's the nine-to-five guy. The others see that it's better to be a nine-to-five guy than it is to do your job.' " Clearly, the most efficient way to avoid doing your job is to spend minimum time and effort on it.

Perhaps that is the upper end of frustration. But it is only different in degree, not kind, from such motivation-killing, bottleneck policies and "traditions" as the familiar "That's the way we've always done things here" or "Oh, no, we never do it that way" or "The client will never buy that" or, most common of all, "They'll never approve it upstairs."

"It's great being able to tell magazine readers what I think they want to know," says Richard Burgheim, *People* assistant managing editor, "not what a senior editor thinks they *should* know." Before Burgheim joined *People* he was an associate editor at *Time,* and the inherent importance of that job, he felt, was diminished if he could not do it the way he thought it should be done (an echo of the chairman of U.S. Steel's warning in chapter II). The substance of what Burgheim reports now may be less momentous, but the process is more satisfying, the *job* (not just his title) more important. And today he is careful to let subordinates tell it their way.

Clear away *all* bottlenecks to show your people that you think what they are doing is important. And when they have done it well, show them you think that is important too. Recognition—the right kind of recognition—is vital to your program.

For starters, it must mark real achievement. "You have to be very honest," says William Bernbach, founder of Doyle Dane Bernbach, "so when you praise the praise means something." It is a common error to imagine that if you tell people they are doing a fine job when they are not they will take heart and start doing it. This is a sugared version of "crying wolf" and will typically produce the same results: People soon will not listen and, worse, will not believe your praise even when it is justified.

"But when you do praise," Bernbach adds, "praise in a very open way. If I see a great piece of work, I get very excited. I run out into the hall and show all my other workers what this person did and tell them why it's great, so we all learn from it together."

The lesson is not only how to do something better. It is also that doing it better is important enough to occasion public pride and rejoicing.

There is no substitute for recognition. "If you keep a guy in a back room and never let anyone know what a great job he's doing," says Ford VP Louis Ross, "it doesn't matter how well you pay him. He wants somebody to say, 'Gee, you did a good job!' " What's more, "you" has to be a singular to mean much. Accomplishment may be the result of team effort, but recognition has to be personal. That fellow in the back room will not be mollified by a mimeographed memo starting, "To all of you who contributed to our splendid showing . . ." In fact, any form of recognition that does not single out people is one of those "nice gestures" barely worth making. What people want, what excites them and can help motivate them, is personal recognition.

It does wonders for people who are already well motivated, so you can imagine what heady stuff it is to those who are just beginning to see the possible delights and rewards in doing their best.

The nearly uncanny power of personal recognition is a large part of what Robert Lund relied on when he first got a chance to run a division at General Motors. As general manager of Cadillac, he had the problem of trying to get dealers who were making a lot of money with minimal effort (since they usually sold all the cars they were allotted) to push for bigger sales. One of his most memorable programs turned on Cadillac's sponsorship of the Masters golf tournament, with Arnold Palmer as spokesman. "I suggested we have a Masters tournament among our dealers," Lund says, "to choose the Master Dealer from each zone. We ended up with twenty or twenty-five and we invited them to a conference. Arnold Palmer came down to play golf with them, and we had special green jackets with the Masters symbol for them. In fact, the label on the inside said, 'This Masters Jacket was personally presented to so-and-so by Arnold Palmer.' And I'll tell you those faces got *pale* when Arnold Palmer put that jacket on each man and we declared him—a Master Cadillac Dealer!"

Big deal? Yes, as a matter of fact, along with other personal-recognition programs for men who, after all, had everything else. Under Lund, Cadillac broke all sales records—and that was in '73 and '74, a bad time for the industry and the Dark Ages for big cars. Lund got recognition, too, in the form of promotion to general manager of Chevrolet, a post *Fortune* calls "a traditional launching pad for GM's presidency." If he makes it, the only drawback to the job may be a seriously diminished chance to achieve much *personal* recognition.

Is it *really* that important? Consider the case of Edgar Speer. As chairman of U.S. Steel, his job has much built-in importance, but that is not the same as specific personal recognition for a one-man, unshared, job well done. Behind his desk is a waist-high credenza, with an amazing-looking trophy. Speer does not go in for executive memorabilia, so the top of the credenza is nearly bare. But even if it were a littered knick-knack shelf, that extraordinary item would dominate. It is a gleaming tube that looks like a piston, about 18 inches high, its base fixed in a handsome chunk of polished wood. Ask Speer what it is, and he smiles happily and tells you about the time the government decreed new safety standards for how much impact automobile bumpers had to take without crumpling. He immediately sketched his notion of what sort of shock absorber would do the trick and showed it to Delco. A grateful Delco chrome-plated the first one off the assembly line and turned it into a funny-looking trophy. Just a way of saying, "Good job, Ed." But that is what he has behind his desk, not a framed copy of U.S. Steel's earnings report.

That is how important personal recognition is.

There is just one thing: as we shall see in the next chapter, it may be equally important *when* you give recognition.

# 15 *Something New: Positive Reinforcement*

It is a hallowed business precept that "the squeaky wheel gets the grease." But any maintenance man who took it to heart would soon be out a couple of bearings, then a job. Look at it from the wheel's viewpoint. What lesson is it being taught? To run with smooth efficiency or to squeak?

Business consultant Aubrey Daniels is teaching bosses to stop greasing squeaky wheels, an action he calls by its more academic name, "reinforcement of negative behavior," and to start reinforcing positive behavior at the right time in the right way. You can get marvelous results if you do it with your subordinates, Daniels says, and he has the company and data to prove it.

The company is Behavioral Systems of Atlanta, Georgia. Daniels, a Ph.D. in psychology, is president; Fran Tarkenton, a QB in football (also, it appears, a psychology buff and astute businessman), is chairman. The company employs some sixty people, including a professional staff of forty-five. They have helped nearly 100 companies in over 250 plant and office sites, with a success record (of customers who declare themselves anywhere from satisfied to exuberant) that hovers comfortably around 95 percent. This may be the cutting edge of a new mass movement in motivation.

Not that Daniels would quarrel with anything in the preceding chapter—just that a paraboss program might not do enough for his particular constituency. After all, it presupposes jobs that *can* be restructured and made more interesting, whose specifications are not cast in concrete. But some jobs are entirely rote and mechanical. A production-line boss may not have the leeway to make a paraboss program work for enough people; the supervisor of especially low-level paper shufflers will not, either.

Besides, Daniels argues, there may be another, surer way to get people to want to do their best, in factory *or* office. "The approach we take," he says, "is that to the extent you can make a job more interesting, do it. But don't spend forever trying to do it. I mean, where does it end? This friend of mine is convinced he's got the dullest job in the world. He goes to work, sits down in front of his machine, cuts it on, operates it all day, can't get up, can't smoke while he's working—only on occasional breaks. Then he cuts it off and comes home at night. What's he do? He flies a 747 from Los Angeles to Hong Kong, Tokyo, Manila and back. So how interesting can you make a job?"

Instead of worrying about the intrinsic interest of a job, the method of positive reinforcement—PRI, let's call it— focuses on making the consequences of doing a good job more interesting and more rewarding for the worker. It is based on the behavior modification techniques of B. F. Skinner, which the Schick centers for smoking and weight control have popularized. The difference is, PRI is the positive, upbeat side of behavior modification.

At Schick the subject is wired in and zapped with a mild electric shock whenever he takes a puff or a bite. Soon the body, no dummy, gets the message that smoking or eating certain foods has unpleasant consequences; the mind accommodatingly develops a distaste for the undesirable behavior.

PRI is Schick without wires or tears. Instead of discouraging unwanted behavior, it rewards—reinforces—desirable behavior. When subordinates work the way they should, the boss makes them feel good about it. There are four distinct phases.

First, you must identify a specific behavior you want from each worker. It is not enough to say, "I want more production." You must figure out *exactly* what someone can do that will bring about the specific result you want.

Second, you establish a base line of performance, so you can measure behavior improvement, which you faithfully and ostentatiously chart.

Third, you must change the consequences of the worker's behavior and give positive reinforcement to the specific behavior you want.

Fourth, you evaluate the results and maintain the changed, positive consequences.

See how the four steps work in a typical case. Let's say the company is a textile mill and the problem is quality control. The three things that most often mar weaving are broken threads, slubs (never mind what they are; they are *awful*) and jerked-end fillings (ditto). The loom may shut itself off if one of these horrors occurs; then again, it may not. And a weaver is often responsible for fifty looms or more, so if one does not stop automatically, a lot of cloth may be woven before the flaw is finally spotted, all of it salable only at discount, as seconds.

If seconds are running high, here is how Daniels and his people would teach a mill supervisor to handle it, using the PRI method.

1. *Behavior.* In this instance, the specific behavior needed to raise quality is more frequent patrolling of the looms, looking

for defects. If a weaver looks at a loom every ten minutes instead of every half hour, maybe only 10 yards will run as seconds instead of 50 or 100 yards.

2. *Data.* You see a particular weaver patrolling the "alley" only twice an hour, on average, and you figure six times an hour will do the trick, so those figures are the base line and target of a chart. Data on the average number of yards the weaver now runs as seconds are the base line for another chart, with whatever you consider a reasonable target also plotted.

3. *Consequence.* Here is the crux. The PRI answer to our original motivation question is that people want personal attention and recognition, and that once they learn they can get them only by doing a better job—in terms of some specific behavior —they will do a better job to get what they want.

"So during the day, I'm going to check," Daniels explains, "and every time I see the weaver patrolling, I'm going to attach some positive consequence to that behavior. I'm going to go by and say, 'Hey! that's good!' or stop and chat for a minute about something that interests that individual. When the patrolling gets up to three times an hour, maybe I'll say, 'Come on, I want to buy you a cup of coffee,' and I'll make a big thing of charting it at the end of the shift. But whatever I do will be contingent on that weaver's behavior, *period.*"

"Contingent" is the operative word. Do not give grease to wheels when they squeak, but only when they are running smoothly. Do not lavish time and reinforcing attention on people when they perform badly, but only when they are performing the way you want them to.

There is nothing startling about the basic proposition. Erik Jonsson, founder of Texas Instruments and a widely acknowledged genius of motivation, says he always told his people, "Look, we want to pay you better than our competitors pay their employees. But to afford that, we have to ask you to produce something of more quality, perhaps, or do it more quickly; in all, to do the best you know how." In other words, he voluntarily gave them all he could, contingent on their behavior. And TI became the miracle of the industry.

But Jonsson operated by instinct, an innate sense of timing and (face it) charisma. PRI teaches less gifted bosses to achieve similar motivational triumphs by system and plan.

4. *Evaluation and maintenance.* The desired behavior and its result should be plotted on a chart every day. In our example, it would be the average number of times per hour the weaver patrolled and the number of feet per shift the looms ran as seconds. One goes up, the other goes down, and both boss and subordinate have graphic evidence of progress—which itself is a potent positive reinforcement.

As for maintenance, obviously it takes less effort to keep the desired behavior going than it did to get it started. "But you do have to continue," says Daniels. "People ask me, 'How long?' Well, how long do you want to keep succeeding as a boss?"

For all its reliance on accurate data, specific behavior patterns, plans and systems, PRI is still an art. The crunch comes in selecting the right reinforcement.

Those who object to behavior modification on principle envision it as unfailing button-pushing that implacably turns subjects into manipulated zombies. But for PRI purposes, people have no buttons you can push, only preferences and predilections you must winkle out by attentive listening and observation. Results will be greater or less, depending on how reliably you identify what each subordinate finds reinforcing. It is not enough to know that people generally like being talked with; what does *this* person want to talk about: children? car? problems? hobby? What kind of tangible recognition does *this* person find most compelling?

Daniels confesses he is continually astounded at how simple the most effective reinforcers are. Some of his staff were running a program to increase attendance at one plant, and they proposed a banner for the department with the best record, plus a pennant for any section that could get 100 percent to show up. "When I heard that," says Daniels, "I thought, Oh, no! That's Sunday-school stuff! Well, that was the most successful attendance program we ever conducted."

Another time, a factory supervisor being instructed in PRI methods was illiterate. He took the manual home for his wife to read to him, and he memorized each lesson. That way he was able to pass the audiovisual tests. It took a 90 to move to the next unit, and there was a wall chart to mark progress. As each person passed a test, a gold star was put against his or her name, with a red paper background for anyone who made a perfect score. On the fourth test, this sixty-six-year-old supervisor got 100.

The instructor gave him his gold star *and* red pastie and told him to post them. The chart was near a door, and the man swung the door open, hiding himself and the chart from view. He stayed there one minute, two, five. Finally the instructor went over, making a joke about whatever could he be doing there in that corner, and pulled the door back.

The man was crying.

It was the first time in his life he had ever gotten recognition for doing something on a level with everyone else, with no allowances made, no special help or easy grading because he could not read.

Well, yeah, but . . . gold stars?

You bet. Gold stars, or whatever else works. "A lot of managers are so sophisticated," Daniels claims, "they sophisticate themselves right out of business." Especially with programs to improve attendance, the hardest part is convincing supervisors that a pat on the back and a "Hey! Coffee and doughnuts are on me!' will mean anything to someone who makes it to work four times this week instead of the usual three. Over and over PRI instructors hear the same question: "You mean to tell me someone who won't come to work for fifty dollars in wages will come for a cup of coffee and a doughnut?" Daniels answers, "Yup, that's where it's at."

Because everyone craves personal recognition. And it is a technique of incalculable power to tie that recognition to some improved behavior and show the person the progress being made. It can produce prodigies of motivation.

But only if you seize on clues as to what each person finds reinforcing, then *use* the knowledge. Herbert Patterson, former president of the Chase Manhattan Bank, points out that the toughest motivation cases are those who feel they have gone as far as they can or want to. He found that such people would perform adequately if given stimulating work, fair pay and a feeling that the boss took some personal interest in them. "But for all you know," Patterson says, "they may get their real joy out of painting landscapes on weekends. As long as they're productive and don't think about painting on the job, that's fine. Of course, if they set up easels by the desks, that's another matter." Sure is, Daniels would say. Once you have found out what excites someone, use it. Let an employee set up an easel, or maybe an exhibit, in your office and drop by to chat about it with you—contingent on some improved behavior.

That is essentially what happened in what Daniels describes as their classic case. In the story of Johnny Mack you can see all the elements of PRI come together.

Johnny Mack was hired by a North Carolina textile mill as a "doffer," which meant that when the warp was full he was to cut the cloth and take it—doff it—off the loom. It is not an exacting job, but it seemed to elude Johnny Mack. Daniels says he apparently had some psychomotor problems. "He didn't walk real straight, and when you looked at him you didn't count on him for much." With an annual turnover of more than 100 percent, the mill could not be choosy, but there were limits, and he was it. The standard number of doffs per shift was eighty; the most Johnny Mack managed all by himself was six.

After a few weeks the supervisor told one of the PRI instructors, "We're gonna pay up Johnny Mack and tell him he's through."

"What's the problem?"

"Well, the guy won't work. He doesn't care. You talk to him, he looks at you kinda bug-eyed, like he just escaped from somewhere."

The PRI instructor convinced the supervisor to try something new.

"What they did first," says Daniels, "was explain each step of the job again so they were sure he *could* do it. Then the supervisor posted a chart in his office, and at the end of each shift Johnny Mack would come by and the supervisor would graph his production, and if it improved the supervisor simply spent a little time talking with him.

"They knew he loved to talk, and they found out he had two special reinforcers. He knew an amazing amount about the Bible and loved to discuss it. The other was, he had an Indian artifact collection—arrowheads and others things he'd dug up locally.

"The supervisor let him keep a paper bag of them in the office, and when he'd done well they'd talk about it: 'Where'd you get that? What's this thing? Where'd you find the other?'

"The guy got to one hundred percent of standard in around two weeks, and then he went higher, helping other people."

They had a follow-up about eight months later and, when they asked the supervisor about Johnny Mack, he said, "I wish I had a hundred of him."

There is no question that PRI works where Daniels and his people have tried it; they have the records, the satisfied customers and the ongoing consulting contracts to prove it. But will it work where they have not yet tried it extensively? Outside the South? Off the production line? With other than hourly workers doing jobs in which the specific behavior desired is reasonably easy to isolate? Will it work just as unfailingly in offices, with more sophisticated workers doing more complex and integrated tasks?

Daniels is convinced it will and is now gathering data and experiences to prove it. As a hopeful sign he cites the bracing reports he gets from people who learned the PRI method at work and now use it outside, with their family and friends. A few claim it changed their lives.

One man called Daniels to tell him PRI had helped him with his daughter, a nine-year-old unreconciled and unruly diabetic. They had to ban her from the school lunchroom because she was always trying to trade off for Twinkies and other proscribed goodies. At home they had to padlock the pantry to keep her from sneaking down to gorge after everyone was asleep. Nothing seemed to help; she was always on the brink of ketosis.

Enter PRI in her father's life.

He took the principles home from the factory and set up a chart of his daughter's acetone level. Each morning she would take her own acetone reading and they graphed it. She earned points, depending on each day's reading, which could be used to have a friend stay overnight, to go to a movie, or to stay up and watch TV.

"There was a dramatic change," says Daniels. "And the guy—oh, he wanted us to go on national TV; he said there are thousands of parents who have this problem.

"I believe it's the wave of the future," he concludes. "Of course, you'd expect me to believe that. But I think I've got the data to support it."

It has to be worth a try. And who knows? You may find yourself riding the crest of the wave.

# 16 *Evaluation and Compensation*

You may wonder what evaluation and compensation have to do with motivation. Evaluation was covered in chapter 13 as part of the section on Control. And it is an accepted dictum that money does not motivate.

Well, here we shall examine a different sort of evaluation, conducted expressly with motivation in mind. As for the motivational aspects of money, when people say money does not motivate, they really mean small change does not. And it is true that the amount of money you can usually command for raises is apt to be peanuts when considered as a percent of your people's salaries. Its motivation is unlikely to survive their cashing the first new paychecks and realizing they still live beyond their means. Even so, money is a superb way to keep score. Used correctly, it becomes spendable recognition, immensely useful in your program for motivation.

As boss, you have a responsibility to evaluate and compensate all your immediate subordinates in a way *they themselves* consider fair. It is also up to you to see that your subbosses, at every level, do the same for their subordinates. Perceived fairness is everything. "People will generally accept your inability to pay them what they want," says Roderick Hills, "or accept the fact that you can't give them as much of a raise as they want, but they won't accept the fact that somebody else is getting even a tiny bit more if they think their effort is just as good."

In theory, that applies to all compensation. In practice, people understand how base salaries become skewed: the going rate for newcomers fluctuates, seniority intrudes, people get raises and then goof off, others blossom just when conditions dictate a freeze, overly rigid formulas or contracts mandate pay differences for jobs the workers themselves do not consider different. All that is all right. Given your evident desire to smooth out inequities, your people will forgive unjustified disparities in basic salary.

Merit pay is different. Here you have maximum control, which is good because, as proximate recognition for good work, merit pay has the greatest impact on motivation. When inexperienced bosses come to this realization, they gleefully sharpen their pencils and draw wonderfully nice distinctions between their people in order to make raises "fair." Their activity ignores both human nature and the purpose of merit pay. If you give one person a $1,000 raise and another $1,050, you beg each to be dissatisfied. Is there *really* a measurable 5 percent difference between their performance? The first is sure to think they are equal; the second will be positive he or she is at least 10 percent better.

When we discussed evaluation for control, remember, there was a substantial reason to place your people along a curve. The purpose was assignment, improvement and weeding out. The purpose of evaluation for compensation is different. It is to recognize and reward merit, not to compare performances, except grossly. You must make merit awards indisputable.

Limit yourself to three categories and resist further elaboration. If you name the groups, use a letter or numerical designation—even a nonsense syllable—rather than "average," "superior," "blah" or any other value-judgment tag that can only evoke side arguments over what *is* "superior" or "blah."

Whatever you call the groups, the biggest one should include those who have displayed perceptible improvement in work, attitude, growth, interest, effort (or any combination thereof) since the last review; those who have made some progress, somehow. You hope the next largest group will be the stars —those who plainly exceed anyone in the first group by such a margin that no one, not even those in the first group, can cavil at the distinction. In the third group are the place-holders, doing enough not to be fired.

Who decides who's where? And how is the decision made?

Whoever reviews a person's performance should also evaluate for merit pay and publish its award. That should be an individual's immediate boss. "Nobody else can perceive the problem as well," Roderick Hills says. "The man or woman at the very lowest level of supervision must feel responsible to see that subordinates are treated fairly. Nobody higher up can do as good a job." There is another reason. Abrasions are inevitable during a performance review, since its purpose is to correct and elevate performance. You help heal the wounds (or twist the knife, in the case of a no-progress evaluation) if whatever progress *has* been made is immediately rewarded. General Mills chairman James McFarland points out that, however hard it is to criticize the performance of subordinates, "having done that, the most exciting way to create better people and eliminate frustration is to have the person who criticized give the raise."

Deciding who is in each group is simple and should also be done by each immediate superior. The boss asks one question about each subordinate: "Is this person better now in any way than the last time I asked myself this question?" If yes, that is progress; if no, it isn't. The outstanding will announce themselves (that is what *outstanding* means).

Almost all will be clear-cut. Borderline cases—which means any people the boss does not automatically toss on a particular pile—should be thrashed out with you (if the immediate superior is one of your sub-bosses; if you cannot decide, use *your* boss as a sounding board). Anyway, you should review all evaluations by sub-bosses before the formal session and demand instances of progress. You do have to watch out for compulsive easy marks. "In almost every company there are differences in raters," says George Foote, McKinsey & Company director and a compensation expert, "so the shrewd boss knows enough to rate the raters." You're fighting a familiar escalation. Some sub-bosses feel others are overly generous and do not want their own people "penalized" by more honest ratings. Or they figure it is a reflection on them (either way) if they have more or fewer people in a particular rating group. You must make it clear that part of *your* evaluation of them will turn on the perceived accuracy of their ratings, no matter how many people end up in each group.

Now, how much should merit raises be?

In number of dollars, as much as you can manage. But number is not important; ratio between groups is. It should be 2:1:0, with the stars getting twice as much as those who made some progress and the deadheads getting nothing.

Should it be a percent of salary or the same lump sum in each group? On one hand, you are recognizing present progress and performance, not longevity or past performance (good or bad). On the other hand, higher present salary argues greater responsibility and contribution. So, on balance, a set percent of salary is more appropriate if the money is an identifiable profit-sharing fund, a lump sum if it all comes from the corporate kitty. It does not matter too much either way, as long as you are consistent and explain your reasoning.

The hard part is steeling yourself against merit raises for those who, indeed, do not merit them. The trouble is we are not talking about basket cases. They are people who do their jobs. And since they have managed to weather another six months or a year without bringing destruction down around them, it is almost assumed that they deserve an increase.

They do not, except when the company decrees a cost-of-living increase, with everyone getting the same. That is inflation, not merit. Giving merit raises to those without merit is doubly destructive.

First, as George Foote points out, "It waters down the impact of what the better performers get. If you're giving the average performer seven percent and the above average ten percent—and then you say, 'Well, we've got to give the below average five percent to keep up with the cost of living'—how does that make the person who got seven percent feel? He did a lot more, and only got two percent more increase. And the outstanding guy only got three percent more than the average." Equally bad, it encourages the unworthy recipient to disbelieve what the boss has just said about lack of progress. That means it spikes one of your biggest guns in the battle to lift the group's overall performance.

"We'd like to encourage a little more turnover," says Robert Hinman, commenting on Gillette's "nobody leaves" reputation. He sees tough-minded refusal to grant automatic raises as essential. "We'd like to get managers to put more of their salary dollars into key employees and maybe let some of the less successful ones go without a raise, hoping they might move on." It is not the same as firing. If long-standing employees are content to vegetate, they may. If they want an increase, it is waiting for them to claim by appropriate effort. But after you have tried everything you know to motivate them, and they still show no interest in doing more than a minimum, you owe it to the group's morale not to reward indolence. You certainly owe it to the people who are trying harder, who are improving, not to diminish their reward.

Maybe money does not motivate. But it certainly can help people get the message to shape up. Or ship out.

# VIII  *MISTAKES*

*You might not win the debate, but you would find it a
readily defendable position to hold that the most revealing
aspect of you as a boss is how you handle mistakes.
Competence and coolheaded grace when things come unglued
indicate a steady ability to perform well under any
circumstances, whereas mishandled mistakes can put you
down the tubes.*

*Of course, you did not get to be a boss without
knowing how to handle your own mistakes. But dealing with
those of your subordinates is harder for the same reason that
control of their work is harder than control of your own is:
because you must act at a remove, sometimes a substantial
one.*

*What should your attitude be toward mistakes by
subordinates? Should they ever be ignored or tolerated? What
should subordinates do to correct their mistakes? What part
should you play in the process? When? How should you judge
mistakes and those who make them? What can you learn
about your people from the mistakes they make and the way
they try to handle them?*

*It is a shame mistakes have to happen. But it
compounds shame not to use them to advantage.*

# 17 *How to Think About Mistakes*

The most important thing about mistakes is not whether your people make them or even how serious are their consequences, short of liquidation; the most important thing is your attitude about the mistakes and those who make them.

One of the more tiresome and misleading clichés is that "mistakes are inevitable." They are not. But the measures necessary to eliminate them guarantee stagnation. You would have to avoid doing anything unless you were totally covered—and then let in on the action only the most experienced in your group. Yet, to stand out, a boss must regularly let less adroit members of the group do things, and must consistently lead the group into new areas, undertaking venturesome new assignments—a kind of double inexperience that actively courts mistakes.

So if you are running your group right, mistakes *will* happen. It makes no sense to say you intend to decentralize, to push decision, authority and initiative as far down in the group as possible, then add, "But don't you dare make a mistake." It means nothing to urge your people to take risks, experiment, grow—and then pounce on each mistake with "Well, you just blew your raise," or "Ever do that again and it's your job." Not that you have to say it. Your people are close students of your expressed moods and, more to the point, actions. They know your attitude toward mistakes and will act accordingly. "You strike a punitive posture at risk of making people shy away from any progress," warns J. C. Penney chairman Donald Seibert. "And at that point you've clearly lost a lot of the energy out of your business."

Another trouble with the "mistakes-are-inevitable"

style of thought is that it suggests the boss's attitude toward mistakes should be one of sour, exasperated resignation. That manages to be at once too begrudging and too complaisant.

First, a modest profusion of mistakes is actually a welcome sign of organizational health. "If a pattern of growth is evident," says bank chairman Mary Roebling, "then a concurrent record of some mistakes probably indicates an optimum level of individual and company striving." Indeed, you should be suspicious if no one in your group makes a mistake. If they never stumble, it is probably because they are standing still.

They probably are not learning much, either. It is much harder to learn from successes than from mistakes. Like being hanged, being wrong concentrates the mind wonderfully. It makes people realize they have to do something different; they focus with intensity and receptive spirit on processes that end badly, whereas they barely notice whatever turns out tolerably well.

So, for a good boss, the only sensible attitude is reflected in what happened to William Spoor when he was in charge of Pillsbury's New York office and made a half-million-dollar mistake. The brass from Minneapolis descended on him for a three-day seminar on the topic, "What We Just Learned About What We Should Never Do Again." When it was over Spoor went to the president and said, "Well, that was certainly instructive. Now, am I fired?" The president gaped incredulously for a beat and then answered, "Bill, we just gave you the most expensive education this company's ever heard of. We *can't* fire you until we get it back!"

The numbers may be smaller with the mistakes you confront, but the underlying philosophy should be the same: Mistakes are not to be suffered; they are to be used. They should be immediately followed by a constructive review with everyone involved, and the review must be legitimately for learning, not recrimination. That means you must investigate processes, not dwell on horrible results. Analyze, don't agonize. After all, what will postmortem wailing accomplish? You will end up with the same bad result, anyway, plus heartburn—and a cowed employee determined never again to take a chance.

All of this may sound sensible, but it is another thing to remember the right attitude in the heat of the moment. Trouble is, the most notable characteristic of any mistake is not its potential as a learning device but its immediate havoc. You want to *get* the deranged cretin who disordered your plans and maybe put you in a pickle. Righteous anger can be deeply satisfying, but you must not indulge. You must not let natural dismay over bad results induce you to consider both the person and the mistake equally hateful. Your attitude, rather, should be like that of a conscientious clergyman toward sin and sinners: You love the mistaken, but hate the mistakes.

You *do* hate them! Remember that one of the twin perils in "mistakes-are-inevitable" thinking is complaisance—figuring that since they are bound to happen anyway, you simply will not bother about them.

There is a similar danger in the right attitude. Once you have mastered the urge to blame and punish those who make mistakes, you must not allow your constructive attitude to degenerate into a soppy permissiveness about the mistakes themselves.

Furthermore, you must differentiate between the right and the wrong kind of mistake. The right kind are those that might be called "honest," made by someone who is trying and thinking, but is inexperienced or overreaching or simply (as we all are, from time to time) wrong. The wrong kind of mistake is made through carelessness, inattention, sloppiness or indifference. Your geniality and understanding should not extend to them.

And even the right kind must never be overlooked, ignored or (worst of all) condoned. While you must convince your people that making mistakes is no reason for fear and trembling, you must never allow them to think that mistakes themselves are ever "all right." Otherwise, mistakes become first unremarkable and then a habit.

That is what had happened at Dictaphone before Lawrence Tabat took over as CEO. The company had made the monumental mistake of supposing they were so far ahead in the dictating machine field that no one could catch up. Then IBM entered the market, bought a company with advanced magnetic tape technology, better than Dictabelts, and suddenly it was Dictaphone that had to catch up. By the time Tabat got there, the demoralized staff had reached a point where, he says, "they just let mistakes go, even recognizing they were mistakes—and as a result they lost their share of market." Drastic action was needed. So Tabat insisted that every identified mistake, every consumer complaint, would henceforth come to him for review, maybe handling. It was a forceful demonstration of his "strong feeling that you can't ignore little mistakes, because they grow into large ones."

Not that Tabat became an arbitrary Tartar about making mistakes; he did not penalize the kind that showed initiative or growth. But he firmly established the point that mistakes do matter, that none may be allowed to slip by uncorrected. For instance, he once discovered that their ad agency in London had run an ad with the headline, "There are a lot of dictating machines, but only one dictaphone." "Just like that," Tabat explains, "spelling Dictaphone with a small 'd.' I immediately phoned the agency manager. He said, 'Well, Larry, old boy, that's not so critical, is it?'

"I read him chapter and verse about trademarks and said, 'Colin, old boy, it is goddamn critical. Now withdraw all space advertising until you fix it.'

" 'But we'll be without an ad next month.'

" 'That's right, you'll be without an ad.' Suddenly Colin-old-boy knew it was critical."

That was plainly the wrong kind of mistake. But how can you always tell the right from the wrong kind?

# 18 *Mistakes: Tolerable and Intolerable*

The kind of mistake someone makes has nothing to do with the relative horrendousness of its outcome. There are mistakes with fairly shattering effects that anyone could be proud to call his own; others, with trifling consequences, are inexcusable and automatically urge thoughts of severance. The difference is in the evident care and thought that went into the mistake.

As a U.S. Steel salesman, Drummond Bell made a mistake that carried, for someone of his age and weight, an awesome price tag. He had sold some coil steel that the customer claimed could not be flattened.

If nothing was wrong with the steel, it would be totally the customer's problem; most likely, something was wrong with the process or equipment or application. But this was a good customer and Bell was inclined to help. Of course, he could have covered himself first by having the steel tested. "I should have had the metallurgic people involved," Bell says, "but one of them was ill and the other was out of town, and I felt I had to make a decision." It turned out to be the wrong one. He found another customer for the material, getting the first customer off the hook. But after a while the new customer had problems too, and now it turned out that this was one of those bizarrely rare cases where something had gone wrong in smelting and the steel was defective. The new customer had suffered some loss and settled for $17,000.

To Bell's way of thinking, that was not so horrible. He figured that there was actually less loss to the company the way he had dealt with things; the customers, while less than ecstatic, were not especially disgruntled. "But not everyone agreed with the way I handled it," Bell admits, "and there was that seventeen thousand with my name all over it. But I didn't get into a shooting match with the mill or anyone, because my boss agreed that what I had done wasn't all that bad."

Of course not. He had displayed initiative, decisiveness and not terribly bad judgment. Maybe he should have realized that something was inherently wrong with the steel after the first customer had problems. But there is almost *never* anything wrong with steel—so that is like saying everyone should always think of everything, in which case there would not be mistakes. Or humans. Contrast Bell's kind of mistake, though, with the one made by Dictaphone's London ad man, who evidently thought of *nothing* and did not seem to care.

"It never bothers me for people to make a mistake if they had a reason for what they did," says Exxon's Frank Gaines. "If they can tell me, 'I thought this and reasoned so, and came to that decision,' if they obviously went through a reasonable thought process to get where they did, even if it didn't turn out right, that's OK. The ones you want to watch out for are those who can't even tell you why they did what they did."

Naturally, you modify your standards according to the level of the subordinates. Lower down, you accept nearly any independent thought and active reasoning as mitigation, grateful that they are thinking at all. From a sub-boss or someone contemplated as supervisory material, you rightly expect more: more intense thought given to decisions, more exhaustive research of problems, closer reasoning. Even through plans and projects that go seriously wrong, there should run a visible chain of ratiocination, a kind of mental audit trail.

With those you peg as potential stars, be even more demanding. Since "hindsight" has a bad name, let's call it "perspective." When all the facts are in, you can peer beneath surface plausibility to determine if the subordinate exercised due care and thoroughness and brought to the problem the exacting analysis that was needed.

At the time of his interview for this book, American Airlines senior VP Robert Crandall was pondering a recent mistake made by a high-ranking subordinate. The man had hatched an idea to eliminate a number of steps and paperwork connected with boarding passes. The plan looked like a winner on paper; in the air it turned out to take more steps, not fewer, to waste time and to bollix up several important activities. "The guy gets credit for coming up with the idea in the first place," says Crandall, "and for doing the staff work necessary to sell it to the rest of us and get it started. But now I'm going back to see if, really, he should have been able to foresee the difficulties and realize why it was impossible before we put it in practice. Were the flaws ones he should have been expected to catch?"

It is not a matter of second-guessing. You are not trying to prove the other person wrong and yourself right. You are not establishing constructive guilt in which "proof" of negligence is the fact that, after all, something went wrong so someone *must* be to blame. All you are doing is dispassionately reviewing a subordinate's thought processes to determine whether an analysis was made with satisfactory rigor or whether a promising idea became so entrancing it obscured unpleasant realities and even visible storm signals. If you decide ultimate failure was merely a concatenation of unfortunate and opaque circumstances, or imponderables breaking the wrong way, the subordinate's credit should not be diminished at all by that failure. With that kind of mistake, the thought *is* the deed. It is a tolerable mistake.

Of course, as was stated in the previous chapter, all mistakes are *in*tolerable in that all must be handled expeditiously. Furthermore, it is eventually up to you, as boss, to make sure every mistake is dealt with. You should, however, hold back yourself until the last possible moment in order to observe how a subordinate goes about clearing up a mistake. That will tell you as much as any other single factor about that person's quality.

"If he faces up and is fearless and finds a solution and

does something about it," says Arthur Larkin—who knows something about mistakes, having been whipping boy for a $46-million dilly when he was president of General Foods, a circumstance we shall examine soon—"if he does that, you've got yourself a pretty good guy. If he tries to cover up, to put it aside and ignore it, chances are he's a fellow you don't need."

The first thing to look for is ability to recognize and admit one's mistakes. That is often the hardest part of handling them. They are inadvertent parts of workaday routine; no tocsin sounds, no light flashes "tilt." Since there is comfort in proceeding according to plan, it is always easy to rationalize mistakes as "not really" affecting the plan. What fractures routine is acknowledgment, not the commission of the mistake. So why bother the boss with something likely to be straightened out by next week, next month at the latest? Why call attention to the lamentable fact that one was wrong?

Even after Lawrence Tabat got the troops at Dictaphone out of their dreary "mistakes-are-inevitable" thinking, even then he encountered the inertia of mistake-making that impels subordinates to dismiss the need to "bother" the boss over "trivialities." In 1976 Dictaphone was introducing a new model of their basic machine. It was gorgeous—except for a small rod incongruously jutting up through the top, marring otherwise sleek lines. It seemed cunningly positioned to achieve the maximum mischief, looking silly and infallibly spilling any coffee cups placed thereupon (which, if you know anything about coffee cups, is exactly whereupon they would be placed). "I blew my stack when I saw it," declares Tabat. "I called the designer—he's head of the design school at Syracuse, and a very good industrial designer—and I said, 'Art, how in hell did you let those guys talk you into putting that goddamn pin there?'

"He said, 'Larry, your engineers said they wanted to use a standard counter as a price concession, and the only way they could fit it in was with the reset pin coming up through the top.'

"I said, 'Arthur, why didn't you call and tell me?'

" 'Larry, you're the president of the company. I shouldn't bother you with these things!' "

Tabat's conversation with the chief engineer was equally unedifying. Given that they had to use a standard counter, why couldn't the reset pin emerge from the front of the unit, along with the other controls?

"Well, I don't know, Larry. You'd have to put two more links in to put it where you want it. You can't do that now."

"But you could have, couldn't you?"

"Yeah, but it would have cost more money."

"How much?"

"Well, another ten cents a unit, and—"

"Les, you ought to have your head screwed on again!"

Notice that everyone had a splendid "reason" for not recognizing the mistake and doing something about it in season. One man wanted to save money; another wanted to save the president worrisome involvement in mundane problems. The result? He ended up hip deep in a serious problem and had to spend more money to correct, late and partially, a mistake that could have been corrected early and totally. Tabat insisted that they at least shear off the reset pin as close as possible to the surface. That helped quite a bit. But, as he remarked darkly to the hapless designer, "That's going to cost you first place in the international design competition!"

You have a two-stage defense against that kind of thinking. First come awareness and vigilance. You know your subordinates will tend to submerge mistakes, and you must guard against this by announced policy and your own forthright example. Second, make it clear to subordinates that the *real* mistake, from the standpoint of their careers, is not the substantive mistake but their response to it.

Once you see that subordinates are recognizing mistakes and ready to do something about them, the next thing to notice is specifically how they handle them.

What is the best way to correct mistakes? Whenever

possible, cut your loss clean and sharp. "The first licking is the best one," as Nathan Cummings, founder of Consolidated Foods, puts it. It is hard to do for the same reason that recognizing mistakes is hard: it runs counter to human nature. People tend to struggle along unpromising paths simply because they have already invested so much time, trouble and ego. But it generally takes less effort, time, talent, tears and treasure to start over than it does to retrieve seriously flawed situations. It sounds somehow wise and mature to "make the most" of bad results. But your best subordinates will, instead, make the least of them—and begin again on a better track.

Even when that is not possible, the approach to correcting a mistake should be as decisive and thoroughgoing as can be. "There is no other way to handle a mistake of large or small magnitude," insists Arthur Larkin, "except to face up to it, bring the best brains you have available to focus on the problem and take whatever action seems indicated, regardless of consequences."

As he points out with considerable pride, that is exactly what he did at General Foods. The problem was overstated real estate values of their acquisition, Burger Chef. They had shelled out potfuls for those hamburger stands. It would have been a dangerous situation in flush times; with a slumping market it was a disaster. When Larkin found out what had happened, he summoned all the advice he could from people who knew about real estate and the fast food business (not, unhappily, the same people who had initiated and guided the operation, which was the problem) and decided on heroic measures.

"We had to convince our board that we should take an extraordinary loss of forty-six million dollars," says Larkin, "and over a fifteen-year term write off those leases, sell them, sublease them, whatever; maintain the stores that were viable and shut the ones that were not—and so on. The board accepted the recommendation and took what was, by far, the biggest loss in the company's history.

"Of course, as I took the action I didn't recognize that it would cost me my job. It did. So be it. At least I did carry out my principles about what you do to correct mistakes."

Offhand that may not seem exactly a storybook denouement or a convincing advertisement for the suggested method. He faced the mistake, took counsel, cut his loss—and got handed his hat. But consider the alternatives both for the company and for Larkin, personally. From the company's point of view things could only have gotten worse. What was a huge (but bearable) loss could have been nursed into a terminal one.

The same goes for Larkin's career. There is considerable question as to how much he was to blame for the Burger Chef debacle. He'd had no direct responsibility for the acquisition (though, he says, as president he should have insisted on being enough involved so he could have done something about the situation early enough to have some effect), and some observers think he was simply taking the rap. In any case, there is no dispute that he took leadership in cleaning up the mess. So, yes, maybe he got canned as a result, but he went into the presidency (now chairmanship) of Keebler at least partly because the Keebler board was impressed by the vigor and uncompromising toughness with which he faced the General Foods problem and brought it to the best possible solution—regardless, as he says, of consequences.

It is the right way to handle mistakes. And when you come right down to it, that was not such a bad result!

# IX  NEW SITUATIONS

*When you go into a new situation as boss, there are two possibilities: you will follow someone who was the effective and successful head of a successful group—or you will step in to clean up a mess. It is a toss-up which is harder.*

*In both cases, though, the very fact of being in a new situation means it is fluid, offering important possibilities. What are the opportunities characteristic of new situations? What are the dangers? If it was a good situation, how can you set your own course without rocking the boat? If it was a disaster, how clean should a new broom sweep? Whom can you trust in either situation, and how can you get them on your side?*

*Above all, how do you show them that you are boss when (on one hand) they just lost the boss they really want or (on the other hand) they doubt that any boss can help them survive?*

# 19 *A Tough Act to Follow*

The most usual new situation is when you are brought in from another group (or company) to succeed the boss of a successful group who is being promoted. It is a tough act to follow.

Someone promoted from within the group also has problems, but they have nothing to do with new situations. Rather, they are problems of familiarity: how to get established as The Boss, having lately been one of the gang—especially since the best of the rest of the gang now include disappointed rivals. (We will look more closely at that problem in the next section.) The strains can be intense. But at least the corporate mustang was part of the group's success, his or her efforts added to their luster and the accession holds some promise for their future promotion. If one of their group made it today, why can't they tomorrow? Furthermore, since the new boss must have been a logical contender for the top spot, the legitimacy of the promotion is manifest; he or she just has to make it stick.

You have a harder task. Far from sharing the group's glory or being reckoned an ornament to its reputation, you are an inferential reproach. They did everything right: worked hard and well, made a splendid record, even promoted their boss. And what did it get them? You. The better their record, the sharper their resentment. It is not mitigated by your general acclaim in the company or the world. No matter how good you're supposed to be, how come they were passed over in your favor? What does someone have to do around here to get promoted, anyway? Given many corporate promotion policies, it is a very common cry.

"It was a very compact group with a lot of esprit de corps, and they had been doing very well," is how Edward

Robinson, deputy controller of Exxon, describes Esso-Africa, an Exxon marketing company. Management had staked out the top job in Esso-Africa as an ideal spot in which to give young comers a taste of running things. Fine for the corporation and for the young star, but how about the company's senior staff? "Almost everyone had been there ten, twenty or thirty years," Robinson says, "and here I was a new boy coming in at the top. A lot of them weren't sure they wanted a new boy—and particularly at the top."

Robinson concluded that his first job was getting the organization to accept him. When you take over a successful group at any level, that is your first job, too, excluding all others.

Unfortunately, that means you should start in a passive role, while career logic screams for the most vigorous, positive exertions, pushing the group to ever better results. You know that a linear continuation of the group's success will ring no bells. To keep career momentum, you must lead the group to unexampled heights, and you are anxious to get on with it. Instead, you must repress the qualities of leadership and innovation that got you the job in the first place.

This goes against the grain. Still, it is essential. However sure you are of what should be done to improve the group's already impressive performance, you must not come out swinging. You may know more about the group's specialty than any of them; but they know out-of-mind more about how *they* function, what they consider success and how to attain it. What's more, they have the record to prove (at least to themselves) they are right and the confidence of that record to confirm their resentment at interference from any newcomer.

So what do you do?

"As I arrived on the scene at Maxwell House," says Arthur Larkin, "things were going very well." His first post at General Foods was as head of marketing for the corporation's largest division—testimony to his acknowledged marketing savvy. Despite that formidable reputation, he approached the job with the lightest possible tread. "I felt the most important thing for me to do was learn the business and the people. For almost four months I felt my best position was not to make a whole lot of decisions, but to maintain a very low profile and to learn what makes Maxwell House tick."

Notice the stress on "making decisions." It is the characteristic duty of a boss, without which you are little more than moderator of a debate. But shrewd decisions comprehend the abilities and resources of the group, plus the personalities, agendas and bents of the individuals involved. These are unknown quantities for you at first, and you are better off making no decisions—keeping the low profile Larkin favors—until you know enough about the group to make the kind of decisions, with the kind of facility, expected of the boss.

Do not try to slide into office. The temptation may be strong at times, particularly if your assignment is part of a broadening program. For instance, if your specialty is finance and you are made boss of a sales group, you know better than to meddle into strictly sales matters for a while; but financial, control or accounting questions are different. Certainly you would dispatch them with ease, even with ego-gratifying flashiness. But to the group you will not so much be displaying your strength in an area where they are weak as you will be underlining your weak hold on the main lines of their effort. You do better to forbear in all areas.

It is also a mistake to tip your hand about any plans you have. Almost at once you will spot areas where the group's performance can be improved, people who should be groomed for better things or moved into functions more congenial to their evident talents. Keep it to yourself. Telling people what you plan dissipates the drama of those plans when you get around to their execution and gains you nothing, since people dismiss what you are going to do for them "someday soon" as vainglory. Wait until you are ready.

How long is that? Until you feel you *know* the game and the players. Certainly a month, probably longer. It is not wasted time. Besides letting you learn what makes the group tick, this hands-off period acclimatizes the group to the fact of your presence as their head. A figurehead, true; but not ever a bumbler or a disappointment. You will still be an unknown quantity when you make your move, but not unfamiliar, and certainly not a figure of fun.

When the time for your move does come, announce yourself in resounding, unmistakable tones.

Although Arthur Larkin joined Maxwell House in November, and the General Foods fiscal year ended in March, it was not until April that he distributed his first noteworthy communication. He titled it "Monkeys." "I complimented the Maxwell House marketing people on a tremendous job in the previous year, but ended up, 'The monkey is now on our back; what do we do for an encore?' "

The beauty of this approach is the natural progression from "You did well" to "For your own sakes, *we* must do better." You do not ask to join the group. You permit the group to join you in their necessary search for better results. In the shadow of last year's superb performance, they may not be certain they can do better; it is unlikely they immediately know how to. They need leadership. They need you to show them the way.

Now establish yourself and consolidate your position. Larkin suggests that, if possible, you take your people "off campus" for a meeting on the subject of where you are, where you are going and how you will get there. At a suitably lofty level, you might go to some resort for a weekend seminar. On a more modest scale an extended lunch or dinner meeting will do fine. Even nine o'clock in the conference room is better than nothing. The idea is to contrive a break in office routine—getting everyone away from the scenes and roles they are used to, off to where you are the undoubted stage manager, scenarist, producer and director. You set the agenda. In fact, as the only one who really knows what's going on, you are in complete control, exerting unquestioned leadership. You might assign topics ahead of time for study and report, and start with your own keynote report that says, "Here is what our operation looks like to someone who lately had the detachment and fresh eyes of an outsider, but who also has the rapt interest of an insider informed by growing knowledge." Invite discussion and criticism of your views, touching on the group's strengths and weaknesses, its potential for improvement and plausible targets of opportunity.

At the end of the meeting, parcel out tasks that have been agreed on as most promising for further study or action.

Up to this point, your people have been going along in their old way. From now on they will be going your way, acting at your instance and direction. Suddenly you *are* the boss.

Now you can start to reveal and implement the ideas you hatched during your novitiate. But it should be step by step. That is especially true with any morale-boosting plans for promotion and job assignment. Although we will look more closely at specific plans in later sections (IX and XIV), the thing to remember about their application in new and favorable situations is their power—if used properly—in winning people to your cause. You can have a firm determination to establish a promotion-from-within policy in your group (as far as company policy allows) to make your group a launching pad for leadership of other groups; you can decide to mix up portfolios to keep people interested. But play it close to the vest. Implement any program person-by-person, making each seem an individual dispensation rather than the execution of a set policy—a singular reward as each person accepts your leadership and shows an interest in hitching his wagon to *your* star. Soon members of the group will realize that superior personal performance equals decidedly personal gain.

The message you put across is clear and simple: To-gether you will all prosper—more than ever before.

# 20 *Turning Things Around*

It is both flattering and daunting to be chosen to go in and clean up a mess. Careers are quickly made by successful troubleshoot-ing; but that is because it is tough. Your raw material, after all, is failure, and if the opportunities are obvious, so are the risks.

Maybe the greatest risk is that you will go into a bad situation so sensitized to the group's failure that you will con-front the people in it presupposing all their works, qualities and ideas to be inadequate, their suggestions suspect and their abili-ties untrustworthy. You would really like to announce your administration with a fragmentation grenade.

That, as a French cop once said, would be worse than a crime; it would be a blunder. "By and large, most people in even very bad situations are pretty good," says William Roesch. He should know. From Jones & Laughlin to Kaiser Industries he has specialized in turning around situations that have ranged from bad to spectacularly rotten. "You'll generally find that the thing has survived at all," he insists, "because most of the people are doing their jobs and doing them well."

A lucky thing. Because to turn a loser into a winner you must get some answers that come best, maybe only, from com-petent people who have lived through the problems. So you would not want to fire everyone and start fresh even if manage-ment let you.

The first step in setting things right is to determine the shape and dimensions of the disaster. It is not what they said it was upstairs. Whatever particulars made management un-happy—lousy production, low profit margin, slipping sales, outrageous costs, bizarre turnover or other such shortfalls—they are not the real problem. They are only symptoms. The real problem is the failure of the group to give other groups whatever goods, services and support they expect and need. The heart of it is blasted expectation.

What is expected of you and your people? What should your group be doing? How? And how did it fail to do what it should in the past?

Start with people in the groups that depend on yours for any goods or services. Not just the leaders of the group: key people at every level. Ask two questions. What do you expect from us? How have we disappointed you up to now? Remember that the least expert are absolute authorities about what they want and expect, no matter what any manual, chart or SOP says. So even if they are demonstrably "wrong" or blatantly unreasonable, what they say *is* what they want. Do not argue, listen. And keep listening when they volunteer notions on how to turn things around in your group. You may get some usable ideas, and it is good public relations to be respectful of their opinion.

The next step is finding out the same things from your own people. How do they see the problem? What do they think they are supposed to do for other groups, and how have they fallen down in the past?

Only rarely will simple misunderstanding emerge as *the* problem; life is seldom that neat. But you may turn up some disparities between what your people think their job is and what other groups actually expect. You may also isolate some expectations that are frankly unrealistic, considering your group's resources. The exercise will unfailingly clear the air, and a huge source of exacerbation is avoided when both sides agree on what is expected.

There are two more possibilities to watch for. First, it is possible that your group has a reputation for not doing a good job because the job should not be done at all. The mission may be a holdover from other times, other market and corporation conditions. Then you must suggest and preside over the group's dissolution or radical reorientation. It is not a major probability, true. But in pondering the group's purpose, you will generally spot at least a few activities and functions overdue for scrapping or streamlining.

Second, there is a possibility that the problem is largely mechanical. Survey your group's logistics: physical surroundings, equipment, communications and technical personnel. If reports never seem to get out on time, for example, it might be largely because there are not enough typists—or typewriters. Again, this will seldom be *it*. But here, too, there are often adjustments to be made.

Exxon's Edward Robinson found one that is not uncommon when, like most young comers, he was put in charge of a group in trouble. Robinson concluded that one controlling factor in the Exxon corporate planning group's sorry esteem was geography. "At that time, headquarters was split among two or three locations," Robinson explains, "and corporate planning was in one of the remote spots. I realized that if we were going to get anything accomplished, we had to be physically available to the people we were supposed to be serving, which was top management. So a high-priority thing, although it may sound like a simple housekeeping item, was to move to where the action was."

Keep all these possibilities in mind. But chances are you will finally discover that, yes, your group does have an important, relevant function, and they simply have not been pulling it off very well.

The next question is what to do about it.

There are no pat formulas, no surefire remedial actions or programs. Happily, though, bosses who have been through it agree that this is an area where to define the problem with reasonable precision is virtually to solve it. Rely on your own observations, conclusions and ideas, after close consultation with your people. For one thing, they ought to have some pretty good ideas, having long dwelt in agonized intimacy with the problem, and they certainly have a compelling incentive to help dig for solutions. There is also the question of morale. Theirs has been buffeted by failure, and what you are about to do requires reserves of goodwill and enthusiastic cooperation, commodities more easily evoked from people who feel they have some say in events.

The hallmark of a shake-up, after all, is that it leaves people shaken. No matter what your diagnosis of the group's problem, obviously there will be some changes made. They may involve radical surgery (effective change usually does) with resulting group trauma. Harold Johnson, VP for employee relations at INA, says, "Ralph Saul was brought in here to change things, and I am one of the people he brought in to help him change them. Well, the line organization that had been here two hundred years doesn't like it. You're talking about whole new sets of accountabilities, new responsibilities, new ways of doing things. It is trite to say, 'Change is tough,' but it is goddamn tough here."

It is tough everywhere, and will not get easier with time. In fact, since healing cannot start until the bleeding stops, the time to effect change is the instant you are sure what it should be. Your people will never again be so amenable (tractable, anyway) to the inevitable dislocations of change as in the beginning.

"When I took over at Jones and Laughlin," says William Roesch, "I figured it was the ideal time to take the job. Even the sweepers knew something had to be done. When the situation is bad, people are inclined to agree with any change you want to make." In their early desperation they will tolerate, even welcome, a degree of efficient high-handedness that would incite mutiny and obstruction in sunnier times. Make your most thoroughgoing changes early, and in wholesale lots—all of them at once, if you can—because, ironically, the more effective your earlier changes, the harder later ones are to institute. As your people warm to success, they will chafe at further change and begin to resist. "Coming in here, I was forced to be a kind of dictator," says INA chairman Ralph Saul. "I had to get certain people in certain places, and initially I could use the diktat to do it. Now that luxury is gone. I have to go through more explanations now, and each move takes more work."

As Saul suggests, the touchiest area of change is personnel. The fact that you did not start by assuming all your people were incompetent boobs does not mean you are blind to the need for new blood or tonic for the old. While you are surveying the situation, soliciting ideas and mulling over options, size up your people. By the time you know what the problem is, you should have a good fix on which people can help you solve it, and in what jobs. Then recruit new people from groups with which yours deals. That helps upgrade your group's standing in the company. And, as Edward Robinson puts it, "Their good reputation and proven ability to work with others in their former functions will help improve relations with other groups and help yours get the job done."

Internally, see if good people have been misused. One school of thought (whose chief professor is Peter Drucker) holds that groups should be built around the strengths of the people in them. That is nonsense—unless those strengths coincide with the group's mission. If your area is engineering, it does not help that one of your people exhibits strength in finance. Or if you need a financial analyst, *that* is what you need, even if the incumbent is a whiz at job costing.

What does make sense is to be sure, within limits of the mission, that individuals do whatever they do best. "What a man doesn't know will never earn a nickel for the company," says William Roesch. "One of my best men literally couldn't write his name. But he knew more about morgoil bearings than the engineers did. It would have been wrong for me to take him off the job because he couldn't write. And it would have been just as wrong to make written reports part of his job."

In this commonsense way, concentration on the strengths of your people means something. As nearly as possible, the effective boss accommodates his people's talents, even preferences, and does not cram people into table-of-organization molds. So, in a financial planning group, the thing to do with the wizard cost accountant is find him a suitable spot in another group (or company), not force him to struggle in an uncongenial calling—or torture your group's mission so as to "build around his strength." Following Robinson's advice, maybe you can even swap him for an ugly duckling financial analyst in accounting. That way you have two more partisans in both groups.

No matter how masterfully you arrange things, though, do not look for clear sailing all the way. "Invariably, at least one guy is going to test you, to defy you," William Roesch warns, "and it's impossible to back down." Early in his career Roesch was put in charge of maintenance at a plant notorious for downtime. The foreman of a large shop in the plant had failed as maintenance superintendent and had been demoted. He was in his sixties; Roesch was not yet thirty. The bitter ex-super kept bucking Roesch until it all came down to one issue on one day. Roesch had instituted a work order system that the older man flatly ignored. "He called in an outside contractor," Roesch says, "and gave him a maintenance job. I sent the contractor back out of the plant and told the man he was going to have to do it the right way. And he said, 'Well, if that's the way it's going to be, let's go up to the boss's office.' I said, 'That's OK with me. But I'll tell you now, when we come out, one of us won't be here. That's the only condition under which I'll go to the boss with you. Either you're working for me or you're not. And if not, the only way I'll stay is if you're gone.'"

The man's ardor for appealing decisions suddenly cooled.

This sort of challenge also occurs in good situations, but it is likelier in bad ones because people chagrined at having failed are bound to resent you, even (maybe especially) as rescuer. Good situation or bad, your response should be unwavering determination to assert ascendance. Pick an issue where you know you are right, then make it a matter of "you or me." Whatever the substance of dispute, going to higher authority is never the solution. Your authority is what is at issue, so going higher only subverts it.

The distinction is clear in what once happened to Stanley Kieller at Ford. He took over a department that had been leaderless for awhile. Section heads had been reporting directly to the division boss, and one continued after Kieller's arrival—though on an informal, stopping-him-in-the-hall basis—even when asked to stop. Going to higher authority was the crux of defiance. So Kieller finally put it to him: If the section head kept it up, they'd *both* go to the division chief one more time—but *one* of them would never be going again. It would take a subordinate of manic confidence not to realize whom the big boss would have to back in such a case. Kieller never had another problem of insubordination in the department.

# X  KEEPING GOOD PEOPLE

*You cannot always promote people as fast as they (maybe
you) would like. You cannot always raise their salaries.
Probably you cannot keep them forever churned up and
challenged and motivated to a peak; maybe you cannot even
keep them always interested. The question is, can you keep
them, period?*

*The ideal is that everyone in your group should be
describable as "good." At different levels of ability and
capacity, to be sure—but good at what they do. The problem
is that the better someone is, the more prey to discontent, the
more quickly challenge evaporates and boredom sets in, the
greater the impatience at lack of progress. So you must be
able to recognize who the good people in your group are, what
makes them good, what the characteristic discontents are of
different sorts of good people—and what to do about it.*

# 21 *Who They Are and Why They Might Quit*

We are talking about *good* people—not only the best. The tendency is to cater to superstars, worry about the "merely talented" only when they mutter, and assume that useful plodders are grateful to have steady jobs. But a team needs stalwart linemen as much as it does flashy backs, and will falter as surely for lack of one as the other. So you must be aware of the probable sources of disaffection for all in your group who do the kind of job you would miss if they left.

First, there are the "promotables" whose talent should move them (at varying speeds, for varying distances) through the corporation. Their unhappiness is almost always a function of how tortuous or delayed their progress seems to them.

The most obvious group of promotables are disappointed rivals for promotion. They figure to be the best people in the group, if you go by proven ability and experience (if not, always, talent and promise); their loss would be a sure blow to efficiency. It is natural to be exercised over the danger of losing them if you are the one just promoted as boss. It is harder to remember that every time you promote a subordinate, he or she will have disappointed rivals who must be mollified. Yet—as we shall see in the next chapter—it is the bigger boss, not the newly promoted, who plays the decisive role in keeping disappointed rivals happy.

Ironically, you may soon have to worry about the one you promoted, too. You can move people only so far, so fast. That means the better someone is, the greater the lag between accomplishment and reward. Especially to the young and impatient, six months since the last raise or promotion can mean they no longer feel loved and had better start putting together résumés.

You can have the same problem, if less acute, with nearly all promotables from time to time. Very good people may have to go a long while with only token raises and no substantial promotion when money is tight and there are no vacant slots. After long enough, even the patient get restless.

Finally, there are "undetected promotables." These are people stuck in relatively low-level jobs, not because they lack the native ability or intelligence to progress (though they often are light on education and formal training), but because they have somehow become inextricably identified with the job in their boss's mind and (worse!) their own. So they stay secretaries, file or stock or billing clerks, machine operators and the like, never aspiring to anything more. They do their jobs very well but are bored silly because the demands of the job are so far below their powers. Like their more obviously able brothers and sisters, their problem is lack of progress. The trouble is, nobody knows it—including them. They know they are unhappy, though, and if something is not done to detect their potential, and their hidden frustration, they will suddenly up and quit, as often as not for the same job in another company.

The other class of potential malcontents includes everyone who might be considered part of the permanent professional staff. It has nothing to do with rank. These are people, at any level, who have found their niche, do not want more responsibility (they may already have considerable), and have come to terms with ambition. They do their particular jobs splendidly; indeed, they keep the wheels turning and are proud of it. They should be wonderfully happy. Then, suddenly, they become furious and want to quit.

The sources of their unhappiness are harder to pin down, being episodic, cranky and even irrational. For instance, they will usually resent a newcomer as boss even more than do the contenders who were finally reckoned not ripe enough for the job. Basically, the problem with the permanent professionals is the very static contentment of their position. They are happy and proud of their limited expertise, yes; but they know it is limited, and so is their station. Nothing is going to change for them, and they dare not try to change it for fear of losing their power base. The knowledge is periodically galling and cause for occasional despair.

The phenomenon is even more unsettling for those permanent professionals who still have vestigial stirrings of ambition. They really have gone as far as they can or ought to (maybe a bit too far). Yet they feel they should be doing more. Certainly they will never be finally content, no matter how great their satisfaction with the job they are doing, until they find out for themselves that they really have reached their limits.

# 22 *What to Do About It*

There are three basic things you can do to convince good people that their future is with you: *Ask them* what they want, *tell them* honestly why they can't have it (if they can't) and *show them* why—and what they can have instead. Any specific technique may be effective with all kinds of good people, but some are patently more appropriate for certain problems.

1. *Ask them.* The greatest untapped source of vital information is the direct question. You can deal with what people want, if at all, only when you know exactly what it is. Even if you know roughly that ambitious comers want growth and promotion, you cannot divine the paths they hope to take or come up with acceptable substitutes unless they tell you. Maybe the ambitious will. But why take a chance when asking is sure and when it pays the handsome dividend of showing your interest in them and their careers?

And if it is wise to ask the ambitious, it is essential to ask the undetected promotables (which means you must ask everybody about their goals, since you will not know who the undetected promotables are until you do ask). They cannot volunteer their ambitions because they are either unaware of them, as practical possibilities, or too diffident. They will not risk derision and rebuff. But they can tell you two things. The first is whether or not they are happy.

"We had a secretary who was *so* good and *so* bright, it was hard to believe. And beautiful, too!" says Paul Charlap, chairman of Savin Business Machines. In fact, the secretary was so bright that Charlap got worried. "Finally, I asked her, 'Tish, are you happy running that machine?' She said, 'Uh-uh, it's boring.' But all she could think to do about it was quit. Finally, I got her to say, 'Hey! there's a job I think I'd like in this company!' Bright as she was, she couldn't spot the possibility without pushing because she had so formalized her position in her own mind. Once she broke out of that mold, she was fine. We shifted her to sales, training customers to use our machines and helping salesmen close. A few weeks ago she told me, 'Paul, I'm bored; I'm not learning anything anymore. I want to be a salesman.' I said, 'Tish, that machine is too heavy for you to lug around and demonstrate.' I was only teasing; we have a girl in Philadelphia who weighs ninety-four pounds and manages to get one around. Tish said to me, 'See the way I look? Some fella will carry it.' " Charlap gladly made her a salesman immediately.

The second thing people can always tell you—if asked —is what they picture themselves doing in a few years. That is the key question for undetected promotables who do have an inkling of their own worth but do not have enough confidence in themselves, or you, or maybe just The System, to push forward. "It's necessary to be continuously aware that, just as the company has one- and three- and five-year plans, so do the people working for you," says *New York Times* director of special projects Leonard Harris. "They ordinarily don't get a chance to tell you their long-range plans; you have to ask them. If we keep people in particular jobs without allowing them to make the progress they've planned for themselves, we won't have happy or productive people." Matter of fact, we probably won't have them, period—not for long. So it is not a matter of losing a superb secretary or billing clerk; you'll lose them anyway. But you may be able to find and keep talent.

The basic principle is that whenever you notice people functioning markedly above the level necessary for the job they are doing, you had better find out if they are happy and if they can see themselves still happy doing the same thing a few years from now.

2. *Tell them.* Of course, the answer may be "yes" on both counts.

Some people who do a fine job either do not want more responsibility or will not exert themselves to qualify for bigger jobs. You cannot do without them; the permanent professional staff is the backbone of any group, providing a continuity of expertise. Unfortunately, like the best backbones, they tend to be unbending. They stake out their empires and jealously guard their functions and authority. They bridle whenever new people are brought in, especially on their own level, because they assume newcomers mean change (which they resist) and will automatically usurp their authority. Besides, why is anyone new needed with *them* and their expertise available?

You can do little about their basic apprehensions. But you can defuse their resentment by what you tell them ahead of time when you recruit new talent.

First, make sure the permanent professionals know that the new people have indisputable credentials, at least on a par with their own. Next, make it clear why you need the new people, and what their presence will help the group accomplish. "It means telling people of the detailed logic behind any 'people-move' decisions," says INA chairman Ralph Saul. "If there's a real business reason about the decision, that will be accepted; people can take that." When Saul contemplates radical personnel moves, he first has a corporate strategy group prepare "the logic paper" explicating the unassailable necessity for whatever he has decided to do. It works. And, of course, these measures also placate those who are ambitious but who are not yet qualified to take over. It is harder to resent superiors who are so manifestly *superior*.

Disappointed rivals are a different problem and must be told something else. The person doing the promoting has the more important message, but the person who has been promoted also has to speak his piece. The experience of Thomas Plaskett, senior VP for finance at American Airlines, is illuminating.

When Plaskett's predecessor resigned, chairman Albert Casey called a meeting of eligible candidates and announced that he intended to try to fill the job from within the company. He promised he'd try to keep everyone informed at every step. "What impressed me most," says Plaskett, "was Al's completely open approach. We went back to him two or three times for interviews. Each time he told me who he was talking to and what his timetable was. 'I'll be back to you by Tuesday of next week,' he'd say, 'and I want to have a final decision by August first.' And he did the same with everyone else. Then, when he made the decision, he personally called all the people involved and told them first, told them why, and asked for their help in making the thing work."

That was just about perfect. Let people know what to expect and when. Tell them the bad news as well as the good (*tell* it, do not write it; certainly do not leave it for the grapevine). Make sure they hear it first so they have time to compose their minds—and faces—for the world. Give them a decent explanation for your decision. Then enlist their help.

The final step is to make sure disappointed rivals know that this defeat in no way blights their future. "One of the three people in final contention knew a hell of a lot more about the airline than I did," says Plaskett. The man had sixteen years' experience in finance, scheduling and marketing. "The problem was to convince him that he is still a very valuable asset to the corporation, that he does have a good future, and maybe other assignments will be more in line with his career path. Only Al Casey could do that." He did it by telling the man of his continued high esteem and bright future.

Equally, only the person promoted can say some things that must be said. There was irony in this case. Plaskett had come to American as an assistant controller after a promising start in finance at General Motors. When the controller left, about six months later, Plaskett and another assistant controller were front-runners for the job—and the other one got it. Plaskett was carefully told why: His financial background had been in the more arcane areas of budgeting and planning, not the nitty-gritty of accounting; the other candidate was a strong technician, which is what's needed as controller.

Now the shoe was on the other foot. The new controller was one of the three finalists, but his narrower background counted against him for the more expansive job as head of finance. Even so, he was invaluable to the department, the company—and the new officeholder. "Bill and I had several talks," Plaskett explains, "and I laid it all out, what I felt. In some areas I needed him more than he needed me. But in other ways I could help him develop and become less specialized. I told him, 'I can give you more exposure to the airline, open up some additional opportunities for you. In return, I need your cooperation and support.' And there was absolutely no problem."

It is not only in such identifiable crisis moments when openness pays off. Periodically, the best of people, comers and permanent professionals alike, may fly off the handle. Deadlines are missed and the people drag about, chronically down-in-the-mouth, beset by a sense of ennui and futility, a free-form longing for "something better." The only treatment possible is a frank discussion—sympathetic, but unequivocally realistic—about their prospects in the company and out of it. Maybe promotions and raises are not so abundant here as they would like. But what are the opportunities for learning? What are the ego gratifications in the kind of work they are doing? What are the working conditions? The benefits? And, honestly, what are the chances that things would be better for them somewhere else? A little discussion goes a long way.

However, as they say, actions speak louder than words.

3. *Show them.* Irrational dissatisfaction most often afflicts permanent professionals whose jobs lack the innate excitement of growth and advancement (they have become so adept exactly because they keep doing the same thing). It is not always enough to point out to them the advantages of staying, or the fact that most of the time they like what they do. They know all that. But they are unhappy *now.* You must do something about the built-in stagnation of their position.

One thing is to run lean enough so everyone has plenty to do. The most pernicious boredom is caused not by dull work, but by too little work. "And there is a multiplying effect of boredom," says Nicholas Mercurio of Benrus. "The more bored they are, the less they want to do, and the more bored they get. Soon everyone is bored stiff."

The second thing you can do is what Edward Robinson of Exxon calls "shifting portfolios." Of course, you cannot take a professional accounts payable clerk or supervisor and shove that person into the advertising group, doing display layouts. But the gap between, say, receivables and payables is not unbridgeable. In fact, even more minor exchanges of assignment chase boredom without disturbing efficiency. "Lots of jobs have so many facets," says Robinson, "you'll always find three or four people capable of doing something. Mix those portfolios up and get people working on this or that special project. It's exciting for them."

You must also deal with those who have advanced too far. Usually, such people either are overwhelmed and quit or they are fired. There is an alternative. You can at least *offer* them discreet demotion to duties you know they can cope with, back to a level where they can comfortably exercise the ability that unfortunately led to one-too-many promotions. "It's very difficult, and you have to think about title, responsibilities, money and so on," says Robert Tisch, president of Loews, "but I'm proud of what we've done in keeping some good people like that, moving them back. Because, you know, it's not altogether their fault; the company is at fault, too, that they were pushed over their heads." Your responsibility, as boss, is making the offer and contriving it (with title or transfer) so they can accept with minimum loss of face.

Better, still, arrange matters so people do not end up in that fix. That means constructive action with those who have reached what you consider the limit of their potential. "I have a situation right now," says Stanley Gondek, controller of Sara Lee. "She's been an accountant here for ten years. She's bright and competent but lacks the imagination and confidence to be a manager. She's been doing the same thing for three or four years and wants to know where she goes from here.

"I've given her the job of reorganizing duties among the accountants—giving her complete control. What I'm saying to her is, 'Here's the sort of work you'll have to do if you go ahead.' I'm forcing the issue. After ten years she's going to have to find out whether she's got it or not. She's got all the resources necessary, so if she fails, she'll know it's her failure, not the company's.

"But you've got to give them a shot at it. Not to convince yourself so much as to convince that person. 'Look, you've been tested, and here's the evaluation, and I'm sorry but you had better resign yourself to the fact that this is as far as you're going to go.' It's a difficult thing for a person to accept, and they won't if you just say it. But showing them helps. It clears the air. They've had their chance."

As a happy bonus, sometimes people will surprise you. But if they falter, as you expect, make it clear that this is not their last raise or interesting assignment, or even last chance at a bigger job. The important thing is that they've had their shot, their access to hope. They have shown themselves what they would not believe if just told: that they are better off doing what they do well. With that demonstration, they may be able to be content; without it, never. We most poignantly regret things never attempted, chances not taken, while we can generally come to terms with reality, even if it includes failure.

Then there are those in your group who would not fail no matter what the assignment. The comers can be even harder to deal with than the professionals. There is no question about the roots of their dissatisfaction. Just as failure is not in their vocabulary, neither is gratitude for past raises and promotions. Nor patience. Today's challenge is tomorrow's tedium, and they cannot understand why they should not forge ahead. The trouble is, they are right. They are chronically underpaid and underpositioned considering their contribution and promise. Still, there is an organizational limit to how far and how fast you can push them. What else can you do to keep them happy?

Start by being certain that the only impediment to their progress is rational company policy—not the nervous, repressive resentment of any intermediate straw bosses. Also be sure *you* are not blocking them. It does not have to be intentional; with all goodwill, you can block people simply by not noticing their needs. If you have a comer in your group who is plainly growing faster than the structure of your group can accommodate, promote him or her out of your group. Sure, it means that you personally will lose the star's splendid services. But as with undetected promotables who stay undetected, you will lose them anyway—and a lot sooner. Better to lose the services to another group within the company than to another company. Better for the company, and for your own reputation.

"There were two such cases here very recently," says Ford executive VP Donald Petersen. "The general manager heard about them first from a more junior manager—and duly noted that here was someone willing to give up talent in the interest of the company rather than the personal, short-term interest of getting a super job out of them, but only for a few months until they got disgusted and went somewhere else." Petersen feels so strongly about the subject that he has formalized the process of identifying and listing such comers. "We tell managers, 'If you have people who are bona fide producers, yet you can't do anything for them, please get them on the list.' We distribute it to all general managers so we can alert them to availability and the need to find places for these people." Formally or informally, you can do the same for your own comers, and to help your subordinate bosses with theirs.

That does not mean you automatically spin off your most promising personnel. It applies only to those whose talents are so palpably underused and underrewarded it is a wonder they have not already left. For what might be called the run-of-the-mill stars, less urgent solutions are appropriate.

As in thinking about motivation, begin by asking yourself, "What do they want?" (Besides more money and bigger jobs, that is.) For both disappointed rivals and comers who are not moving as fast as they would like (which describes most of them), there is an attractive alternative. Give them responsibility. Not just titular authority, mind, but what the chairman of Pillsbury calls "the freedom to exercise the power you give." For the best people that is more important than titles or any but epic raises. Giving it means you must be prepared to surrender some of your own power, but it is in a cause that radiates self-interest because it keeps good people doing a good job for you, even in the face of objective disappointment or serious frustration.

At J. C. Penney, for example, management was facing growing discontent among some of their best people, the general merchandise managers who work directly under store managers. Their pay was great; in fact, a general merchandise manager in a big store would make more than the manager of a small store. But in the Penney tradition, store manager was *the* job everyone pointed toward, and there just were not enough such jobs to go around. If 200,000 feet of floor space was built fifteen years ago, that meant ten stores with openings for ten managers. Today that space is one store, with one manager—and a lot of general merchandise managers.

"So, as a percentage of the managerial population, the opportunity to be a store manager today is actually less than it was fifteen years ago," says chairman Donald Seibert, "though the opportunity for a big, better-paying job is better." The "big, better-paying" part cut no ice. "What it came down to," Seibert says, "was a desire to be a *manager* in a literal sense. They were saying, 'If you can assure me that in a big store the job will carry its own well-defined responsibility and authority—and I would not have to run to the store manager all the time—if I really had a piece of the store to run under the general direction of the manager, I would find that a very satisfying, rewarding job. I know it pays well. But what I really want is to be a manager.' And I think that's true of most people who have what you're looking for: they want to manage something."

It is your ultimate weapon. It is how you keep the good people, the best people. After all, isn't it how they are keeping you?

# XI  *MOVING ON*

*This is the other side of the coin.*

*Remember that all the way up the ladder you are somebody else's "good people." Everything discussed in the previous section applies to you, and your management may be concerned about keeping you. But there are times when you should not let yourself be kept.*

*Certain conditions can develop in a company that are simply intolerable, no matter how avidly management tells you they treasure your services and do not want you to leave. What these conditions tell you about the company is so fundamental that it means they cannot change without the company's ceasing to exist as the company it is. How do you recognize such conditions? What should you do about them?*

*How can you tell that the time to move on has come? What are the signs and circumstances? When you do move, what kind of move should it be and how should you arrange it? What should you look for and how can you tell you've found it? What should you look out for?*

*Maybe most important of all: When should you not move? And why?*

# 23 *When to Leave, When Not to, How and Why*

Whatever time you spend with a company is an investment whose dividends are repute and stature within that company, assets only minimally transferable. Even if you leave for an objectively better job, you largely write off your investment with each move.

That fact leads to a number of important conclusions.

Your moves should be made early in your career. After ten years a move should herald extraordinary circumstances (for choice, moving into a top or near-top position). Early or late, moving on should be a defensive response to plainly terminal conditions. There are several impelling, even imperative, reasons to leave a company, but only one proper mood: more in sorrow than anger. Sorrow that you cannot stay after your investment of time and talent; sorrow over the failure of your most strenuous and imaginative efforts to contrive a way over, under or around any obstacles to your continued employment. Being in the same job too long *is* deadly. But there is no such thing as being in the same company too long.

Recognizing that fact arms you against the meretricious temptations of "résumé-building." Nothing could be worse for your career. A few years' "exposure" with all the more plangent corporate names in your field may wow some entry-level personnel type; those who do important hiring are not impressed. "People who consciously build résumés are making a *terrible* mistake!" insists Sara Lee president Thomas Barnum. "It looks good for a while—'two years at Procter, four at General Foods' —but when you're looking for a senior officer, you want to see stability. If a fellow has been a few places, I'm not against that.

But if I see a regular cycle of change, I wouldn't want him."

It does not matter that each company hop is upward. It is the inordinate number of them that makes a prospective employer nervous. "We need a chief actuary," says Gordon Crosby, chairman of USLIFE, "and I've been interviewing two men who from a technical, professional point of view are qualified. But in fifteen to eighteen years, they've been with maybe eight or ten different companies. Well, how do you know? Are they now coming here for a career? Or only until the next guy waves an extra five thousand dollars at them?"

None of this means that when you join a company you enter peonage. In fact, you must keep yourself perpetually ready to leave if need be. The secret ingredient is money. "I always want to feel freed up enough to leave if I run into an environment I can neither tolerate nor change," says William George, president of Litton Microwave. "That's why I do *not* spend most of my income. It's important as to how I think about my job, today and tomorrow." Family-budgeting experts say you should set aside six months' pay "for emergencies." It is good advice, but the real reason is so you can avoid any feeling of economic pressure when you weigh a decision about moving on. With enough financial cushion, you can leave without sweaty palms.

But don't go away mad. Or, if you can help it, with them mad at you. This is another aspect of being ready to leave. Your absence will be their loss, right? That is punishment enough. So make sure your group's affairs are in good order before you go, with your successor trained to a degree that does you proud. And leave on a note of reasonableness and expressed regret. If exit interviews are not already company SOP, request one yourself, as far up the hierarchy as possible. It accomplishes two things. It is a final stab at setting things right before you call it quits. As the ultimate corporate protest, resignation commands attention. Now they *know* you are serious about your complaints and may be more disposed to consider them seriously. But in any case, a rational, measured explanation of why you feel you must leave, along with your lack of rancor and your punctiliousness about leaving in good order—these will mean you are remembered (and, more important, referred to) as someone of exemplary responsibility.

Understand, you will likely leave anyway, even if the exit interview is a love feast. Since you should contemplate moving on only when conditions nearly guarantee a dim future, those conditions are apt to be central to the company's way of operating. Management may agree with you and still not be able to change things without, in effect, changing the sort of company it is. They may not figure you are worth that.

Fortunately, there are not too many of these irretrievable conditions.

The most common one—as well as the most intolerable and dangerous—is when you are stymied and smothered by an extravagantly dumb superior. Maybe he was good once and burned out; maybe he was promoted over his head; maybe he is someone's nephew. Never mind how he got there. Trouble is, position in many companies develops a life of its own, and management automatically ratifies those they've set in power by backing them against challenges from below, even given evidence of palpable incompetence. In fact, an inadequate superior's bankrupt esteem is the greatest single hazard for a subordinate. You recall the chairman of American Airlines saying, in chapter 7, "Promote your boss"? Well, he went on to say, "But you've got to have a promotable guy as boss. He must be secure and competent, someone you can help move along without his viewing you as a challenge." Management is unlikely to trust a nonpromotable boss to oversee momentous projects (which means you and your group will not get any); they will be bored with someone so stagnant and may not bother looking too closely at the people under such lackluster leadership. At the same time, your boss's quite justified sense of inferiority will impel jealous suspicion of everything good you do, and the most inert incompetents somehow unearth wellsprings of talent and vigor when it comes to artful malevolence and repression of those they fear as a threat.

"Now, you have to give it time," warns Thomas Barnum. "You can't say in the first week, 'Gee! I hate this s.o.b.' It takes, minimum, a year to make that kind of evaluation." Furthermore, it has nothing to do with mere liking or disliking. If they have things to teach you, it is not at all necessary to enjoy yourself while you study under prickly superiors. In fact, the better you like them, the more watchful you must be. Are you continuing to learn and grow, or are you simply luxuriating in an easy relationship? "You can't just stay with a person you're compatible with and still expect to learn a lot about how to run a business," says William Roesch, president of Kaiser Industries. "Look at how many people have gone to work for Geneen! Probably every one of them learned a lot. I know I did. Geneen was controller of Jones and Laughlin when I was a superintendent, and I learned an awful lot from him."

There are other flaws in a superior that, while less automatically terminal, are so inhibiting you must either find a way around or leave. If your boss will not talk to you: to discuss or review your performance, to let you know anything beyond the bare essentials of your immediate task. If your boss refuses to let you take on new projects and responsibilities, and maybe interferes with your present authority. In short, if for any reason your boss is ill-disposed toward you and plainly does not want you to grow.

In all cases it is worth forcing a confrontation—a peaceable one. That is, you should not get into a debate, much less a shouting match, over the merits of your grievance. Do not accuse and do not threaten. Say what's bothering you in equable tone and diction and ask that he change. He probably won't, even if he can—but at least you tried, and that will score heavily for you in the exit-interview situation mentioned earlier. Management will regard you with greater respect for having made a firm, calm effort at accommodation. They may let you out from under that superior while staying in the company. Then again, they may not. As noted, they will probably feel they must support the superior in the name of "channels" and good order. It will be company policy.

That brings us to the next sort of intolerable situation: wrongheaded policy, pigheadedly maintained, that fatally compromises your progress.

Actually, any adamant, unshakable policy is bound to be wrongheaded. Policy has an honest role. It assures coherent, predictable decision; it makes desirable activity routine, saving time for the bright while keeping the dim from creating disaster. But policy should be the servant of decision, not master. Elevated to Holy Writ, it is deadly.

As soon as you discover the dead hand of policy set against you, find out how committed the company is to that policy. Is the inviolability of policy itself company policy? If so, you should probably move on, depending on the sort of policies the company holds sacrosanct. The important factor to examine is not the degree of discomfort you feel over a specific policy, but what the policy tells you about corporate mind-set and its portent for your long-term future.

After fine progress up several corporate ladders, Evelyn Berezin found herself at Digitronics as a product planning manager. "The next level would have been vice-president of engineering," she says, "and I wasn't going to get that. I don't know if it was entirely because I was a woman, although I'm sure that was part of it, but I realized that was the end of the line. I knew I had to start my own company if I wanted to be at the top." So she started Redactron.

The policy was not carved in marble, or even anywhere explicit (that would have been illegal). But discriminatory policies of any kind (including subtle ones like "engineers don't become managers, here" or "the sales department *owns* the executive committee") are easy to pick up with even moderately sensitive antennae. What's more, a company policy does not have to exclude you permanently to make you consider moving on, if it clashes with your life or career plans.

Thomas Plaskett, who became a senior VP at American Airlines at age thirty-three, grew up with General Motors. He went from high school to the GM Institute. In 1968, after an MBA, he started a succession of GM jobs that were interesting, challenging and flattering in what they said about the company's opinion of his potential. By 1973 he was staff assistant to the treasurer, often working directly with the chairman. It was swell. And yet "I realized it would be some time before I achieved a level of responsibility I wanted," he says. "I didn't want to wait until I was forty or forty-five for major responsibility. Traditionally, GM has not pushed young managers— though they're doing it more now. Still, leaving was a tough decision because GM had been very good to me and I had progressed very well."

He knew that the amount of responsibility he might eventually achieve by staying would be awesome. So would the money—eventually. "If you prove your commitment to the General," Plaskett says, "you get gigantic money when you're, say, fifty-five years old. But I don't need a half million a year. I'd rather be turned on by what I'm doing now." For him, more responsibility *now* outweighed lots more (of everything) someday. He was not willing to wait ten or fifteen years, not even for the moon.

Paul Charlap was not willing to wait even a few months —but for a different and highly instructive reason. One of his first jobs was in the fabric business, with United Merchants and Manufacturers. "It was a fat company," Charlap says, "with college graduates running the mail room. My second day there, I asked why I had to spend four months delivering mail. The VP in charge said, 'It's so you know the executives, where they are and what they do.' That night I took home lists. Three days later I went back and said, 'Ask me anything.' "

The company's response at that point was OK. They immediately skipped Charlap to the next idiot training stage, cutting swatches of material. "Everyone had to spend six to eight months there," Charlap says. "A salesman would call, you'd cut a swatch and drop it down a chute. The idea was, that way you'd learn the line. So I made myself a swatch book and I memorized everything. Then I went to the VP and said, 'OK, I've learned everything I'm supposed to in there.' He asked questions, and I'd tell him, 'For that material we buy the gray goods here for so much, it's converted in this plant in North Carolina at such-and-such a cost and we sell so much a year in this price range.' He couldn't believe it! But he had to. And I said, 'I want to move out of there into sales.'

"He said, 'I'll talk to you about it tomorrow.' He obviously talked to other people and they all decided, no, I'd have to keep cutting swatches the 'usual' length of time. I went right upstairs, took a whole bolt of cloth and dropped it down the chute. When it hit I called, 'Can you hear me, sir?'

" 'Yes.'

" 'I quit.' "

It was not the number of months he would waste; it was what that demonstration of mental rigidity told him about the company. Delivering mail and cutting swatches is arguably a valid way to learn what the company wanted its new people to learn. As policy it has at least the color of reason. But it is simply gaga to hold swatch-cutting, itself, important training. It signaled that the *real* policy was a controlling fear of subordinates going too far too fast—an intolerable one for Charlap or any other comer.

Not that a policy even has to be objectively "bad" to be intolerable. Kenneth Monfort saw a "nonvalue" policy clash from the corporate viewpoint. He still regrets (though not inconsolably) the loss of a former VP in charge of Monfort of Colorado's international operation. "The man wanted a more formal way of doing things than we're comfortable with here,"

Monfort says. "He wanted a set procedure for reporting to me, and didn't want me answering phone calls during his appointments. Well, my calls are from customers, and to me that comes first. And I prefer people just dropping in—and coming back if I'm tied up. But that didn't suit him. In fact, his style and mine were just so different he felt he had to leave." Similarly, if you quarrel with a company's basic idea of how they want to do business—low price and high volume versus quality; discounting versus fair trading; open versus closed atmosphere or some such other fundamental difference in outlook—chances are you should leave. It is not, notice, a question of right or wrong, but of mutual intractability on a central point.

There are other reasons to move on that do not involve intolerable conditions. Indeed, they are hard to recognize as terminal exactly because there is no telltale sense of contest or faction, no moment of clash.

You should move on when you have played out your string.

The most common such situation is when you are too long in the same job. "I think a three-year learning curve is about right," says William Roesch. "After that, I always made up my mind to be somewhere else." Of course, there is no magic in "three years." Roesch is a fast learner; you may be even faster or a lot slower. Moreover, some jobs are so complex and varied that it takes a lot longer to crack them and extract the meat, while you can exhaust the possibilities for learning and growth of other jobs almost at once.

It took Louis Ross just over a year to realize he should leave the testing department at General Motors. "We got some test requests that looked like what I'd seen the year before," Ross says. "One of the pros told me we did it every year. 'The same test cycle?' I asked. 'Yeah—ninety, ninety-five percent,' he said. Well, I could see that if I were there five years, I wouldn't have five years' experience, I'd have one year's experience five times. I wanted to move." Unfortunately, GM was pretty inflexible in that particular area at that time, so Ross had to leave the company. He would have stayed if he could have had another job. It is obviously better to stay, and is often possible. Roesch kept changing jobs, as he said—but within Jones & Laughlin—all the way to the top. You have to be forthright about what you want, sending up immediate distress signals when there is nothing more for you in your job.

You may also have played out your string in a particular company when you find yourself passed over for promotion. That does not mean rejected, of course. There has been a consideration of your merits and a conclusion that, however impressive, they are not what's needed for some greater post. Or, even more vaguely disquieting, you may simply get a feeling that you have lost your momentum in a company. It is a situation that calls for profound introspection and nice judgment. Are they right? Or is it merely that some insuperable shifts of favor and fashion have conspired to cramp you? If you decide the company's assessment of your potential is wrong, you must make a move. The first one should be to clarify the situation. "You should go to your boss," says former Chase Bank president Herbert Patterson, "and say, 'What's my future?' The boss may say something like, 'You've got a bright future with the company. I know the guy who was promoted is two years your junior, but Joe's going up a special column; you're more of a generalist and need more experience.' Then you have to make up your mind about the accuracy of that—and the boss's honesty."

Then again, you may be told the company thinks you have reached your peak. At least that sharpens the issue. There is also the possibility that the boss may not be able to say anything useful about your future. "In many disciplines, a company—especially a major company, such as Ford—tends to hire far more super talent in, let's say, financial analysis, than can possibly rise to the top of their company's financial organization," says Ford executive VP Donald Petersen. "In that case it's entirely appropriate that people who see themselves closed out, leave."

"If," adds Exxon's Leonard Berlin, "it's early enough in your career." Berlin sums up from the young comer's point of view: "Do the job the way you think is right, and if you're good you'll advance—at least you will in this company. If at some point your career stops, and you think there's more in you, that's the time to move." Before, that is, you are either trapped by the mortgage, orthodontia and college tuitions or seduced by accreting profit shares.

But watch out for the tendency, when jumping from a frying pan, to land not in a fire (because you are not stupid) but in another frying pan—because that is, after all, what you know best, having just come from there. Be wary of a new situation that looks "comfortable" and familiar, one you *know* you can handle. If you must move, move to a challenge. In fact, one of the urgent reasons for moving on is a sudden suspicion that just maybe you *can't* handle something new. At that point, you should try something new at once!

Albert Casey's career touches almost all relevant bases of moving on correctly. He never left in a huff; his replacement was ready to take over. When he left it was always at the right time for the right reason. "I worked for Southern Pacific for thirteen years," he says, "until I felt they didn't need me. I was handling short-term investments where success was making half a percent more than the next guy; it wasn't personally rewarding. What's more, the management team had great depth and competence; my boss was sixteen years from retirement.

"So I went to Railway Express, where everything was a disaster. They had been losing thirty-eight to forty million dollars a year. Bill Johnson—an outstanding guy who now runs IC Industries—let me run everything but the express business itself: purchasing, real estate, insurance, negotiations for subsidiaries, everything! In eighteen months we turned it around to where we made a four-million-dollar profit. Then the board of directors—presidents of the railroads that owned Railway Express—demanded that we pay a four-million-dollar dividend. Well, I refused to go along with it and quit. I felt it was a violation of representations I had made to banks—besides, it showed that my future there, and the company's future, was limited if the board was going to drain the company."

Casey next went to the Times-Mirror Corporation, working mostly with acquisitions. That was fine—except that he was Number Three and he had a hankering to be Number One. He was offered the job of running the bankrupt railroads, but it was just at the time of Watergate. "The Senate wasn't going to give Nixon anything unless he gave up the tapes, so my confirmation got hung up," he explains. He would not take the job without full authority, which he could not have without Senate confirmation. Same with the next offer, from American Airlines—to be sort of Number One-and-a-half,—with the ex-chairman still around. "He'd look over my shoulder and give me his wisdom and counsel. This is no reflection on C. R. Smith. He's a brilliant executive and a hell of a lot better guy than I am, but I feel a company can have only one boss." And he was going to be it—or why bother moving on? It would have been a variation on the frying pan theme. Casey waited until he was offered the job at American with no strings.

It comes down to this: Know what you want to move *for* and make sure it is what you are going to get. Stay where you are if you can arrange what you want there. And when you move, do not drift—*move!*

# XII  *HANDLING TALENT*
       *AND TEMPERAMENT*

*You may have the problem without realizing it, because you do not think of people in your line as having the sort of talent that suggests problems of temperament. You may think it is confined, in business, to advertising, architects, design engineers or research scientists.*

*Actually, a dedicated stock analyst or actuary or cost accountant—or anyone bright and talented enough to be capable of total absorption in the processes of any job—can be as much a problem in temperament for the boss as the flightiest artist or monomaniacal researcher.*

*It is an unexpected problem.*

*To be proprietor of a group rich in extraordinary talent might seem like a picnic in the Land of Beulah: Just sit back and let the rascals at it! Their abilities should rocket the enterprise along with minimum direction.*

*But no. There is nothing automatic about the fine performance of potentially fine performers. It must be elicited by patient and clever direction from a boss who understands the problem. "I'm amused," says the founder of the supertalent ad agency Doyle Dane Bernbach, "when other agencies try to hire my people away. They'd have to 'hire' the whole environment. For a flower to blossom, you need the right soil as well as the right seed."*

*When you provide the right soil, though, the results are spectacular!*

# 24 *Unexpected Problems, Exceptional Solutions*

The kind of talent that can be a problem is the province of every very bright employee whose passionate interest in technique is so intense it effaces every other consideration. These employees are zealots about their work, whatever it is, inclined to perfectionism and apt to get wrapped up in the unraveling of some little problem they consider fascinating. It engrosses them to the exclusion of any other calls on their time and energies—including the group's needs.

If what these zealots want to do happens to coincide with what the group must do, fine; if not, the group's goals go hang! And even when undisciplined talents go in the group's direction, it is generally the way a broken compass points in the "right" direction: only while you are headed north. Chances are, people like this will want to pursue some line of investigation long after the group is going somewhere else.

This is unexpected. You would think such bright people would surely make an analytic connection between the group's success and their own interests, especially since their luminous abilities promise that a good share of that success will come their way. But they do not care about such things. They have no self-interest, only self-absorption—which is total. The only thing that interests them is whatever details of their work catch their fancy, not the work's utility or rewards. In fact, doing it is the only reward that moves them.

A few years back, when Fairchild Camera and Instrument ended a totally permissive attitude toward research, one worker said (according to chairman Wilfred Corrigan), "From the company's viewpoint what you're doing is probably right:

having a more structured environment, with a clear statement of where we're going, keeping track of what money is spent and for what, and so on. But I liked working on whatever I wanted to all these years. Now you say what I work on has to have an economic result. So I'll probably look elsewhere for a job."

People with that attitude (the above sample is an extreme version, but sounds a typical motif) plainly present their boss with some totally unexpected problems of motivation.

Francis Sweeney sees the phenomenon all the time. As a doctor himself, and hospital director at Jefferson in Philadelphia, he orchestrates the talents, interests, directions and demands of many highly talented and fiercely independent doctors, a position with striking similarities to that of a boss in any business who encounters the highly talented. "They all wonder," says Sweeney, "why the entire focus of the institution isn't on the care of *their* patients, their projects. They don't think of themselves as necessarily being part of 'management' of this hospital even though they may be full-time staff."

That is often the basic attitude of the exceptionally talented in any group. It is a problem of too much dedication too narrowly directed.

What you must do is redirect their dedication. You must channel their talent to harness it for the group's goal.

None of the usual motivational techniques to get people interested in their work mean much here. Exceptionally talented people are already interested. The problem is: in *what?*

The way to get them interested in *your* work, as their boss, is to mix intimately in what they are doing, get excited about it and communicate your excitement to them. Your authority as their boss is not enough to compel their interest, but you *are* a figure of command, and they will find your enthusiasm stimulating, your involvement and attention flattering, your interest an official endorsement of their importance and the importance of what you want them to do.

"Too many companies get stuck with a sexy idea that

has no practical application," says Savin's Paul Charlap. "I get with my people and say to them, 'Now let's take this idea and see where we can go with it.' Then I start to play it back and forth with them, and before you know it one of them has turned it into an idea with real business potential. Just the fact that you get in and get interested and talk with them about their ideas —that stimulates them and excites them about what they're doing."

From your side, the excitement is in the incredible results that can come of the collaboration, from your interested involvement. "I am always surprised and dazzled by what a talented person can do," says George Cukor, Academy Award–winning film director, "and they surprise themselves, too, if you encourage them and free them." Which you do by that energizing interchange of ideas. "In one picture with Jack Lemmon and Judy Holliday," says Cukor, "they were supposed to be having a row. And I said, 'That was very well done, but I didn't believe it. What do you do, Jack, when you're angry?' He said, 'What I do couldn't be used—I get a stomachache.' I said, 'Try it!' So they were having this flaming row, and in the middle of it he sat down and had cramps while he kept up the fight. It was marvelous!"

You also free inventiveness by being willing, always, to at least consider seriously whatever talented people come up with. In another film, Judy Holliday was supposed to spill champagne down someone's back. It was a technically difficult scene normally requiring many takes because the glass had to be held just so or the champagne would not catch the light. At that point, the prop man announced he had only four shirts on hand. On top of normal tension, that did it. "Judy was so nervous," says Cukor, "she said, 'I know I'm going to laugh.' I said, 'If you laugh I'm just going to kill you, that's all I can tell you.' So she did the scene, and it was perfect—the glass tipped at exactly the right angle. But, sure enough, while she poured it, she giggled. The man's line was, 'Did you do that on purpose?' And she said, giggling again, 'I don't know!' It was absolutely realistic—and *awfully* funny. I had been totally wrong." When the director saw that what her talented instinct told her to do worked, he instantly accepted it.

"You must not cut off inspiration," Cukor concludes. "You build on their ideas and they build on what you tell them."

The only problem in handling talent by means of such collaboration is that as a boss you may feel diffident about working at close quarters with gifted people. If they are better at what they do than you are, will you lose your edge of authority? Will they show you up?

Don't worry. You are not competing with your talented people; you are firing them up and channeling their zeal, directing them—essential functions if anyone, including them, is to realize the full benefit of their ability. "I had a boss once who was really a genius," says Redactron president Evelyn Berezin. "He had ideas in such profusion! Unfortunately, he was president of the company, so they *all* got carried out—which was *terrible*. He should have been locked in a room where you'd take food in and bring his ideas out, and somebody else would decide whether each idea should be used or not."

You can perform that function despite great disparity in natural ability, or even knowing very little about the intricacies of their work. Because the best way to evoke their talent is to ask questions, not give answers, even if you can.

William Bernbach, perhaps the top all-around creative man in advertising, is supremely qualified to give any of his people answers. But he has always been careful not to. "I remember one of my *great* art directors saying to me, 'You never told me how to do *anything;* you asked me questions and my answers told me how to do it.'"

Besides, your people need you, no matter how brilliant they are, to supply the overview and direction to exploit their potential and give coherence to their performance. "You do a scene," says George Cukor, "and you have an enormous advantage over the actors because you're not involved. If they're smart they ask, 'How was it?' Not that you're so smart, but you see it, and you have a sense of the whole thing—whether the scene itself works, and how it fits in. It may be a bravura performance yet not fit in with the whole movie."

There is also the factor of discipline. Cukor points out that the old-time movie moguls, for all their faults, played a decisive role in making many Hollywood films masterpieces. "They were not cultured men," he says, "but they had a sense of showmanship and great business sense; they enforced restraint and responsibility in the artistic effort and they saw to it that stars did not burn out their careers with overexposure. Furthermore, they genuinely respected talent and knew how to use it. If you had something to give, they would encourage you." All of which exactly sums up the proper role for anyone who is boss of talent.

When you get your talented people on the right track, working toward usable ends, the remaining problems of handling them are relatively simple. But they are also unexpected.

For instance, you might suppose the brilliant would be secure in their powers and not prey to self-doubt. Not so. The sequel of each triumph is gnawing fear that *this* time they will not live up to their reputation. "The whole world has talked about their campaign," says William Bernbach. "What if the next one is not so good? They get uptight and resort to technical tricks instead of basics."

With ordinarily talented people you would buck them up and assure them of their ability. With the supertalented you must take a sterner line. "I let them know I'm aware of what's bothering them," Bernbach says, "but I tell them the surest way *not* to do a great job is not to be themselves—to be so concerned about their egos and their reputations. I'll say, 'Look, don't worry about your execution of this campaign. You are so talented anything you put down will be provocative. But if you start thinking only of how you're putting it down, you're liable to forget fundamentals, the *purpose* of the campaign.' When they see I'm aware what's going on inside them, they come right along."

Another control problem involves perfectionism. The talented find it hard to end an effort short of some ideal solution. "Their attitude," says Evelyn Berezin, "is *always* 'I can do it better—just give me another two months.'"

You might jolly lesser talents out of it, telling them what they have done is perfect. But the supertalented know better. So lay it on the line with them. Evelyn Berezin tells them, "I know you can do it better, but the exigencies of the whole program are such that it's more important to get it out on time than that it be the very best possible." Then she tells them the reasons—an essential part of the process.

That kind of honesty is especially important whenever you must say no to the highly talented. A complete discussion of your reasons will assure that you are right to say it.

"It's important that you don't say 'no' where it ought to be 'yes' or 'maybe,'" says Francis Sweeney. He had been allotting space in a new building at Jefferson Hospital and was besieged by requests for last-minute changes. Some were inevitable, like total redesign of the coronary care unit to accommodate a new aortic pump. But one role of the boss is making distinctions and making it a firm no when appropriate.

"If they become obdurate," says George Cukor, "you flatly tell them, 'No! It's not going to work.' It's a collaboration, but they must always know that when it comes to the nitty-gritty, your decision stands."

Another group at Jefferson Hospital wanted a vacuum outlet at a certain spot in their unit. To redo the plans would have cost a lot and held things up. "I said, 'Absolutely not!'" says Sweeney. "After they've occupied the space, if they still must have a vacuum outlet at that spot, and nowhere else will do, we'll core the floor and put it in." But the fact that it was an oversight indicated it was not all that vital. After discussion, Sweeney knew the group just thought it would be "nice" to have the vacuum outlet there, saving users an occasional trip around the corner. "For the ten thousand dollars it would have cost to change it this late, they can walk. It's good exercise."

The group's response was what it usually is from talent to a firm, honest and *justified* no: "Oh, well, we tried."

But, more often, full discussion will let you find inventive alternatives to flat rejection. And the boss who does not enlist talent in searching for alternatives fails to use an important resource. If nothing else, having them try with you to find ways around refusal disarms their feeling of rejection and convinces them that you could not decide any other way.

When you are saying no to a project already under way —when it is time to scrap it and start over—you must be extra careful to turn off the project without turning off their enthusiasm. Because of their talent, their defeats have the potential of being personally devastating. It depends on how you treat the defeat. "When it turns out that they've come to a closed door," says Paul Charlap, "I don't say to them, 'You dummy!' I say, 'Oh! Did we learn where not to go!' We set up a maze and we learned, 'Don't go down there.' We *learned* something." Together.

If all this seems like a lot of trouble, or like mollycoddling, reflect on the rewards of doing it right. Remember, these *are* talented people. Handle them right, get their zealots' temperament working for you, and you can achieve exemplary results. Also, you can have more fun.

"Better soft, yet firm, hands on a hard-driving team," says First Boston chairman George Shinn, "than always having to whip up sluggards."

# XIII  *MARGINAL EMPLOYEES*

*The previous subject was important because, although the number of the supremely talented is small, their impact, good or bad, is likely to be enormous. The same goes for marginal employees.*

*Marginals either do not have even ordinary quantities of talent or are steadfastly refusing to use what they do have. In either case, their impact is disproportionate to their number (which, unhappily, can be pretty high, depending on what business you are in). They do enough to justify their continued employment, especially if you are far from hopeful about the chance of replacing them with anyone better, but their lack of contribution is what causes a large part of the notoriously low production of white-collar departments.*

*What can you do about marginals?*

*If they are simply not able, is there a way to get more out of them? If they are not working up to capacity, is there a way to get them there? And get them to stay there, even after you have walked away?*

*It is not a matter of turning marginals into world-beaters, but can you get them at least to pull their weight?*

# 25 *An Expanse of Marginals*

Marginal employees are those whose habitual performance is enough this side of incompetence not to automatically inspire the ax, yet so far from praise that any idea of promotion is laughable. Their unedifying records may result from inability or indifference. They may be young or old, green or veteran, individual performers or supervisors, in high position or low. All that counts is how close their performance comes to unsatisfactory.

"Unsatisfactory" is your indispensable benchmark. You cannot take the performance curve you plot for control and arbitrarily declare the bottom twentieth or tenth or fifth (or whatever fraction seems to you suitably stern and exacting) to be your group's marginals, then treat them accordingly. The indicated ways to handle marginals involve kinds of remedial motivation that people inaccurately stigmatized as marginal will surely resent. The least adept performer in a group may be, objectively, splendid; it depends on the group—both its quality and, perhaps, its kind.

"It's a question I've never had to deal with," says Ted Cushmore at General Mills, "because my career has largely been in marketing, and marketing is an 'up-or-out' kind of thing. I can't 'career' even at my level." If you are in the same position, count yourself lucky for now—and tremble for the future, because one of the things success surely brings is the problem of handling marginals. Cushmore knows he is on the brink. "What happens at the next level," he asks, "when I'm managing functions that don't have that 'up-or-out' philosophy? It's tough—because in any large organization you need those kinds of people."

So you do. Not every job is so attractive that a tumult of competition lets you choose among eager, gifted candidates for it. Not every employee is animated by a drive to excel. For that matter, not all of them could excel even if they wanted to; there are a lot of only marginally equipped people in the world, and one mark of the high executive is a certain resignation. "You have to use them all," says Charles Pilliod, chairman of Goodyear.

It is not that Pilliod is personally less hard-driving or demanding than some section head dispensing easy cant about how "in this outfit excellence is the only acceptable standard"; it is just that he has more responsibility for more people. There is nothing like enlarged responsibility to teach rhetorical and functional restraint in the face of limited talent and to show that, indeed, you do have to use them all. The art of the boss lies in using as many of them, even the relative defectives, as well as possible, getting the most out of those without much to give.

If you can get someone now performing at 20 percent up to just 30 percent, you have half again as much production. That is the essence of handling marginals.

There are three distinct types. Each presents a different problem and must be treated differently. The first includes those who are willing, even eager, but lack native ability. The second type could do better if they wanted to but will not make the effort. The third type are veterans who, having gone as far as they are apt to, have surrendered to apathy.

You might imagine that marginals of the first type are hopeless. They cannot give what they do not have, and you should not even try to extract it. "Probably the greatest tragedy," says Edgar Speer, chairman of U.S. Steel, "is to challenge a guy who can't meet the challenge—because then he's a disaster. You challenge those who are not performing up to their capability, but you have to know enough not to challenge that guy who *is* working up to his capacity."

The first type of marginals are doing their best, and their best is none too good, stacked against the requirements of the job. They wrestle with their duties, go flat-out and achieve . . . bare adequacy. They can drag on forever, never hearing "Well done." Considering the meagerness of their returns, the wonder is that they try as hard as they do. You cannot challenge them further. Yet the tonic effect of stretching people's abilities is a commonplace.

Ironically, the trouble started because they were given assignments someone thought they could handle—and it turned out they could. In fact, that is the usual way of making assignments, and for people with potential it works well: They start out behind in experience, but their ability, focused by hard work, lets them first cope with the job, then master it. Marginals are at full stretch just coping, with nothing left over for mastery.

The solution is to switch to what might be called "zero-based assignments" for marginals. You ignore their proven ability to handle a certain level of assignment and give them something to do that they can, by stretching, master—something they can end up doing *superbly.*

This is standard technique for the more enlightened and effective bosses of production lines. Take Benrus Corporation, for instance. Mass production of wristwatch cases is not exciting. Machinery for every step from stamping globs of molten metal to milling surfaces is automatic, but not automated. Someone must press buttons, turn levers, lubricate and clean, mount and dismount material; above all, someone must observe what's happening and make adjustments. It is not *quite* mindless work, but close enough to bore most people silly.

So Benrus director of industrial engineering Walter Goldfarb rejects all the usual personnel-department blather on the lines of "getting the best people we can." His conscious policy is exactly opposite. "You look for low-qualified people," he says, "and you stretch them." They are not bored. The job engages their full interest; indeed, absorbs them. At the same time, they are not overwhelmed. By applying themselves, they can know the delight of striving that ends in success, not just survival. They are content—and it shows up as high morale and efficiency. You turn marginals into willing *and* able performers by changing the one flexible factor: their assignment. Make it one they can master, not just manage.

Why bother? Why not simply sack the marginals and get better people? Two reasons.

First, "better people" do not always do a better job. Let's say you need someone to operate a computer terminal, entering orders and invoicing data for processing by the main frame. Give that job to someone who has the ability to eventually be a programmer, and before long you will likely have a mightily bored, discontented employee given to the woolgathering that results in careless error. Give it to someone barely up to being a bookkeeping entry clerk and you will have a job done conscientiously by someone pleased and proud to do the best job possible.

That leads to the second reason. It should be your policy to treasure *and* reward willingness, both for the sake of abstract justice and as an example to the group. While you may, anyway, treasure the willingness of a high-hearted but floundering marginal, you cannot plausibly reward anyone who flounders. But you can reward a marginal who masters a suitable assignment —to the instruction of all (see what willingness gets you in this group!) and probably their pleasure, since such willing marginals are usually appealing and popular figures.

Of course, you cannot expect to effect the necessary changes overnight, or with a wave of your hand. There may not be enough jobs at your disposal, or all jobs may be so demanding that excellence in them is beyond the most fervent efforts of your marginals. Then the best solution may be transfer. You should easily find a home for people eager to do their best.

Even if you do have a suitable job, there is still the

problem of punctured pride. To meet it, talk in terms of "reassignment" and announce that the marginal is "concentrating" henceforth on certain important aspects of his or her specialty. Avoid the atmosphere of demotion. In truth, willing marginals have not done anything to deserve demotion—except be born (relatively) inept—and you owe it to them to be tender of their sensibilities, especially since you require their continued enthusiasm and all-out effort.

An effective piece of face-saving legerdemain is to have two marginals switch jobs ("general reassignment," you call it) with some duties of each sloughed off ("restructuring of assignment") and given to a young comer. In fact, note how neatly your program for type-one marginals fits in with paraboss programs for the more gifted. You end up, overall, with a unit in which everyone is happier and more productive, in which each job is done better because each is being done by someone at full stretch, on a note of triumph.

Unless, that is, some jobs belong to marginals of the second type—the ones who are not willing to do the best they can, or anywhere near it.

That does not mean they are people of vast potential. Their best might take them no further than a step or two more up the ladder. But they could do better, right now, if they wanted to. The tip-off is their uncanny ability to calibrate the effort needed to get by: They deliver not a discernible erg more.

The technique for handling such people is clean-cut and simple. "With that type, first and foremost, I nail them," says Keebler chairman Arthur Larkin. "I tell them, 'Hey! If this isn't fixed, and real quick, we're going to part company.' That includes managers, secretaries, everybody."

The ultimatum should be delivered the second you decide people are type-two marginals, and the earlier in their careers the better. If you do not make it an immediate issue, you are in for endless mediocrity, since such people have already shown indifference to improvement and advancement. Even if they are "doing the job," they are occupying space that would be better filled by others (reassigned type-one marginals, say) who would do their best.

The confrontation may turn the trick. It certainly has the shock value of novelty. "There's a great hesitancy to tell a guy, 'You're not doing the job' or 'You're mediocre,'" says American Airlines' Robert Baker. "But doing that is a key element in motivating them. We need to tell people, no matter how high or low, to what degree they are or aren't doing the job. You've got to come right out and tell them, 'You're perceived as marginal; now you have the opportunity, and we think the capability, to do a hell of a lot better.'"

If that does not do it, you should find out as soon as possible. It is one thing to fire the invincibly lazy when they are young, another thing after they have grown old in the service (however middling) of the company.

How about when the once vigorous and eager turn lazy? The third type of marginal, the veteran slackers, are in many ways the hardest people to handle. The difficulty starts with identification—making sure you really are dealing with type-three marginals, as opposed to valuable, venerable senior performers. To the casual observer they look alike in most particulars: age, experience, unflappable style, their contented (or resigned) recognition that they have gone as far as they are going to go in the company. When a job is done so effortlessly as to seem almost haphazard, is it because a thoroughgoing pro always makes things look easy? Or is it because a drained and disappointed marginal is putting out no more effort than minimally needed?

The question is especially hard for the young, dynamic achiever, who is instinctively antipathetic to anyone who, for any reason, accepts a plateau of achievement. For this boss, stability looks like regression. Anyone who is not still visibly striving to get ahead is suspect. The thought is epidemic among young comers. Ted Cushmore speculates that "those kinds of people may be operating that way because they've made some trade-offs or concessions, and as a result are better able to accommodate the fact that they're not going to move ahead."

True enough; but such people are not necessarily marginals. "In some situations," says Stanley Hunt, "people have simply reached their level. They will stay in the job and be relatively happy. I think you must recognize that they are doing good work in their niche." The niche can be at any level and may be a matter of preference rather than lack of further ability. Hunt himself is an example. At age fifty-one he is assistant controller of General Mills, has considerable responsibility, is highly regarded and does an excellent job. He is anything but marginal (as Cushmore would be first to tell you). On the other hand, he is no longer driven by ambition. "At some point," he says, "we all find our rut. Sometime you have to come to a realization of what you want and what you don't want—and be relatively happy with what you do achieve. You know, I don't want McFarland's job. I've been in many meetings with McFarland. We're different people with different interests. People have eventually got to find peace with themselves and with the world."

And their bosses have to differentiate between such valuable producers and care-nothing marginals. For all the similarities, there are even more striking differences. The main one is work product. Keen old pros may not seem much busier than fatigued marginals, but somehow they keep turning out an impressive body of fine work. If they are supervisors, things somehow always seem to be churning around them, though they stay serene.

Not so with marginals. Even if their own identifiable work load seems to be in hand, casual inspection and a moment's reflection will show it always to be minimal. Nothing much around them seems to move forward, either. Such people are interested in getting by, not getting on with it.

Remember the test of how nearly unsatisfactory a mar-

ginal's performance is. If the quality and the quantity of someone's work are good, it does not matter with what negligent ease
it appears to be accomplished. If quantity or quality is marginal
(or just lackluster and uninspired), so is the performer.

If so, what do you do about it?

First, ignore the fact. Stop treating such people like the
marginals they are. The tendency—especially for aggressive
young bosses—is to look at marginals, fleetingly despair that
everyone does not share their own endocrine balance, then
dismiss them as incorrigible time-servers. At least they cause no
trouble; they do get the job done, however desultorily.

For their part, they quickly gauge how little is acceptable to keep the boss off their back. No more is expected and
they have no reason to deliver more. It is a self-perpetuating
and woefully common plan for mediocrity.

"I have one section that works for me," says Ford's
Gary Tessitore. "People in their late forties, early fifties, who
have gone as far as they will go. The previous manager took no
interest in them. They did the job, there were no problems—
so he didn't involve himself. The supervisor of that section
rarely saw him; the analysts in it *never* did."

Tessitore broke that cycle of mutual indifference. He
says he just did not know enough about these people to ignore
them. "I had to find out what this section was doing, so I sat
down with the supervisor regularly, and with things he couldn't
explain I'd say, 'Well, who did the work? Bring him in!' And
the guy would come in and explain what he was doing." Suddenly they were no longer faceless drones. Tessitore then in-
jected the section back into the mainstream of company activity
with such psychologically bracing assignments as field audits.
Obviously, people perceived as marginal are not going to be sent
out from under their taskmaster's eye.

The program made a difference. "I don't mean I've
gotten these people to work all hours for me," admits Tessitore.
"But I have gotten something more out of them."

With type-three marginals, that is stunning success! Instead of reinforcing their feeling that horizons have closed, do everything with older marginals that you would do if they were still young and promising. The elements are familiar: performance reviews, job enrichment, broadening, a leavening of novel assignments—even career-planning talks (just because they are not going higher does not mean there is nowhere else in the company they want to go). You let them know that you are interested in them and what they do, and that you expect more than threshold performance from them; at the same time you show that there are rewards for extra effort besides promotion.

As a matter of fact, one of the most gratifying rewards belongs exclusively to older marginals. "Generally you find that this type of person gets a great deal of satisfaction from contributing to someone else's success," says Edgar Speer. "If you make them feel responsible for training people with potential, it gives them more than the routine, day-to-day job they can do off the back of their hands. They want to say, 'So-and-so was my protégé; I trained him!' "

The future success of their pupil is validation of their own less distinguished careers. What's more, the attention they get from an obvious future star, the respect, the feeling of importance and responsibility—all these are specially sweet to people whose own careers have gone flat. They typically throw themselves into the instruction, and their newborn enthusiasm carries over into the rest of their work. After all, they are anxious to show their protégé how it *should* be done, not how to soldier on the job.

The young comer gets a lot out of the tutorial, too. Remember that what makes it possible for type-three marginals to slack off is their undoubted expertise, however narrow. In their special field they have a lot to teach and can be an important resource for the sort of training we'll examine in the next section. They often become single-minded and wholehearted teachers. "It's a strange thing," says Exxon's Frank Gaines, "but some of the very best developers of people are not people who, themselves, have high management potential. They've accepted their niche, and they concentrate on delegating responsibility and bringing along young people."

Gaines points out that while the very cream of the managerial corps are those who both advance themselves *and* train others, many great performers are lousy developers of people. "They want to make all the decisions," says Gaines. "They don't necessarily pass this responsibility down." Older marginals are torn by no such conflict. Their triumph will be their protégé's success, and they will eagerly arm young comers with all they know. Both marginal employee and potential star shine brighter.

# XIV  PICKING AND TRAINING
## SUCCESSORS

*This brings us full circle.*

*Fact is, if you were a computer, the subject of successors would not be worth discussing. You already know everything you have to about both phases of it—identifying the likeliest candidates and bringing them along. Even if you have never done it yet, you have been on the receiving end, an attentive observer.*

*Why and how were your merits recognized? Or not recognized? What should have counted that did not? What skills and qualities were overprized and turned out to be irrelevant? How were you brought along? What should have been added to your training? What was a waste of time? A moment's reflection—and maybe a review of subjects I through III—should be all you need.*

*Except for human nature. As we'll see, the whole process of picking and training successors is a constant resistance to the urgings of human nature—your own and that of your subordinates.*

*You must know what to look for and what to look out for; how to train subordinates not only to take over your job but to train their own subordinates to do the same someday. And how to train them, in turn, to know what to look for during that training cycle.*

*So your interest is in what* should *make people stand out now as bosses. And how to make sure they know, too.*

# 26 How to Find Good People Despite Yourself—and Them

Start with an easy question. Which statement is more nearly true?

    1. "Future managers are relatively easy to identify. Their work is a marked step above that of their peers. Everyone I get interested in, other managers are already interested in."

    2. "You have to look at the whole universe of candidates and systematically examine each one. Otherwise you could miss someone who doesn't pop right to the surface because of characteristics that can be improved."

    The answer is "all of the above." What's more, both statements were made by the same person, Edward Hess, deputy marketing manager at Exxon, a company where finding and training talent are done with a zeal popularly thought to be reserved for the fight against divestiture and price regulation. No sooner had the current chairman and president taken office than they received a note from former chairman M. J. Rathbone: "Your job right now," it warned, "is to develop more Garvins and Kauffmanns." They take succession seriously at Exxon.

    So this is not some politic trimmer platitudinizing out of both sides of his mouth; it is a thoughtful executive enunciating what experience shows are equally valid sides of the question. Yes, the stars are "known by their performance," as the chairman of General Mills puts it, "and everyone wants them." But *also* yes, some important talent does not so obligingly announce itself and must be winkled out.

    The problem is human nature. *Of course* good performance commends itself to you, while indifferent performance leaves you cold. Nothing could be more human or natural—or dangerous. "The danger is in making too quick an observation —positive or negative," says Sara Lee president Thomas Barnum. Also, too-hasty judgments easily become immutable, a generally overlooked aspect of favoritism.

Most people suppose favoritism means only that Joe is promoted because he toadies to the boss or went to the same school or is marrying the boss's daughter. Actually, the most common and pernicious form develops because Joe has done a bang-up job—once or twice—and suddenly Joe is *the* boy. It is damaging to the group; it can destroy Joe. "I once had a boss," says Redactron's Evelyn Berezin, "who either hated you or loved you. Either you were a good-for-nothing or you could do anything—then he'd put you in a job you were no damn good for, and when you failed, you suddenly couldn't do anything right."

The hard part is deciding what constitutes true, repeatable superior performance, especially since most jobs are cooperative team efforts. It remains a judgment call, with many subjective elements. "We all have people that we have better chemistry with than others," observes Thomas Barnum. "And that can cloud your judgment. You like the person; you like the style. But there are a lot of other things more important."

Yes, there are, and a depressingly large number of them are further snares set by human nature. For instance, how can you resist giving high marks to a subordinate who does things the way you do them? Especially if it is not a matter of guileful flattery but of deep and plainly sincere persuasion that your way is best. Anyone who does things the same way must be doing things right. Right? Well . . . "I feel the biggest mistake executives make is picking successors in their own image," says First Pennsylvania chairman John Bunting. "They always pick someone who has practically the same background, same methods, same attitude on every question, everything the same. It's almost always a tragic mistake."

It does not materially help to be in a field, such as sales, where precise measurement seems available, because the precision is illusory. Steadfastly considering only uncontestable numbers allows bosses to flatter themselves on their fairness—and shirk the task of probing for talent. It is what Union Carbide's Warren Anderson calls "the danger of picking winners." At higher levels there is always the question of whether you are looking at the results of leadership or irrepressibly effective followers. And, at any level, an evident whiz, turning in brilliant results, may simply have been lucky, while someone else's objectively meager results were achieved in the face of circumstances that would have turned the whiz to jelly. The rest of the organization is probably on to the true situation. And as Anderson also points out, little promotes disenchantment with leadership like a pronounced and insistent talent for rewarding the wrong people.

That is what Edward Hess was talking about. You must not be bemused by surface glitter; you have to look at all your people with an open mind and consider their merits long and hard.

It helps if you resolutely refuse to identify a successor until you are practically clearing your desk for your own move upstairs. Construct the largest possible (though plausible) pool of candidates, not only for immediate succession but also for some undefined managerial role in some unspecified future. Such a policy automatically pays a number of handsome dividends. It impels a wider, and deeper, talent search. It mandates advanced training and recognition for *all* your best people (including those you do not instinctively rate at the pinnacle) and engenders healthy competition among them without the spirit of cabal that is otherwise inevitable against the "heir apparent."

It also avoids your embarrassment and their more acute disappointment when none of them succeeds you, which is an increasing likelihood the higher you go. "We tend away from

'Who is your replacement, Plant Manager?' " says Fairchild chairman Wilfred Corrigan. "We want really diffuse recommendations." And, though the incumbent's recommendation carries great weight, it may be overridden by other considerations. "That job may be a key one from a training standpoint," Corrigan continues, "and we may have someone somewhere else who we feel strongly should pass through a particular job."

Ponder the implications of that. The clincher is not results, or even superior on-the-job performance (since the newcomer has none), but a quality we can call "boss potential." The temptation is to ignore this quality because it is so elusive. Yet it should be the most important component of anyone's equipment for promotion, even to posts with *no* supervisory duty. Every job above entry level inherently involves boss potential. At the very least, your successor must someday select and train a successor, two quintessential functions of the boss. So considering successors must always be a two-step process: You must weigh any candidate both as immediate performer and potential boss.

That is hard to do, especially at lower levels before you have seen a candidate supervising anyone. How much easier to declare boss potential an imponderable and examine only performance. And then, if the person promoted fails, how easy to blame it on the ineluctable workings of the Peter Principle.

The Peter Principle (in case you have been in hiding since 1969) states, "In a hierarchy every employee tends to rise to his level of incompetence." It is claimed to be a nearly inevitable process, and unpredictable; examples given show someone going in a single sudden step from praiseworthy competence to unpromotable static ruin.

That is nonsense, a bugaboo, an imposition on people who should know better—and, indeed, do know better. Everyone in the business world acts as though there were no Peter Principle, while solemnly assuring each other that there is. How did such a grotesque situation come about? And what difference does it make?

To start with, there is a virile tough-mindedness, an attractive cynicism about claiming that most everyone (except *us,* of course) ends up incompetent. Also, it is an easy excuse for wrong promotions. And there is an apparent logic to the proposition that, endlessly promoted, any employee will sooner or later run out of competence. Hence Peter's Corollary, which insists, *"In time, every post tends to be occupied by an employee who is incompetent to carry out its duties"* (authors' italics). And that explains the book's subtitle, *Why Things Always Go Wrong.*

But the fact is, things emphatically do not always go wrong, or even almost always. Shortly after Laurence Peter and Raymond Hull published their book, C. Northcote Parkinson, promulgator of "Parkinson's Law," wrote a refutation. It was bad-tempered and querulous, giving the impression that Parkinson mostly resented some upstart working his side of the street, but it was devastatingly accurate. Parkinson ran through modern instances of things that go amazingly *right* despite their fearsome complexity, then nastily (if plausibly) suggested that Peter's peculiar outlook derived from his professional background in education. Immersed in the world of normal schools, one might understandably conclude that incompetence is all around, the rule and not the exception. If Bernard Shaw was right that those who can, do, and those who can't, teach, what of those who teach teachers?

Actually the whole issue is phony. The surface logic of the Peter Principle turns on such key phrases as "given enough time" and "enough ranks in the hierarchy." In the real world, most people run out of time or ambition or room (they reach the top) before exhausting their abilities.

Besides, even if the Peter Principle were valid, what difference would it make? Given that someone must be promoted, who shall it be? "You pick people who have had a good record other places," says David Packard, chairman of Hewlett-Packard. "You don't take someone from the bottom of the class, but from the top of the class, with enough energy and interest to do well." Of course! And maybe there is no surefire way to know that your choice will continue doing well, but as Packard says, "If people do a good job here, they're likely to do a good job one step up." Surely more likely than those who did not do a good job here! Common sense wins again.

Still, there is a distinct danger in the style of thought represented by the Peter Principle. It directs attention away from what should matter in selecting possible successors— away from the telltales of boss potential—and focuses on mere performance, its underlying assumption being that performance alone is the desideratum for promotion. That simply misses David Packard's message. Good performance is not the controlling factor in selecting managerial possibilities; it is only the *sine qua non* for consideration.

Put it another way. "I've never seen a guy who was a lousy assistant product manager," says Ted Cushmore, "about whom I could say, 'He's going to be a good manager.'" Once a candidate passes the "performance test," then the real scrutiny should start, the close search for signs of boss potential apposite to the job.

Take the star salesman who ends up as a disastrous sales manager, a situation regularly advanced as stunning "proof" of the Peter Principle. What has really happened? The issue is not truly the salesman's level of competence but the type of boss potential needed for the job. "It's not capabilities, but how they're applied," says Harry Farnham, Los Angeles regional manager of Savin Business Machines, a star salesman who became a star manager. Selling ability only starts the duties of a sales manager, who must be primarily an organizer, an administrator, a motivator and, above all, a teacher of salesmen. When a star salesman fails as manager, it is largely because of a lack of ability to transmit knowledge. "You give them 'B,' 'C' and 'D,' " Farnham says, "before they've got 'A.' " Certainly salespeople must *know* before they can teach; that is why you first assess their performances. But it is up to you, as the boss, to be sure they *can* teach (and motivate and administer) before they are made managers.

You had also better be sure they want to manage. As Farnham's boss, Savin retail national sales manager Abraham Ostrovsky, points out, "Most of the time, for good salesmen to step into management means a substantial demotion in dollars." Temporarily, at least. So candidates must crave the more psychic rewards and satisfactions being boss affords. "If they go home every night," says Ostrovsky, "saying 'I'm manager, but damn it, I'm not earning enough!' they'll be rotten managers because they won't approach the job with a 'want-to-be-successful' viewpoint." In short, they must have what IBM director of management development Edward Krieg calls "an interest in the process of management."

What are the signs that candidates do or do not have it? All the qualities discussed in the first three sections are significant; some are essential. First, there must be an implacable urge to command. You want people who will push what power they have to the limit. "In a hierarchy," says Exxon's Frank Gaines, "it's easy for young people to ask their boss for a blessing on every decision before they make it. But the real good ones take all the authority they can and are willing to be judged on results." That demonstrates a healthy impatience with the organizational restraints that diminish as one ascends. Such people want to get to the top so they can run things more *their* way.

The next most potent evidences of boss potential are the ability and constant inclination to examine all questions with originality. "I like to hear the unexpected, not the pat, answer," says William Howell, J. C. Penney western regional VP. "There are a lot of pat answers in this business, and someone who isn't his or her own person tends to pick them up and repeat them without much thought. What typifies and sets apart the future stars is that they've done their own thinking." If, for example, markdowns are increasing, Howell may ask a subordinate why. "A pat answer might be, 'It's a result of overstocks.' A more analytical answer, from a guy or gal who's thought it through and done some research, is, 'Our problem really was a lack of understanding by our store people when we introduced the Inventory Allowance System . . .' and they'll go on." The specifics are not important; the thought process is. It bespeaks those who can recognize the important issues and ponder their consequences in their own sphere.

Likely candidates will also be exceptionally fast to spot key issues without your having to belabor each point. "The executives with potential are the ones who pick up just the hint, just the lead," says INA chairman Ralph Saul. "They don't need to have everything spelled out; they might even resent it if you try because it's an insult to their intelligence." That sharpness is indicative of a probing, sensitive intelligence, the antennae always out and receptive, the computer always on-line. In chapter 2, when the chairman of Pillsbury wanted to characterize one of his young comers, the story he told involved exactly that kind of acuteness.

It is part of a general manner of assured confidence that you should expect to find. Such a manner comes of being prepared, which in turn suggests hard work and effective application of energies. All to the good, of course; but just the manner itself is important. Someone could be a miracle of hard work and shrewd judgment and yet be so slight and shrinking as to hopelessly compromise any probable usefulness as a leader—at least until you work on it together (a perfect example of what Edward Hess means by "characteristics that can be improved" masking otherwise valuable talent). It is easy to tell whether candidates have the right manner. "Watch them as they present to you," advises Ted Cushmore. "If they are confident and assured with you, chances are they're going to be with the people working for them." The reverse is also true. "If people are tentative and nervous with their boss," says Cushmore, "chances are they're going to have difficulty with subordinates, too."

Candidates for promotion will certainly have trouble unless they are both articulate and fluent. But with these qualities the situation is somewhat different. Like an assured manner, they are important in themselves, for compelling operational reasons. "Today in business there are always a lot of meetings and presentations," says William Spoor, "a lot of selling situations." That is reason enough to insist on an ability to speak both clearly and well. But even more important for your talent search is the significance of such ability. "Articulateness may be symptomatic of something deeper," says Edward Hess, "the ability to organize one's thoughts, which means problem solving as well as good communications." So the ability to express one's thoughts convincingly tells you something about the quality of those thoughts.

The characteristics discussed so far are absolute; lacking any one, a candidate must overcome a presumption of unsuitability. The final one is unique in that either its presence *or* absence can be a key factor in deciding whether someone has the boss potential you're looking for. It depends on the person, the company and the circumstances. Glenn White, Chrysler's VP for personnel and organization, says it involves a determination "not to be dominated or to dominate, but to be able to get along as a team member." He is not talking about anything so pallid as mere "getting along with people." He means a sense of team membership so abiding it animates someone even after becoming team captain and impels that person to work for solutions the team can live with even though solutions could be imposed. "It means being able to work on a situation until the other person feels comfortable with it," White explains, "instead of saying, 'Well, here's the answer; good-bye, I'm going.'"

It is easy to tell whether an individual gets along tolerably well with his peers just by observation and passing attention to gossip. And it's possible to get a fix on how well people work for him even before he has formal subordinates. "One way is in terms of project management," says Litton Microwave VP Dick Jackson, "where he is cutting across lines. How much are others' functions involved? How did he get the project completed? Did he go off by himself and do it, or did he get them fully involved? Do *they* come out of it with a feeling of team effort?" The word gets around. And even if a loner was "right" to ignore some peers whose opinions and contributions are highly ignorable, it is a demerit not to be able to handle the situation without putting their noses out of joint. A good boss makes the most of the whole team and leaves even the weak sisters feeling good about it.

So much for team spirit. It is a strong case, but not the whole story.

We come back to the need for looking at every plausible candidate with meticulous care. Some splendid boss material may lack bare civility, let alone team spirit. "These people are an extrapolation of the type of person that ends up being *the* boss," says Wilfred Corrigan. "They have a low tolerance for mistakes in their peers—or bosses. They tend to be autocratic and abrupt, too outspoken, with too visible an ego. They don't worry enough about the 'people' aspects of business." Those characteristics are a hyperthyroid version of the manner a boss should have, and most comers learn to cool it. Most, but not all. "That tends to make them less effective at the subordinate level," Corrigan goes on, "because they subject peers and superiors to attitudes that may be appropriate in *the* boss but are sharply resented down below. I guess we have four or five people like that around here; and to some extent you have to protect them from the chain of command." They will be superstars—if they live long enough.

The need to protect such people epitomizes the difference between performer and boss. Recall, back in section I, that people skills were a decided necessary quality of the boss. They are; and obviously it is better for a candidate to have them. But you, as boss, must look beyond their absence in others and take steps to rescue these people from the predictable results of their ill-advised and premature autocracy.

How you protect them depends on the prevalent threats. You must keep them from being fired, of course, but also from being encouraged to quit, which is especially hard if they are a couple of levels down. Typically, their immediate boss will be reluctant to give them promotions or raises, or even due credit. Someone else will be "really responsible" for the latest coup the upstart has pulled off. You must override the sub-boss's denigration and stinginess. On occasion the only possible protection will be to get the fellow out from under. Harold Johnson, at INA, tells of having to rescue one young Turk who had been shaking up his boss by questioning basic assumptions about what insurance is and how it should be marketed. The older man had had similar notions when he was young but had decided to go along with things as they were and bitterly resented the youngster's implacably (and tactlessly) stirring the embers of his own one-time fire. The challenge was unremitting and the conflict so strong that Johnson decided he had to force a transfer, putting the young man with someone either more secure or indifferent to heresy.

Failing all other solutions, you can always take the talented disrupter under your own wing as "staff assistant" and simply insist that people put up with him. Advanced boss potential is rare enough so that strong signs of it must be seized on and developed. You cannot waste it even for the sake of "harmony," because harmony is not the only point. There is also excellence.

Savin Business Machines chairman Paul Charlap neatly summed up the spirit of the search. "I'm constantly looking," he says, "for the people I call 'on my team' that want to *do* something." When you find them, make the most of it.

# 27 *Planning for Success—Theirs and Yours*

If picking likely candidates is a struggle against human nature, bringing them along is that struggle compounded. You must guard against not only your own nature but also that of the subordinates, plus any intervening sub-bosses.

There is no choice. Notable developers of talent agree on how to go about it. "Both Bill Hewlett and I," says David Packard, "try to identify people we think have ability; then we give them something to do and let them alone, not looking over their shoulder. It's a conscious part of our system." You have to let go—completely—and that is something most people find desperately hard to do.

Then there is the two-fold nature of executive training. When you let go of duties in favor of subordinates, you make them better performers and yourself a better boss. But it is also your job to make *them* better bosses, too, which means getting them to let go of their subordinates. It is hard enough fighting your own urges toward involvement and control; the problem at one or two removes is awesome.

Still, the fight must be fought. And it helps to be armed with a clear rationale for its necessity, both to stiffen your own resolve and so your mandate that sub-bosses let go carries unshakable conviction. There is a persuasive chain of logic. "If you think you're the only one who can do the job," says David Packard, "you're never going to develop anybody else." No development, no pool of plausible successors—which routinely means no promotion. It does not matter that management might have intended all along to bring in someone from outside the group to succeed you; the fact that you had not trained people who *could* step in would count heavily against you because the consequences of elevating *non*developers are notorious. "I've seen companies where the people in charge want to dot every 'i' and cross every 't,' " continues Packard. "It means they can never go beyond the compass of their own ability. Even if I could do something twice as well as anyone else, I sure as hell couldn't do it a hundred times as well." No sensible company will tolerate in high position anyone who would even want to try.

The only rational conclusion is to let go, to develop talent even at the cost of perceptibly (though temporarily) compromised group performance. "I'm not trying to run the most efficient setup in the world," says Leisure Dynamics chairman Bo Polk. "I'm trying to develop people to handle a constantly changing competitive environment." Which cannot be done without letting them into the act. You, however, must decide what role, and in what scenes, each subordinate will play. The key to success for both of you is comprehensive and thoughtful planning. It is the final defense against the pulls and stresses of human nature.

Take the initial broadening process. It must be tailored to each subordinate's needs or it is useless. "I think the worst thing you can do," says U.S. Steel chairman Edgar Speer, "is have a stereotyped training program where everybody gets a little bit of everything, and not really very much of anything." Especially not what the person needs. It cannot be left to the individual, either, because the essence of human nature is to move toward strength. The accountant's notion of broadening is a tour in financial analysis; left to themselves, the marketer will "broaden" into the advertising department, the production specialist into design engineering. As their boss you must look at them and decide what they need. "Maybe," says Speer, "you have to shift them into responsibilities where their weaknesses become a problem. That helps a man recognize that it is a weakness and that he must do something about it." You must also compensate for everyone's tendency to denigrate the unfamiliar, to figure that the things they know nothing about cannot be very important. "The only way you can correct that kind of situation is to put people in where they're directly involved," Speer continues, "where it's suddenly their job. Then they learn something about it and begin to respect the function."

After remedial and educational broadening you must arrange a candidate's step-by-step assumption of your powers. This is not the same as even the most advanced paraboss program set up for the encouragement of lesser talents. Here you are letting go of central parts of your job, and you must be mentally prepared. It is not easy. "Some of my managers I have trouble with," says SEC's Stanley Sporkin, "are those who do not understand that what they are supposed to do is work themselves almost out of a job." Rigorous planning helps. The trick is to make the devolution as untaxing, psychologically, as possible, scheduling so you can let go and he can take hold with minimum fret, wrench and worry.

The size of the increments of duty you transfer, and the tempo of the turnover, will vary with the individual. "It depends on how familiar I am with you," says Charles Kean, staff assistant at Gillette. "How much I know you know"—the only rational approach. You can generally determine ahead of time if you have selected the right-size portions. Before you relinquish any function, say to yourself, "OK, as of tomorrow this candidate will take over all of X; can I envision myself going cheerfully about my other business without wanting to check up every few minutes?" If the answer is no, reduce the dosage.

Of what?

Every function breaks down into two components: the technical/action and the judgmental. You start by turning over technical aspects of any job, and with those, observes Bo Polk, "you need a lot of interaction at first; you have to pretty intimately involve yourself with the person until you're sure the person can do the job." Here's the progression in a reasonably simple, clear-cut situation: turning over accounts-payable duties.

First break the job down into coherent segments. The technical aspects include verification of debt, checking invoices and processing of invoice data, preparation and execution of payment. There may also be technical supervision, if only looking over the shoulder of a payables clerk.

You should transfer the segments piecemeal, keeping close tabs only until you are sure there is no foul-up. At first you want to see everything. Then you will not bother looking at verification, then checking and so on. You go through cycles of release until you are not bothering to supervise the candidate's supervision of the payables clerk.

By then you should be turning over the judgmental aspects of the job: Who gets paid and on what basis. By cycle? To take advantage of discounts? By aging? Should certain accounts *not* be paid? (For material that may be returned, as an example.)

The judgment calls are also turned over gradually, with you at first reviewing every decision, then letting review slip from detail to detail as mutual confidence builds, until the candidate is totally in charge of paying bills, in the most efficient and creatively advantageous way consonant with company policy.

It makes no difference how big or small you make the increments of responsibility, how swift or deliberate the pace of transfer. But when you do let go, it should be all the way. You are still boss, and whatever degree of oversight and control you exercise over every subordinate's duties will be in effect for the candidate's new one. The same, though, not more. (There is no recorded instance, in such situations, of its being *less.*)

A helpful ploy is to contrive some sign that graphically distances you from the abdicated duty. For instance, when Nathan Cummings turned over operational control of two companies, he made a decisive move—literal and symbolic. "After I got Sprague-Warner and Reed-Murdoch running, policy-wise, the way I liked," Cummings says, "I moved my office to the Field Building in Chicago." There were two reasons. He felt he could run what was becoming Consolidated Foods better by following reports. Even more important, he says that by moving out, "I could give the fellows in charge of each company real authority to run their businesses." Still under his overall direction—but not interference, in the absence of egregious goof-ups.

If shifting offices physically is not practical in your circumstances, you can still signalize the cutting of apron strings by pointedly arranging an absence to coincide with the completed turnover of duty. The distance or duration of your removal is not important; the spirit is. Your willingness to go away at that moment, even for a day or two, confirms the transfer in everyone's mind, including your own.

At a climactic point in delegating authority at Monfort of Colorado, Kenneth Monfort decided on a family trip. "We're taking a two-week cruise," he said. "It will be the first time *ever* that I'm not going to call this office for two weeks. It means two things. First, I've got to be relatively satisfied that I don't have to check—for my own peace of mind. And it shows them that I know everything is OK. I'm sure there's an office pool betting on when I'll call in. But I'm not going to." Because by the time he was ready to go off, it was not necessary for his subordinates, his business or himself.

That is the state of mind, on both sides, your training plans should aim for, where you can totally let go and be confident that authority to perform has so devolved to the people you are bringing along that you can rely on them to do the work and bring you the results. "Have you ever seen a pea-sorter?" asks Chevrolet general manager Robert Lund. "They have a raised series of hoppers, and the holes get progressively smaller as the peas drop through them. At the bottom are the tiny holes where the precious, costly, little sweet peas come out. As a manager, it's not your job to do all the shaking and sorting. Give other people the peas and let *them* sort out all the pros and cons, the good and the bad, the difficulties. You give out the problem and they bring you the results." In the process you pretty thoroughly sort out the sorters, too.

That is just performance, though. There is still the second phrase of training: turning good performers into good bosses; getting your subordinates to do with theirs what you have done with them. Again, the enemy is human nature.

Here they are, lately masters of new skills and authority (more probably, still acquiring them), and now you ask them to delegate to less capable hands some central duties for whose outcome they will still be accountable. It is asking a lot of their newborn confidence. Too much. So, since command cannot be gradually learned, anyway (though, of course, the number commanded and degree of responsibility can be gradually increased), it is best not to ask but to contrive matters so your subordinates *must* become effective sub-bosses, must train their own subordinates to take some of the load. "I've seen it work at McKinsey and in line companies," says George Foote. "When you bite off more than you can chew, you have to depend on others. Keep piling the work on your best people, forcing them to bring others along." Of course, he warns, you have to be sure they are indeed passing the work along and not killing themselves trying to do it all (in which case they have failed a vital test). "But it is one way to force someone to develop managerial skills," Foote concludes.

That just gives impetus. Once development is going forward, you should require formal, reviewable training plans from sub-bosses. "We ask the head of each activity at every level," says Chrysler VP Glenn White, "to tell us what is the next logical step for every person in his organization."

What should the plans look like? There are no boilerplate answers. But the important outlines are highly visible any time a good boss turns a good subordinate into a good sub-boss.

Take the case of Robert Iverson, director of marketing for Sara Lee bakery products. "Until recently we had not had a layer below the product manager level," he says. "But one of my guys has just been promoted to group product manager, with a young gal as associate product manager. The key to his success will be how well and quickly he orients her to the job, then whether he gives her meaningful projects with enough direction so she can be really productive."

Note the elements. First he must arrange a solid grounding in the marketing concepts of Sara Lee, plus specific techniques and practices—the rudimentary performance level. Next he has to turn over real duties, not just make-work, planning enough built-in autonomy so she will learn, but not so much as to leave her floundering. "That is the balancing act," says Iverson. "To give the person enough rope to see what he or she can do, yet not back away from giving direction. Don't give so much rope they're not productive." That applies with as much force to the new sub-boss as to his new subordinate. The difference is that you, as boss, must give most of your direction to sub-bosses up front. You will watch how they handle the training of subordinates with consuming interest; but once you intervene, their training as responsible bosses ends. Intervention should not be necessary. Meticulous planning ahead of time will compensate for the natural tendency of sub-bosses to hold back, and the natural tendency of inexperienced subordinates to range between bewildered wheel-spinning and headlong charges down blind alleys.

In the present instance, Iverson's new group product manager came up with a model project and plan of guidance. The project was to develop a theme promotion for a new line called "International Desserts." The contemplated direction included a clear statement of the promotion's objectives, with reasonable due dates and progress benchmarks. There was complete information on budget and timing. Also tentative suggestions for possible tie-ins (for instance, Nestlé Tea had expressed some interest), incentive programs and advertising support. Finally, Iverson wanted to know how, and on what schedule, the group manager planned to follow up with review, criticism and evaluation (and his criteria for evaluation) of the young associate's performance.

From then on it was a matter of Iverson's keeping an eye on both people, making sure they were both learning and performing what was, for each, a new realm of responsibility and skill.

That last sounds simple but is often a sticking point. How do you tell what is working and what is not working a couple of levels down? And (even rougher!) how do you instruct sub-bosses in the art of determining how subordinates are doing? "One of our fellows dubbed it, 'Management by walking around,' " says David Packard. You must move among your people as often and intimately as possible. And you must vigorously urge sub-bosses to do the same. "I think you can 'teach' it," Packard says, "but only by really encouraging your people to do it."

Given enough direct observation, it is not hard to tell what kind of job a sub-boss is doing. "I have one guy I'm pretty happy with in terms of his group's output," says General Mills' Ted Cushmore. "But I have reservations. What happens when his span of control becomes more than one or two people? His people aren't happy. I see them as I wander by their offices, with the computer printouts all over the room. I'll ask them, 'What are you working on?' and learn that it's overkill or not really relevant. I see them in my office with inconsistent points of view, and obviously at times no previous communication. I stop them in the hall and ask them about a project, and maybe they haven't even heard about it. You don't have to be Sherlock Holmes to realize their boss isn't playing a team game. Just make it your business to know what's going on." Which, of course, *is* the business of any boss—a fact you can demonstrate most aptly by showing sub-bosses how closely you do keep tabs on what's going on.

If someone is going wrong, there must be exhortation and lectures. But the greatest force for keeping people going right is the example you set. It extends to all activities. The way you treat, direct, motivate, control and discipline your subordinates is the proximate model for them of how it should be done and must influence how they deal with their subordinates.

And with you. "As I relate to my boss in the presence of my people, I try to operate in the way I want them to operate with me," says Ted Cushmore. "The same with the analyses I handle on my own. I copy my people on them and try to make them as professional as possible so they'll understand the standard I expect."

Also, your subordinates can do a better job of helping you, and more intelligently direct their subordinates to help you, the more they know about what you are expected to produce for your superiors. "I always take the people who did the work in with me," says Robert Baker, talking about his relationship with his boss, Robert Crandall, at American Airlines. "That gives them the exposure they need to understand how Crandall thinks—which is very important because when I turn them loose on a project it changes the way they look at what I told them to do if they see what I'm up against when I go to give the answers to Crandall."

That's "answers," notice, not questions. You should be a sounding board for your people when they need one. But you should insist that when they come to you to thrash things out, they have done all the possible preliminaries. A concomitant of your giving over authority and initiative in certain areas is their eager assumption of it; they have to deliver, not rely on you to do their thinking.

"I would say you can get the best opinions by demanding, when people make their ideas known, that it is always done in a concise, well-thought-out way," says Glenn White. That does not mean they cannot ask for your advice or opinion or help in the more difficult areas of ratiocination; just that you insist they at least have the husk off the corn before they bring it in for advanced shaking. And they must insist on the same degree of preparatory thought from their subordinates. "It cuts down the time the boss has to spend," observes White. And even that is not the most important factor. "It forces individuals to get their thinking down clearly, which is a good development activity." Maybe the best.

The final question is how you make adjustments along the way. That does not mean formal rating. You have already rated these people superior or they would not be candidates for succession. It is a matter of interim criticism made forcefully enough to effect necessary changes, yet in a way that does not discourage.

The enemy is still human nature. Despite the necessary trait of being quick to pick up suggestions, any candidate is bound to have an entirely human reluctance to "hear" bad news, even the remediable sort that is the essence of constructive criticism. They want to be making the sort of progress that will win your unstinted, unmodified praise; they are unlikely to welcome evidence that it is not all roses and may tend to tune out negatives. So you must make it clear you are talking about improvement to a good product. "Anyone you are going to criticize this way you think well of, or you wouldn't bother criticizing," says Arthur Larkin, chairman of Keebler. "So you sit down and talk positively about his progress, then you say, 'But now, Joe, there are a few things you need to correct.' He then is thinking positively and is in a mood to take criticism because he knows you're for him."

Whatever the regular performance-review schedule in your group, it is not frequent enough for these purposes. "Moving pictures show a lot more than snapshots," as George Foote puts it. "It's easier to tell an individual right at the time, 'I don't think you carried that off quite well; what did you learn from it?' And do that on an ongoing basis."

Your criticism should never include trivia because of everyone's natural tendency to put as good a face as possible on their own acts. Even if subordinates do not tune out criticism, they are apt to concentrate on whatever part is least derogatory, most effortlessly corrigible—and flatter themselves that they have then "taken care of the negatives." "If it's going to be a nitpick," Foote advises, "you are better off not even bringing it up. If you have five things you want to talk about and only two of them are really important, the other three being 'if-I-could-design-the-perfect-person' kinds of things, get your two points across and leave the others, if you bother with them, for another time."

You are never sure the training will take until the candidate has actually taken over—either for you or for some other boss. But you can give all the candidates, and yourself, and the company, the best chance of successful successions if you make your training a matter of painstaking planning and then slow, sure transfer. Of knowledge. Of authority. Of power.

# XV WHY BE BOSS?

*The questions asked each executive naturally varied depending on the flow of the interview. But after the interview was over, almost all were asked the same question:*

*"Why did you, why do you, like being and want to be a boss?"*

*You will notice that a few people do not have answers here. It is not because they would not answer, but that for some reason they were not asked. A couple of times interviews were interrupted before the end; in one case, the tape ran out, unnoticed, and the answer was lost.*

*But everyone who was asked found it an intriguing question, one that few of them had ever been urged to think about. They did think about it, and they gave thoughtful answers, some quite long and detailed. In the following chapter, general themes are grouped together, so an individual may seem to be giving several reasons, while actually all are part of his or her total reason for wanting to be and liking being a boss.*

*"I imagine you would get a lot of fascinating answers to that question," said William Roesch when he was asked it.*

*He was right. And here they are.*

## 28 *What a Boss Is, and Why Bosses Want to Be One*

Curious word, "boss." Can you think of another that at one moment connotes admirable qualities and the next moment, describing the same person or activity, connotes qualities that are irksome and oppressive, even downright evil?

In its upbeat use, "boss" suggests the sort of person everyone wants to be: the sort who can always show 'em who's boss, to whom others meltingly admit, "You're the boss."

But let that person start to boss you around, and he or she is . . . "bossy." If that person is a politician, a Boss Tweed, you send for the cops.

The word's origin is the Dutch *baas,* meaning "master," which is still its likely connotation when used by a Kaffir in South Africa or a prisoner on a Southern chain gang (recall the movie *Cool Hand Luke?*). Question is, does that servile spirit linger when "boss" is used in the nearest office or factory?

Some undoubted bosses think so, and they hate the idea. "The last thing I want to do," says McKinsey & Company director George Foote, "is be a boss. There is something about the term 'boss' that implies dictatorship. At least to me it does." He is not alone:

"I think 'boss' has negative connotations," says Leisure Dynamics chairman Bo Polk. "Boss, to me, is someone who is spouting orders all the time, and I don't think that is necessary in order to make things happen."

"I don't look at the thing as being a boss," says IBM director of management development Edward Krieg. "I guess it's because of the connotation of wielding power, et cetera. Supervising others just seems to provide the best approach to personal fulfillment and psychic satisfaction. It's what I've found I could enjoy doing."

Et—as he says—cetera. He likes being a boss, but not being called one. And he has company. People were chosen to be interviewed for this book because of some specially demonstrated insight to a particular subject. Movie director George Cukor, for instance, is noted for his sympathetic handling of talent and temperament. The original concept, though, was to match his views with those of another director, Otto Preminger, whose reputed approach to talent is antipodal. As soon as Preminger heard the book's title, though, he recoiled. "That's a terrible idea," he said. " 'Boss' is a terrible word, and it is an awful thing to be. No one should be a boss; I am not a boss. And I can take no part in this." That was that.

The fact is, even Cukor has doubts about being identified as a boss. " 'Boss' is not necessarily the right word," he says. "It's perhaps more 'head of a collaboration.' " Even so, he realizes the function is important, probably inescapable. "It is reassuring," he says, "for people to feel they have a boss, someone who knows the answers and has charted the course."

That is really the answer to queasiness over any possibly too-masterful connotation of the word. Enterprises need leaders no matter what they are called. Most people need, and want, the reassurance of those leaders. The question is, why do certain people want to be the leader, the boss?

"I suppose the only honest answer," says U.S. Steel chairman Edgar Speer, "is you feel you're making a contribution, and in making that contribution you get more satisfaction than you would in doing other things. Anyone who enjoys his job is saying he has found some satisfaction in that job that keeps him going."

Bosses want to be bosses because they want to run things. It is not a universal passion. Along with "organization man" there is what might be called "organization boss," simply the head flunky who has survived long enough to wheedle promotion. A real boss wants more than the title; he wants the *job*. "There are those who are bosses because of the number of people they manage," says INA chairman Ralph Saul, "and the amount of paper that piles up. Then there are those who are bosses because they feel they *command* their profession." A real boss almost cannot help wanting to be boss.

"I'm just not a good follower," says Savin Business Machines chairman Paul Charlap. "I don't know who said it, but I think it's true that if you take all the people in the world, undress them, and put them in a field, five years later the same ones will be rich and educated. It has a lot to do with genes or drive or *something* that came with that person."

"I don't think I would like being a follower all of my life," says J. C. Penney western regional manager William Howell. "Eventually I would want the challenge of being the leader. As far as how *big* a boss, I'm not hung up on that at all."

"Every social situation," says Leisure Dynamics chairman Bo Polk, "requires somebody to accept leadership, and I'm willing to do it. If someone else is more capable of taking the lead, that's all right with me. Of course, I wouldn't want to stay in that situation forever, when I could be the prime mover in making things happen"

"You have got to do the job," says Kaiser Industries president William Roesch, "because you want to see something built or produced or a service rendered; you want to see it done better, and you are willing to settle the conflicts. It's fun if you can take it. But if you can't take the personal abuse when you think that you are right, then you weren't meant to be the boss. It takes two things: a thick skin and a big mouth. One for defense, one for offense."

Bosses want to see something done—and are convinced they can get it done. So they must want power, must like having it and exercising it. Many bosses frankly say so.

"I enjoy power, no question about it," says American Airlines chairman Albert Casey. "I enjoy not having to refer or defer or be overruled by anybody. I've got to report on my stewardship; but I constantly remind the Board of Directors that if I come in on the representations I make, I expect no criticism. Norman Chandler used to say if he had his way he'd do away with the Board of Directors. I would except for that one essential responsibility: to get somebody else if I don't do the job."

"It's very enjoyable watching people respond," says Chevrolet general manager Robert Lund. "It's like giving a speech. You can watch people move forward in their seats, listening to what you're saying and what you're trying to accomplish. You can make them laugh, cry, do anything you want. It's almost like playing an instrument. That's the way it is leading an organization like this."

Power to bosses also means greater control over events, results, and their own destinies. Some bosses decide they want ultimate control almost right from the start.

"I first got started at General Electric," says Hewlett-Packard chairman David Packard. "I wasn't sure I was going to be able to get along in a big company like General Electric, and I thought that I'd rather be out on my own. So I've been a boss because I started my own company. I never had any ambitions to make a lot of money. It's simply that I wanted to be my own boss; that's what it was all about."

Others get a taste of control and want more—or simply realize they are not going to be happy until they achieve all the mastery of events possible.

"When I was running the European operation and was asked to come back to the States, I didn't want to," says Goodyear chairman Charles Pilliod. "I told the president 'You can call me vice-president of International, but either you or the chairman will press a button and I'll have to get up and run. I've been pressing buttons for years, and I don't want to go back to the position where somebody else is pressing a button and I'm running.' 'Oh, no,' he says, 'that won't happen.' So I came back, and I'd be in a meeting and the secretary would come in and say, 'Mr. Thomas wants to see you,' and I'd have to jump up; the button had been pressed. The only joy I used to get was when I'd be in his office and someone would come in and say, 'Mr.

Thomas, Mr. Dionne wants to see you,' and *he'd* have to jump. So I think one of the motivating factors for me was to get to the point where you *own* the button."

"I like to be in control of things," says Redactron president Evelyn Berezin. "To feel I know what's happening. I was always extremely frustrated feeling I was a cog. Now, you're always a cog at some level, always at the mercy of some forces beyond your control. But as a boss, you have a much greater span of understanding of what they are and how they affect you. And you have greater capacity to control them."

"I think all of us," says Fairchild Camera and Instrument chairman Wilfred Corrigan, "are basically motivated toward getting more and more control over our own environment. I think that you are almost making a statement that that is what you are trying to do when you end up being a boss of a large piece of an organization."

"To be in a position where you can change things you think ought to be changed is a strong motivational factor as far as I've been concerned," says USLIFE chairman Gordon Crosby. "I saw things, and I said, 'Gee, that isn't the right way to do it. If I were to get behind that desk, I would do it differently.' "

"It's easier to see from the top of the hill than it is from the valley," says First Boston chairman George Shinn. "And I guess I would rather lead. There is a limited amount of time in a man's life, I want to accomplish something, and it's hard to accomplish as much if you are a follower."

"I've been able to try ideas one step up that I wouldn't be able to try one step below that," says Ford executive VP Donald Petersen. "At a lower level it would be an interesting theoretical discussion; at a higher level I can *try* something."

"I like having some responsibility for charting direction and course of action," says Chevrolet director of salaried personnel Richard McIlvride. "I like that better than contributing my best idea and having a different course charted. At least you become a tie breaker if there is a difference of opinion."

The sense of the utility of power—people wanting to be boss for what it means they can accomplish—is so strong that many bosses honestly feel they never really did *want* to be boss. It just happened as a result of their intense interest in getting the job done. Even the chairman of Goodyear, who wanted to *own* any buttons being pushed, never cared what size button it was. "I never asked for or sought a bigger job," says Charles Pilliod. "I was always fully occupied doing the job assigned me." But when he had to shift from being in charge in England to being an underling (however highly placed) in Akron, he wanted to get back in charge.

A majority of bosses say they feel the same. All they ever *wanted* was to do the best they could—and that best propelled them to the top.

"I never aspired to be the boss of bosses or whatever," says J. C. Penney chairman Donald Seibert. "Just to be the best of whatever I was doing at the time. When I joined the Penney company my objective was to run the biggest and best shoe department. Well, I had been in the company a year, I guess, when I saw other men in the store running the whole men's department, or the whole floor—not working as hard as I was to run the shoe department, and being rewarded more and getting more personal satisfaction. And I concluded that, if I'm going to work this hard, I might as well work at something a little bigger than the shoe department."

"I believe in the kinds of things we've been talking about as we've gone along," says Gillette chairman Colman Mockler. "I think the result happens to be that I'm a boss. But that was the result, not the objective of the process. I went about doing what I thought should be done, and the result was that I became boss."

"I didn't come into Union Carbide and say, 'I want to be a boss,' " says executive VP Warren Anderson. "People do the best they can. You're given an opportunity. You do what you think is right, and if it's done well, you get another opportunity. I was extremely fortunate in having a number of outstanding bosses who said, 'Get in there and fight; you can do it, I'm with you.' They took a chance and it worked out. If you like to try to get people to do what you know they are capable of, it's kind of fun, and you wind up as boss."

"It never occurred to me that I was going to be," says movie director George Cukor. "I never said, 'I want to be boss.' You grow into it. Maybe you are bossy by nature. I was a stage manager first, and that means that you give a lot of orders. 'Go over there, and move this over here.' You have to learn how to be a boss without being a bully. Yet you must be authoritative. You learn how."

Says Chevrolet's Richard McIlvride, "It is part of being able to work to my capacity—and that involves being the boss. Not because I have people working for me, and I get to direct them, and so on. It's just an integral part of my total responsibility."

A variation on that theme is that some bosses feel driven to the sort of achievement that results in being boss. It is part of their makeup.

"I have impatience for the world and for myself," says Paul Charlap. "The kind that drives you toward success. If you have it, and you're smart, if something doesn't happen the way you want it to, instead of saying, 'Oh, God, what bad luck!' you say, 'How could I have made it better? How could I make it not go wrong?' And then you become the boss."

"I never particularly wanted to be boss," says Texas Instruments founder Erik Jonsson. "I guess it happened to me because of circumstances. I enjoy risk-taking and I keep testing my judgment. It's fun; and if you win a high enough percentage of the games you play, you finally get to be captain of the team. And I think it's having joy in what you do, in part, that leads to this job whether you want it or not."

"I didn't choose to head an organization," says William Bernbach, founder of Doyle Dane Bernbach. "I had certain ideas and very deep feelings about communications and what makes communications work. I worked for somebody else with no idea of being the boss. One client insisted I open my own agency. I said no because I didn't want to take the account away; finally, this man said, 'If you don't open your own agency, I will take the account away from them anyway.' When he made that statement I went into business—not to be a boss but to do the things I thought were great."

"I really don't think of myself as a boss," says INA VP Harold Johnson. "I've got a hundred and forty people in my organization who work for me and I don't mind being 'the boss,' but I don't think I'm on any kind of power trip. I probably have one of the better jobs of this kind around. I want to be a success and run as far as I possibly can. But where in the hell that is, I don't know. I can't imagine myself really doing anything else."

There is another factor. In some ways being boss is almost a duty.

"One of the things that indicates you are proceeding in what you are doing," says Securities and Exchange Commission director of enforcement Stanley Sporkin, "is accepting promotions. If somebody says you are doing a good job and you ought to be doing something bigger, then you ought to at least try to do it."

"It never occurred to me," says Consolidated Foods chairman John Bryan, "that you shouldn't accept the bigger challenges that come along. Maybe it's some sort of ethic that was bred into me."

"I like doing things," says Sara Lee president Thomas Barnum, "and making things happen. The result, if you do it well, is that you get to be more of a boss. I'm here, and I know I'm the head guy, but that's almost irrelevant, relative to getting this thing done that we are trying to get done."

"I did enjoy the individual performance of having a sales territory," says IBM's Edward Krieg. "But then someone interested in my development said, 'I think you would like staff work. Have you ever thought of . . .?' And the next thing you know I was doing some teaching. And somebody said, 'Now that you have a broader perspective, how would you like to go back and manage some of the people who used to be like yourself?' That's the way things happen."

An important subsidiary question to why someone wants to be boss is, "Boss of what?" To many, being boss immediately suggests a certain substance; the size of the organization they head is itself a factor in their satisfaction, in their wanting to be boss.

"I enjoy being associated with a very large organization," says American Airlines chairman Albert Casey. "I like big numbers. I wouldn't like to be a loner, though I think you can probably make more money being a deal maker. That isn't what I like. I like the employee meetings, the staff meetings. I even like the annual meeting where I get chewed up for three and a half hours. I like the interchange with large groups. I like the big corporate life."

It just would not be the same operating, even as boss, on a more intimate scale.

"I get a lot of enjoyment out of taking a big problem and making things change, hopefully for the better," says American Airlines assistant VP Robert Baker. "I don't think I'd like to run a pizza factory or a retail store. Because the challenges are not there, except for taking a loser to a profit. But once I got the store on its feet I would lose interest very rapidly."

"I enjoy doing something that is demanding," says Chrysler VP Glenn White. "I enjoy working with people. Being a boss also conveys the idea of being involved in a competitive business that requires original thinking, trying to do things differently from the way they have been done before. Running a grocery store, for example, might not require that to the same extent, so that's why I would say being part of a big business is much more interesting than something very small."

"The larger the organization one is associated with," says Edward Hess, Exxon deputy manager of marketing, "the more things you see getting done, and the bigger the things that get done that you feel responsibility for. It boils down to the much greater leverage that being responsible for a large organization gives a person."

That "greater leverage," of course, is the essence of being boss in any size organization. Many people want to be boss because their own abilities are hugely magnified, and they can accomplish through their people and their organization so much more.

"I think I have a lot more to offer than I have output capability to deliver," says INA director of financial relations William Adams. "You don't take an IBM 371/95 and put one printer on it and one tape drive. You put a hundred tape drives, forty printers, and remote terminals, and you can utilize the power of that computer. Now someone like a writer can do that without having to utilize fifty people as a vehicle for outputting his capabilities and ideas. He can do it through writing; a businessman can't. He has to do it through the people and the distribution system of the company. And that takes people directly or indirectly influenced by him."

"I enjoy patient care," says Francis Sweeney, hospital director of Thomas Jefferson University. "I miss patient care, and I miss teaching—though I still try to do a little of both. But I enjoy what I do. I enjoy administration. I think that in some ways I'm taking care of *more* patients this way. You get a different perspective on taking care of people running an institution like this. And I enjoy it."

"I want to be productive," says Chrysler manager of securities investment John Knutson. "And as an individual I'm not as productive as a person running the plant with two thousand people. I think that in itself is a reason for being a boss."

Magnification of their personal productivity aside, for some bosses the need to work with and through other people is, itself, why they want to be boss.

"I like people," says Charles Kean, Gillette staff assistant. "Working with people and through people. I like being able to take an organization of people and reach an objective. Organize them so that we come out to where we wanted to be. And have them get some satisfaction from it. That's the kick I get out of it."

"It's a little like: Why do I enjoy football?" says Leisure Dynamics chairman Bo Polk. "I enjoy the interaction with a lot of people in trying to get something solved, or to attain a goal."

For some, what they want to do simply is not possible alone. They need people.

"I get an extraordinary thrill from seeing something—a newspaper, a book, a magazine—that began as an idea come into being," says *New York Times* director of special projects Leonard Harris. "Except when one is an artist, this requires a large number of people and a fantastic number of skills. When you have the joy of producing something good and the additional joy of seeing it succeed in the marketplace, that seems to me to be the greatest kick one can get. And if it's produced by a harmonious group of people, that is a very important part of the kick."

Not that such bosses denigrate those who prefer to operate on their own. It is just not for them.

"To me," says Akzona chairman Claude Ramsey, "being a boss is more challenging, more stimulating, with more variety, more activity, and more feeling of accomplishment. I am not knocking the individual performer. It has to do with temperament as much as anything else; I suppose you are born with it. I know some damn capable people who have no interest at all in being a boss, and hurray for them!"

"I enjoy performing on my own," says J. C. Penney chairman Donald Seibert. "There isn't anything much more satisfying than going in and walking out with an order. But you can accomplish more if you can inspire and lead two thousand people. If you're a salesman, or an accountant working by yourself, everything you achieve is all for yourself. But in business, if you have ability that is worthwhile, and you can transmit it to other people, that is of greater benefit to society—and you get more out of it than just the almighty dollar."

It is even possible to accept the role of boss without being entirely sure you *do* want it. Or, at any rate, to have lingering yearnings after some of the individual rewards of the individual performer.

"Many times I think I'd rather be strictly a lawyer, trying cases," says SEC's Stanley Sporkin. "This year, just to get back into things, I went up and argued a case before the Court of Appeals. I have a good administrative assistant, so I do not get bogged down in determining where this guy is going to sit and that guy's going to get his papers. I refuse to do that sort of thing. When this job becomes a question of intolerable administrative problems, I'll quit."

"I love to go into a plant and sit down with a supervisor and help him work out his problems of motivation," says Behavioral Systems president Aubrey Daniels. "But more, I like to see the growth of this idea. I guess I'm a bit of a missionary, which reinforces me in terms of seeing people change. I know that I can't do it by myself, and that's probably one thing that keeps a lot of people going at this level in a company—because, as boss, the amount of personal positive reinforcement you get is limited. You hear everybody's problems, and try to get people to improve their performances, and you personally don't get that much positive reinforcement feedback."

Anyone who, on balance, decides there is not enough reward in leading to offset the diminished opportunity to concentrate on and exercise his or her own powers as a performer, anyone who actually prefers working alone, does well to stop being a boss.

"I never wanted to be, and I never have been, a good boss," says Bernard Haldane, who remains a consultant to the company he founded. "About a year after I sold my business to the manager of one of our divisions, we had a celebration in the Washington office and I was asked to say a few words. I looked around at a staff of twenty-odd, and I said, 'You know, I had four people when I was running the Washington office. I think the number of you here is a clear demonstration of my *in*effectiveness as a manager.' I believe that. I'm an innovator, a good planner and organizer and writer; I'm a very good teacher. But as far as managing is concerned, I'm no good. I am a very bad delegator; I like to do it myself. And when you like to do things yourself, you cannot do them on a big scale. The organization has doubled in size since I sold it."

For most people who become bosses, though, the satisfactions of working with people, through people—and, above all, developing people—are enormous. Indeed, developing people is *the* reason for wanting to be boss for many bosses.

"I have some definite ideas as to what I want this outfit to be," says Union Carbide executive VP Fred O'Mara, "not only while I'm here. I want to help get these younger guys trained up to the point where it will be even more so in the future. Sure, money goes along with it, and there are perks, but if that's all you had, you wouldn't have anything; you'd be an empty shell. The real reason I like being a boss is the ability to help some of these younger guys come along faster and be better than I ever thought I could be. Because that's what makes the damn thing go, you know. And I can feel maybe I'm part of that."

"Of course I like being a boss," says Keebler chairman Arthur Larkin. "I like responsibility. I like success. I love to see others succeed, especially if I have had a hand in their development. I get more kick out of that than almost anything else. I'm about to be sixty years old. The management of Keebler are men in their twenties and thirties; the new president is forty. I have, in a small way, helped to develop them as managers and I get a big kick out of it."

"I'm very people oriented," says Gillette VP Robert Hinman. "I enjoy working with people, having people to supervise. The biggest kicks in business come in selecting people and seeing them come along. I get a great deal of satisfaction out of watching them grow."

"Being a leader is much the same as being a father," says McKinsey's George Foote. "You want to perpetuate yourself, to develop others and see them have an opportunity. One of the things you can leave behind is that you helped identify some bright young talent and were able to teach them something. When you're through, you can always measure how successful you've been by how much you've accomplished as an individual. But you might prefer to measure it also by what those you've brought along have accomplished.

A living monument is much better. I can't step out from my role at McKinsey until I have people coming along who are better than I am. That's why I like being a leader. Eventually, I hope to be a follower or supporter of people who are even better leaders."

"I guess this is a sign of age now," says USLIFE chairman Gordon Crosby. "You get to a point where there is no longer financial motivation, no more 'rungs up the ladder.' So I get a hell of a charge these days out of the young people. You see them come in as juniors, and you see them move up to executive VP. That's your motivation: to be able to take the product of your years of experience and success and pass this baton on to younger people so that they can capitalize further. You can leverage your own experience through other people, and that's a *big* motivation!"

Actually it is not just "a sign of age." The satisfaction of developing people accounts for why some younger men also want to be boss.

"Beside its being satisfying to my own inner drives and ambitions," says Exxon deputy controller Edward Robinson, "beside its being a certain evidence of progress, it affords me the opportunity to work with people, hopefully having a role in helping them get more out of life. A fellow I had helped realize his potential when I was head of Esso-Africa just got a very nice promotion. He was passing through town, and I committed time I shouldn't have this morning just talking with him because I saw the fruition, frankly, of something I worked very hard at two or three years ago. I saw that his whole life is different. I get a lot of kick out of that. And I feel, being a boss, I have opportunity to do some of these things I wouldn't have if I were just a personal performer, no matter how good."

"The reason I would like to be a boss," says U.S. Steel's Drummond Bell, "is to have some say in what subordinates do— to improve them. I would like to be a factor in training, in giving them the techniques I've learned. I'd rather not have to do everything myself; I'd rather have people who help me do these things. And from a corporate standpoint, to be a boss is the way to go further."

"Making sales is fine for the short term," says Savin VP Abraham Ostrovsky, "and I still get a chance to negotiate large contracts. But there is nothing quite like the satisfaction of looking around you and saying, 'These people are better maybe because they came in contact with me. They are where they are because I helped them get there.' That is the ultimate kick, the real answer to it."

As with most such questions, there is no *one* "real answer." Nor is there any reason why reasons for wanting to be boss should necessarily have to do only with the boss's relationships to other people. A lot of people want to be boss just because being boss is more challenging, more fun.

"What I like most about it is the variety of things you deal with," says SEC's Wallace Timmeny. "You can get stuck on one case as a lawyer, beat one case to death for years and years. But in my position, I'm exposed to a variety of problems. Every one of the eighty or ninety lawyers and accountants that are working with me will have some problems each day I get exposed to. There's a tremendous learning curve; I learn all the time. So the basic thing is the variety more than anything else. I don't want to be stuck in a corner someplace."

"Each step of progression upward," says Ford executive VP Donald Petersen, "the issues get broader—more conceptual and less specific and repetitive. It offers more variety to the activity you're engaged in. I have more interest, frankly, in the strategy of the business than in the specific actions of turning out outstanding sales or manufacturing or whatever it might be."

"I don't like to administrate," says Bo Polk, "and I set my businesses up so that I don't have to. So the distinction I make as a boss is that I'm more interested in problem-solving than in day-to-day matters, and I no longer want to do something on a day-to-day operating basis."

Bosses also like to be bosses just because, psychologically, it feels good—for a wide mixture of reasons.

Ford VP Louis Ross: "I suspect the reason is recognition. People like to be recognized for having done well. And being boss here is one token of recognition."

USLIFE's Gordon Crosby: "People who are running big companies have to be motivated, in part, by ego."

Chevrolet's Robert Lund: "I like the challenge, the opportunity to make the decision. I thrive on competition. And I like to be number one. Put it another way: I enjoy leading the troops. Not only from the selfish standpoint, but hopefully to inspire people to do a better job. That's the fun of working."

Gillette's Charles Kean: "There are psychological rewards and money rewards, and I like to be well thought of by the good people in the organization."

Dictaphone chairman Lawrence Tabat: "I like the challenge, and I like the opportunity of accomplishing something that I know I can accomplish."

Gillette treasurer Milton Glass: "I've always enjoyed my work and enjoyed working with people. And it's financially rewarding to be a boss. So I decided being a boss was my goal."

Loews president Robert Tisch: "I like the feeling of accomplishment and of being a team player. I like working with and developing people. I like big business. I think we can accomplish a lot for ourselves, as well as for the economy, the country and the world."

American Airlines senior VP Thomas Plaskett: "I enjoy being able to do things on my own volition, analysis and decision. Granted, I'm not there yet; you're there when you run a company. So I guess my objective is to be number one. It comes down to two things: I enjoy achievement and I enjoy the power that goes with it. And the money's not bad, either!"

That brings up another reason for being boss: money and perquisites. They *are* considerations, and bosses do not mind saying so. "I think there are a number of reasons I like being a boss," says J. C. Penney's William Howell. "Financial gain is certainly one of them." On the other hand, it is not an obsession. "Life is good at a lot of different levels," Howell continues. "We don't all have to drive Cadillacs and own big homes. They are great, and I enjoy them to a certain degree, but if worse comes to worst, peace of mind, my lovely wife and family—those are more important. I could be very happy managing a Penney store somewhere."

And in the long haul, money turns out not to be all that vital. Especially when you have an awful lot of it.

"I may give the money away," says Consolidated Foods founder Nathan Cummings. "Yesterday I was up at Mount Sinai Hospital about the Nathan Cummings Plaza. This is my fun. I buy beautiful sculpture and paintings and lend them for exhibitions or give them away. I don't expect to die as rich as I am today; I don't need it. What I do, what I've always done, is because it's fun."

The same goes for perquisites—all the famous executive toys. They are fun, but they are not why someone wants to be a boss.

"If I work until I'm sixty-five," says Union Carbide's Fred O'Mara, "I will have been around here forty-five years. And I'm conscious of the fact that when I walk out the door, that's it; there is no more company limousine, no more company airplane, no more expense account. On the other hand, I won't have to shave every day. I'll have done my thing, and I can relax."

Why do bosses want to be bosses? The ultimate answer may not seem of lively interest or pertinence to a young man in the flush of early success, of growing power and privilege, but a longer view of achievement animates the boss who nears the top.

"It's the satisfaction it gives you to put something together and have it succeed," says Pillsbury chairman William Spoor. "I think that's all I'm after. I realize my tenure is short; I want to leave it a very powerful company, so that as I look back on my life I'll say, 'You know, I did something I was proud of.' That's the satisfaction of achievement, leaving it a better place than when you came in."

All the rest is fine and fun, and there is no reason for the boss not to openly enjoy, even revel in, the privileges of office. "I like the prerogatives of heading a large organization," says INA chairman Ralph Saul. "I think it is often difficult to find people who will admit that, but I think most people do." But that is not *the* reason for wanting to be boss. Saul glances around his exquisite office: at the gleaming brass andirons in the Georgian fireplace, the lovely carved wainscoting, the prints, the furniture, the burnished model fire engines—the *works!* "You have to be very careful," he says. "You have to check yourself. Because you can be bemused by all this nonsense and forget what makes the organization go and that all you are is just a steward, just a temporary steward, and it's all going to pass on to somebody else."

He likes to recall that when Napoleon was showing off Fontainebleau to his mother, the crusty old Corsican lady looked around, shrugged and said, "But will it last?"

Of course it will not. Not the money or the perks, not the power or the glory. Nothing. Except perhaps the satisfaction of achievement and the knowledge that the people and organizations you led and served are better off because you were boss.

# Appendix I: List of People Quoted

Titles are as of the time each person was interviewed; for more information, see APPENDIX II.

Ackemann, Andrew, assistant to the chairman, Leisure Dynamics, Inc.
Adams, William, director of financial relations, INA Corporation
Anderson, Warren, executive VP, Union Carbide
Anspach, Ralph, co-inventor and chairman, Anti-Monopoly, Inc.
Anspach, Ruth, co-inventor, VP and secretary, Anti-Monopoly, Inc.

Baker, Robert, assistant VP, marketing, American Airlines
Barnum, Thomas, president, The Kitchens of Sara Lee
Bell, Drummond, staff assistant, U.S. Steel Corporation
Berezin, Evelyn, founder and president, Redactron Corporation
Bergerac, Michel, chairman, Revlon, Inc.
Berlin, Leonard, senior financial analyst, Exxon Corporation
Bernbach, William, founder, Doyle Dane Bernbach, Inc.
Bontempo, Ann, public relations, Loews Corporation
Bryan, John, chairman, Consolidated Foods
Bunting, John, chairman, First Pennsylvania Corporation
Burgheim, Richard, assistant managing editor, *People*

Casey, Albert, chairman, American Airlines
Charlap, Paul, chairman, Savin Business Machines Corporation
Corrigan, Wilfred, chairman, Fairchild Camera and Instrument
Crandall, Robert, senior VP, marketing, American Airlines
Crosby, Gordon, chairman, USLIFE Corporation
Cukor, George, film director
Cummings, Nathan, founder and honorary chairman, Consolidated Foods
Cushmore, M. E. ("Ted"), marketing director, family products, General Mills, Inc.

Daniels, Aubrey, president, Behavioral Systems, Inc.

Farnham, Harry, branch general manager, Savin Business Machines Corporation

Fausch, David, VP, director of corporate PR, The Gillette Company
Foote, George, director, McKinsey & Company

Gaines, Frank, coordinator, compensation, organization and executive development committee, Exxon Corporation
George, William, president, Litton Microwave Cooking
Glass, Milton, treasurer, The Gillette Company
Goldfarb, Walter, director of industrial engineering, Benrus Corporation
Gondek, Stanley, controller, The Kitchens of Sara Lee

Haldane, Bernard, founder, Bernard Haldane Associates
Harris, Leonard, director of special projects, *The New York Times*
Hess, Edward, deputy manager, marketing, Exxon Corporation
Hills, Roderick, chairman, Securities & Exchange Commission
Hinman, Robert, VP, chairman's office, The Gillette Company
Howe, Arthur, director of public affairs, INA Corporation
Howell, William, VP, western regional manager, J. C. Penney Company, Inc.
Hunt, Stanley, assistant controller, General Mills, Inc.

Iverson, Robert, director of marketing, The Kitchens of Sara Lee

Jackson, Richard ("Dick"), VP, finance, Litton Microwave Cooking
Jackson, Richard ("Rick"), manager of business analysis, Litton Microwave Cooking
Johnson, Harold, VP, employee relations, INA Corporation
Jonsson, Erik, founder, Texas Instruments

Kean, Charles, staff assistant, The Gillette Company
Kiam, Victor, chairman, Benrus Corporation
Kieller, Stanley, product quality manager, Tractor Operations, Ford Motor Company
Knutson, John, manager of securities investment, Chrysler Corporation
Krieg, Edward, director of management development, International Business Machines Corporation

Larkin, Arthur, chairman, Keebler Company
Larry, Heath, vice-chairman, U.S. Steel Corporation
Ludwig, Robert, accountant, The Kitchens of Sara Lee
Lund, Robert, VP, general manager, Chevrolet Motor Division, General Motors Corporation

McFarland, James, chairman, General Mills, Inc.
McIlvride, Richard, director of salaried personnel, Chevrolet Motor Division, General Motors Corporation
Mercurio, Nicholas, senior VP, operations, Benrus Corporation
Mockler, Colman, chairman, The Gillette Company
Monfort, Kenneth, executive VP, Monfort of Colorado, Inc.
Mulloney, Peter, executive assistant, U.S. Steel Corporation
Musante, Betty, receptionist, First Boston Corporation

Novak, Alex, senior VP, controller, Benrus Corporation

O'Mara, Fred, executive VP, Union Carbide
Ostrovsky, Abraham, VP, marketing, Savin Business Machines Corporation

Packard, David, chairman, Hewlett-Packard Company
Patterson, Herbert, senior adviser, Marshalsea Associates, Inc.
Petersen, Donald, executive VP, Ford Motor Company
Pilliod, Charles, chairman, Goodyear Tire & Rubber
Plaskett, Thomas, senior VP, finance, American Airlines
Polk, Louis ("Bo"), chairman, Leisure Dynamics, Inc.
Port, Donald, project manager, The Gillette Company
Preminger, Otto, film director

Ramsey, Claude, chairman, Akzona, Inc.
Robinson, Edward, deputy controller, Exxon Corporation
Rock, Milton, managing partner, Hay Associates
Roebling, Mary, chairman, National State Bank, Trenton
Roesch, William, president, Kaiser Industries
Ross, Louis, VP, general manager, Tractor Operations, Ford Motor Company

Saul, Ralph, chairman, INA Corporation
Seibert, Donald, chairman, J. C. Penney Company, Inc.
Shinn, George, chairman, First Boston Corporation
Shriner, Richard ("Rick"), manager of range engineering, Litton Microwave Cooking
Speer, Edgar, chairman, U.S. Steel Corporation
Spoor, William, chairman, The Pillsbury Company
Sporkin, Stanley, director, division of enforcement, Securities & Exchange Commission
Stanger, Edward, senior financial analyst, The Gillette Company

Sweeney, Francis, M.D., VP for health services and hospital director, Thomas Jefferson University

Tabat, Lawrence, chairman, Dictaphone Corporation

Tessitore, Gary, manager of cost analysis, Tractor Operations, Ford Motor Company

Timmeny, Wallace, associate director, division of enforcement, Securities & Exchange Commission

Tisch, Robert, president, Loews Corporation

White, Glenn, VP, personnel and organization, Chrysler Corporation

Williams, James, assistant director of PR, Chevrolet Motor Division, General Motors Corporation

# Appendix II: List of Companies

*Note:* In addition to names and titles of all people quoted in the book, there are listed the names and titles of others in the company (generally public relations people) who discussed the subject of the interview, often sat in on meetings and sometimes contributed by asking their own questions of the person being interviewed. Ages, where available, are given only for those quoted. Ages and titles are given as of the time of the interview. Updates on careers appear in parentheses.

AKZONA, INC.
1 West Park Square
Asheville, NC 28802
     Claude Ramsey, 51, chairman

AMERICAN AIRLINES
633 Third Avenue
New York, NY 10017
     Albert V. Casey, 56, chairman
     Robert L. Crandall, 41, senior VP, marketing
     Thomas G. Plaskett, 33, senior VP, finance
     (Plaskett had been appointed to his post just two weeks before his interview)
     Robert W. Baker, 31, assistant VP, marketing administration
     (Plaskett's old job; Baker had stepped in, promoted from director of ramp services)

ANTI-MONOPOLY, INC. (now DBA Anspach)
1600 Holloway Avenue
San Francisco, CA 94132
     Ralph Anspach, 50, co-inventor and chairman
     (This parody of "Monopoly" was promptly sued by General Mills, proprietors of Parker Bros. Anspach claimed the game is in public domain; the first judge ruled otherwise—which is why "DBA Anspach"—but Anspach has high hopes for the appeal. Meanwhile the game still sells, by court order under the

name of "Anti," and the corporation has come up with a new game, "Choice," which lets you play as either a monopolist or competitor. Anspach says it's the first board game played with two sets of rules simultaneously.)

Ruth Anspach, 40, co-inventor, VP and secretary.

## BEHAVIORAL SYSTEMS, INC.
3300 N.E. Expressway
Atlanta, GA 30341

Aubrey C. Daniels, Ph.D., 41, president
(Has since started his own PRI Company, Aubrey Daniels and Associates, P.O. Box 898, Tucker, GA 30084)

## BENRUS CORPORATION (now, Wells-Benrus)
Benrus Center
Ridgefield, CO 06877

Victor K. Kiam, II, 50, chairman
Nicholas R. Mercurio, 53, senior VP, operations
Alex Novak, senior VP, controller
Walter Goldfarb, director of industrial engineering

## CHEVROLET MOTOR DIVISION, GENERAL MOTORS CORPORATION
3044 West Grand Boulevard
Detroit, MI 48202

Robert D. Lund, 56, VP, general manager
Richard McIlvride, 45, director of salaried personnel
James Williams, 39, assistant director of public relations

## CHRYSLER CORPORATION
12000 Oakland Avenue
Highland Park, MI 48203

Glenn E. White, 50, VP, personnel and organization
John Knutson, 35, manager of securities investment

## CONSOLIDATED FOODS
135 South La Salle
Chicago, IL 60603

Nathan Cummings, 80, founder and honorary chairman
(As he suggests in chapter 28, Cummings has retired to his Waldorf Towers art collection, whence he sallies to give away an awful lot of money; in between

times he keeps busy as a director of General Dynamics and chairman of Magnatex Ltd., London, and answering the phone, which never stops ringing)
John H. Bryan, Jr., 38, chairman
(*See also* The Kitchens of SARA LEE, a Consolidated company)

## DICTAPHONE CORPORATION
120 Old Post Road
Rye, NY 10580

E. Lawrence Tabat, president
(He has since been elected chairman, continuing as chief executive officer)

## DOYLE DANE BERNBACH, INC.
437 Madison Avenue
New York, NY 10022

William Bernbach, 65, founder
(Just before his interview, Bernbach officially retired as chairman of the worldwide organization; he remains a director and chairman of the executive committee—and a tremendous voice in advertising)

## EXXON CORPORATION
1251 Avenue of the Americas
New York, NY 10020

Frank Gaines, Jr., coordinator of organization, planning and executive development and compensation; secretary of compensation and executive development committee (COED)
(As explained in chapter 26, Exxon seemed a good place to inquire about picking successors. Neither the chairman nor the president was in the country at the time, but, as his title suggests, Gaines is intimately involved in the process —and after thirty-eight years with Exxon, he knew the company's views on picking and nurturing comers)
Edward Robinson, 43, deputy controller
Edward Hess, 43, deputy manager of marketing
Leonard Berlin, 26, senior financial analyst

## FAIRCHILD CAMERA AND INSTRUMENT
464 Ellis Street
Mountainview, CA 94040

Wilfred J. Corrigan, 38, chairman
Fred M. Hoar, director of communication

## FIRST BOSTON CORPORATION
20 Exchange Place
New York, NY 10005

> George L. Shinn, 53, chairman
> (He was approached for his views on the topic "moving on," having left Merrill Lynch after 27 years; he was No. 2, his boss was only 56 and he wanted, he said, "the challenge of being chief executive officer." He loves it)
> Betty Musante, receptionist, main executive floor

## FIRST PENNSYLVANIA CORPORATION
15th and Chestnut Streets
Philadelphia, PA 19102

> John R. Bunting, Jr., 51, chairman

## FORD MOTOR COMPANY
American Road
Dearborn, MI 48121

> Walter Murphy, executive director, public relations staff
> John E. Sattler, director of public relations services
>
> Donald E. Petersen, 50, executive VP, Diversified Products Operations
> (He now heads a different division, International Automobile Operations, still, of course, as an executive VP of the corporation)
> Richard Judy, manager of public relations, Diversified Products Operations
>
> Louis R. Ross, 44, VP, general manager, Tractor Operations (part of Diversified Products)
> (He was then the youngest VP at Ford; he is now the youngest executive VP, having succeeded his then boss, Petersen, as head of Diversified Products)
> Marc J. Parsons, director of public relations, Tractor Operations
> Stanley T. Kieller, 36, product quality manager, Tractor Operations
> Gary Tessitore, 31, manager of operations cost and profit analysis, Tractor Operations

## GENERAL MILLS, INC.
9200 Wayzata Boulevard
Minneapolis, MN 55440

> James P. McFarland, 64, chairman
> (A year later he retired, but continues as a director of the corporation, as well as sitting on the boards of many other companies, including Toro and Scott Paper)

Glen E. Gaff, director of external communications
A. Louis Champlin, Jr., director of public relations
(Now, director of consumer affairs)
Stanley M. Hunt, 51, assistant controller, director of accounting
M. E. ("Ted") Cushmore, 36, marketing director, family cereal products

## THE GILLETTE COMPANY
Prudential Tower Building
Boston, MA 02199

Colman M. Mockler, 46, chairman
Robert W. Hinman, 55, VP, chairman's office
Milton L. Glass, 47, VP treasurer
David A. Fausch, 43, VP, corporate public relations director
(He joined the company after 13 years with *Business Week,* having run the Management Department. Part of his reason was a hankering to see what corporate life looked like from the inside. His conclusion: "different")
Charles Kean, 35, staff assistant
(At the time of his interview he had already been named as controller of Gillette-Canada, but had not yet made the move. He's now financial coordinator, diversified companies group)
Donald F. Port, 46, project manager
(Shortly after his interview he received his expected new assignment as director of materials management, Gillette International)
Edward C. Stanger, 38, senior financial analyst
(Now, senior economist and director of civic affairs)

## GOODYEAR TIRE AND RUBBER
1144 East Market Street
Akron, OH 44316

Charles J. Pilliod, 58, chairman
Robert H. Lane, VP, public relations

## BERNARD HALDANE ASSOCIATES
1747 Pennsylvania Avenue, N.W.
Washington, DC 20006

Bernard Haldane, founder
(He sold his business, as described in chapter 28, but continues as a consultant)

HAY ASSOCIATES
1845 Walnut Street
Philadelphia, PA 19103
> Milton Rock, managing partner

HEWLETT-PACKARD COMPANY
1501 Page Mill Road
Palo Alto, CA 94304
> David Packard, 64, chairman
> David Kirby, VP public relations

INA CORPORATION
1600 Arch Street
Philadelphia, PA 19103
> Ralph S. Saul, 54, chairman
> Harold E. Johnson, 37, VP, employee relations
> (Now, senior VP)
> Arthur Howe, III, director of public affairs
> William C. Adams, 29, director of financial relations

INTERNATIONAL BUSINESS MACHINE CORPORATION
Armonk, NY 10504
> Edward Krieg, director of management development
> James W. Hill, senior information representative

THOMAS JEFFERSON UNIVERSITY
11th and Walnut Streets
Philadelphia, PA 19107
> Francis J. Sweeney, Jr., M.D., 49, VP for health services, and hospital
> director
> (Jefferson is one of the country's top teaching and research medical institutions)

KAISER INDUSTRIES CORPORATION
300 Lakeside Drive
Oakland, CA 94666
> William R. Roesch, president
> (During his interview Roesch said that 3 years was usually the duration of his
> jobs; then it was on to clean up another sticky situation. Three years after he
> was called in to turn things around at Kaiser—which he did—he was out,

having given the company, according to *Business Week,* "a strong dose of professional management." His replacement was quoted as approving all Roesch's moves, but was also "expected to be a less abrasive and personally ambitious regent" until young Edgar F. Kaiser, Jr., was ready to step in. He is now executive VP, steel and domestic raw materials, U.S. Steel)

## KEEBLER COMPANY
677 Larch Avenue
Elmhurst, IL 60126

Arthur E. Larkin, Jr., 59, chairman
(He left the presidency of General Foods after taking the rap for the $46-million Burger Chef disaster)

## LEISURE DYNAMICS, INC.
375 Park Avenue
New York, NY 10022

Louis F. ("Bo") Polk, 46, chairman
Andrew C. Ackemann, 31, assistant to the chairman
(Congruent positioning means always being ready to seize opportunity—even when it conflicts with otherwise sound plans. One came along, and Ackemann is now with MBA Resources, Inc., 717 Fifth Avenue, New York, NY 10022)

## LITTON MICROWAVE COOKING
1405 Xenium Lane
Minneapolis, MN 55441

William George, 33, president
Richard H. ("Dick") Jackson, 33, VP, finance
(Now, senior VP, finance and administration)
Richard ("Rick") Shriner, 33, manager of range engineering
(Now, VP, commercial products)
Richard ("Rick") Jackson, 26, manager of business analysis
(Now, director of business planning and analysis)

## LOEWS CORPORATION
666 Fifth Avenue
New York, NY 10019

Preston Robert Tisch, 50, president
Ann Bontempo, public relations

McKINSEY & COMPANY
245 Park Avenue
New York, NY 10017

George Foote, 49, director

MARSHALSEA ASSOCIATES, INC.
555 Madison Avenue
New York, NY 10022

Herbert Patterson, 52, senior adviser and consultant
(Starting as a trainee, he worked his way up to presidency of the Chase Manhattan Bank under David Rockefeller. He will not discuss why he left— "that's between me and the Chase"—but he maintains friendly ties with many people there and is still called by them, informally, for advice. He now heads Stanover Company, 450 Park Avenue, New York, NY 10022)

MONFORT OF COLORADO, INC.
P.O. Box G
Greeley, CO 80631

Kenneth W. Monfort, 48. executive VP
(He had run the family business, the world's largest feedlot operation, for some 20 years. "Then I demoted myself," he says. He thought maybe he was getting too set in his ways. Besides, he wasn't having as much fun as he used to, when he was more intimately involved in sales. "My desk is messier now, and I'm enjoying it more." However, he is currently listed as co-chairman, as well as exec VP, sales division)

THE NATIONAL STATE BANK
28 West State Street
Trenton, NJ 08605

Mary G. Roebling, 71, chairman

*THE NEW YORK TIMES*
229 West 43rd Street
New York, NY 10036

Leonard Harris, 52, director of special projects
(Now, director of corporate development)

J. C. PENNEY COMPANY, INC.
1301 Avenue of the Americas
New York, NY 10019

Donald V. Seibert, 53, chairman

Sylvia A. Dresner, corporate information

William R. Howell, 40, VP, western regional manager
(P.O. Box 4999, Buena Park, CA)

*PEOPLE*
Rockefeller Center
New York, NY 10020

Richard A. Burgheim, 42, assistant managing editor

THE PILLSBURY COMPANY
608 Second Avenue
Minneapolis, MN 55402

William H. Spoor, 53, chairman

REDACTRON CORPORATION (subsidiary of Burroughs)
100 Parkway Drive, South
Hauppauge, NY 11787

Evelyn Berezin, 51, president, founder

REVLON, INC.
767 Fifth Avenue
New York, NY 10022

Michel C. Bergerac, 44, chairman

The Kitchens of SARA LEE (subsidiary of Consolidated Foods)
500 Waukegan Road
Deerfield, IL 60015

Thomas F. Barnum, 37, president

Stanley Gondek, 47, controller
Robert Iverson, 40, director of marketing, bakery products
Robert Ludwig, 25, accountant

SAVIN BUSINESS MACHINES CORPORATION
Columbus Avenue
Valhalla, NY 10595

E. Paul Charlap, 52, chairman

Abraham E. Ostrovsky, 33, VP, marketing, retail operations
(2401 N.W. 34th Street, Miami, Florida 33142)

Harry M. Farnham, III, branch general manager
(P.O. Box 6600, Cerritos, CA 90701)

## SECURITIES AND EXCHANGE COMMISSION
500 North Capitol, NW
Washington, DC 20549

Roderick M. Hills, chairman
(With the change of administration, Hills was replaced. He was shortly afterward elected chairman of Peabody Coal Company of St. Louis, the nation's largest, but has since resigned)
Stanley Sporkin, 44, director, division of enforcement
Wallace Timmeny, 38, associate director, division of enforcement

## TEXAS INSTRUMENTS
Office: Republic National Bank Tower
Dallas, TX 75201

J. Erik Jonsson, 75, founder
(One of four elected first to *Fortune*'s business hall of fame, Jonsson is a master of motivation. He served as mayor of Dallas for 7 years after leaving Texas Instruments, and still keeps busy as an active director of several banks and trustee of U. of Dallas and Rensselaer Polytech)

## UNION CARBIDE
270 Park Avenue
New York, NY 10017

Warren M. Anderson, 55, executive VP
(Has since been elected president of the corporation)
Fred B. O'Mara, 61, executive VP

## UNITED STATES STEEL CORPORATION
600 Grant Street
Pittsburgh, PA 15230

Edgar B. Speer, 60, chairman
R. Heath Larry, 62, vice-chairman
(He since retired from Steel to become president of the National Association of Manufacturers)
Peter B. Mulloney, 43, executive assistant to the general manager, Eastern Steel Division
(Now, general manager—commercial, hot rolled products)

Drummond C. Bell, 31, staff assistant to the VP, sales, Eastern Steel Division
(Now, manager of tire wire, Eastern)

## USLIFE CORPORATION
125 Maiden Lane
New York, NY 10030
Gordon E. Crosby, Jr., 56, chairman

## FOCUS GROUP PANELISTS
Dennis Brown, General Telephone and Electronics
Howard Claus, Western Airlines
Mark Dennett, Western Airlines
James Dintaman, Carnation Corporation
Bill Faulkner, TRW
Rick Haenel, So. California Gas Company
Al Hunter, Transamerica Corporation
Terry McCarthy, TRW
Pat O'Hara, Ducommun Corporation
Ken Olsen, Southern California Gas Company
Dick Powers, Transamerica Corporation
Bill Roberts, Oil Shale Corporation (now, Tosco)
Jeff Rubin, ARCO

# Index